SHAKESPEARE'S ENACTMENT

The Dynamics of Renaissance Theatre

SHAKESPEARE'S ENACTMENT

The Dynamics of Renaissance Theatre

ALBERT COOK

THE SWALLOW PRESS INC.
CHICAGO

Published by
The Swallow Press Incorporated
811 West Junior Terrace
Chicago, Illinois 60613

First edition
First printing

This book is printed on recycled paper

Library of Congress Catalog Card Number: 76-3128
ISBN 0-8040-0695-4

CONTENTS

For Thomas McFarland

I should like to thank The Center for Advanced Study in the Behavioral Sciences, where this study was begun and then some years later brought close to completion. I am also grateful to the John Simon Guggenheim Memorial Foundation, under whose auspices I did some intermediate work; and to the staffs of the Folger Library and the Huntington Library for courtesies extended on my visits there.

My students in a seminar on Shakespeare over a dozen years have furthered these ideas by letting me test them, and two of their number, Dugald McLeod and Thomas Pison, helped as research assistants in the preparation of the manuscript. Stephen Armstrong made the index and offered useful suggestions for final revision, while Sylvia Lane helped prepare the final typed copy. I am indebted to numerous colleagues, but especially to Thomas McFarland; to Father Walter J. Ong, who suggested that I condense a somewhat larger early draft; to Jan B. Gordon; to Norman Holland; and to Angus Fletcher, whose keen critical advice provided the impetus that impelled me to give the book its present shape.

As always I am deeply grateful to my wife, Carol.

Preface

A theory of drama adequate to its subject must be adequate to the best of its subject—to Shakespeare. And, conversely, our critical preoccupations have increasingly brought it home to us that the discussion of Shakespeare will gain in adequacy from having an opening on theoretical questions.

Shakespeare's complexity poses problems that are, finally, theoretical ones; the critic slights such considerations at his peril. To give but one kind of example, the case for a petulant Cordelia, a skittish Desdemona or a meddling Isabella, which is brought forward now and then, cannot be simply refuted by the organized interpretation of a character's speeches; the erroneous case has itself been put together, as often as not responsibly, by just such a procedure. With no theoretical check, such critics in effect maintain by highlighting the negative side not only that these women are complex but that they work deleteriously in the plays where they appear rather than (in the conventional, and correct, view) bravely resisting the deleterious effects of what is happening to them. And readings of their speeches can be slanted either way, with or without Freudian help.

The heroine can be shown to be one, in the last analysis, only by adducing the *response* to what she says on the part of an audience presumed to be normative; Freudian analysis, if brought to bear on the pattern of her actions, must be balanced by a theory of how language works in plays. In throwing attention off the meanings of her statements and onto their impact, one does not of course leave the meanings behind. The impact must be construed as a sort of direction-finder for the designative meaning of her words. This is a circular process in one sense. But such a use of the context of verbal communications may not be surprising when, contrary to normal speech, the auditor of a play cannot answer back. To carry off anything like an adequate reading of "intentionality" under special conditions of enactment, conditions which Shakespeare's practice brought to an unrivalled pitch of intensity, must depend on a scrupulous balancing of many large theoretical questions, especially for so complex a playwright as Shakespeare.

The masterly playwrights in other traditions tend to bring their plays thematically to a unity; Sophocles, Racine, Ibsen, and Beckett are all notable for homogeneity of tone and presentation. But Shakespeare, who works in a panoramic tradition, expands this tradition most powerfully by preserving the heterogeneity of its elements in the complex unity of each of his plays.

It is the central aim of *Shakespeare's Enactment* to account for his thematic coordination of such heterogeneous elements. In his earliest work we find him doing so: the *Henry VI* sequence tries to coordinate a wealth of seemingly heterogeneous action. In *The Comedy of Errors*, for all its rigorous schematism, he has one plot of beating the executioner under way before he begins the other, related plot of sorting out the marital and matchmaking identities. *Love's Labour's Lost* suddenly defers its consummations out of deference to the death of a royal father. The "festive" tradition will not by itself account for the strange intertwining of social orders in *A Midsummer Night's Dream* (the semi-legendary Theseus and Hippolyta, the normal aristocrats, the guild members, the fairies) when each order is given its own particular sphere and mode of behavior. In *King Lear* the words have a gravely pessimistic or skeptical drift, while the actions have a bearing different enough to have produced the most divergent readings of its tone. Shakespeare himself has mastered as well as produced these divergences, and "The Mastery of Divergences," the title of my first chapter, might also have served as a title for the entire book.

The next chapter, "The Sounding of the Theme," studies his handling of one large convention mistakenly labelled by just one of its components, "revenge," especially as his redefinition of this convention bears on *Othello* and on other tragedies of love.

"Dramatic Irony" addresses the consequences for dramatic

statement of Shakespeare's marked freedom in utilizing a practice that was particularly widespread in the theatre of his time. "Play" further analyzes the structural possibilities inherent within the "metatheatrical" practice of presenting plays-within-plays, or combining dumb shows with ordinary stage action for contrapuntal effect.

"Style" reads all these complications back into Shakespeare's remarkable conflation of styles as he enlists for special effect a charged relationship of words to stage action. "Endings" examines the structure of time on his stage by looking at his conclusions, and "Justice" inspects his implied attempts, especially in the history plays, to draw up a balance sheet among the diverse events, each with its own moral implications, that are presented as happening in complex succession and often after long intervals of time. This final chapter, too, could have been called, "The Mastery of Divergences," though it only partially closes the circle my theoretical projections have tried to draw in trying to take the measure of this playwright's Protean universe.

ONE
The Mastery of Divergences

But a moment's reflection suffices to make every man conscious of what every man must have before felt, that the drama is an imitation of reality, not a copy—and that imitation is contradistinguished from copy by this: that a certain quantum of difference is essential to the former and an indispensable condition and cause of the pleasure we derive from it, while in a copy it is a defect, contravening its name and purpose.

Coleridge
"Notes for a lecture on *The Tempest*, 1818"

The spectator is distanced from the actors who are addressing him: he cannot cross the stage line, he cannot speak, and he is addressed in a sort of silent third person. The words, which make sense only if they are conceived of as having an auditor before whom they unfold themselves and their related action, are subjected to the conventional distancing of taking place as though he were not there.

This exclusion becomes a kind of inclusion. In ordinary dialogue Ego and other are not confused, though they may agree on a scale of unification all the way to the sublime union of love's transports. The interchange of language preserves the identity of the speaker. But the auditor of a drama has no identity with respect to the play. Having no identity, his perceptions float free. He is free to recognize, or not to recognize, himself in any of what he sees.

His silence before an ongoing action and his freedom towards it make him somewhat like the dreamer before a dream, an analogy stressed by some psychoanalytic critics. But in one important respect the spectator differs from the dreamer; in most dreams the dreamer figures as a chief participant. The dream is a cryptogram with one figure solved, that of the dreamer. Of course other figures in the dream may also represent him, but the figure he knows to be himself interacts with those other, as they may be, selves he is himself distancing.

But the play is the reverse of a dream—a cryptogram in which all figures but one are solved, having the identities the playwright has endowed them with. The one left out—but necessary in the communicative relation—is the very one, the auditor, who is given as solved in a dream.

Such a communicative relation is present in any tale about persons, dramatized or not. In the drama, though, the exemplary character of the narration, its accessibility to identifications, is intensified by the presence of the auditor, just as a tale is when told *viva voce* to another person. A tale told live wears its exemplary character on the sleeve of its voice. The auditor is being held by another, the live narrator, where the reader only holds himself. In a play live people emit live speeches, as though there were no text and no foregone story.

In a play, we have long easily assumed, one "identifies" with the protagonist. That is, one seizes psychically on the protagonist as centering the events around himself, and thereby as providing a focus for Ego in a dialogue from which he has been formally barred. By taking the protagonist as the self with whom we can solve the cryptogram of who these people are, we can sit back and let the events demonstrate their correspondence to the lives we are living, a correspondence that must be posited for the play to have any sense at all.

But we also tend to measure any speaker by our own assumptions, and thereby to invest with the richness of identification, and also reaction, anyone who may speak up. The servant who leaps forth to stab Cornwall surely accords with, and therefore enacts, our wishes, though we have mainly been identifying with persons of a different class. The protagonist, in fact, tends to be a king or someone with authority not too much inferior to a king's. And if a ruler is present in the audience, of *Twelfth Night* or *Measure for Measure*,[1] he will be given subdued hints of homage, fortifying the obvious fact that the ordinary spectator is not a king. In this sense, then, the spectator is dissociated from King Lear or Hamlet as well as identified with him. As someone from the past, too, he cannot be contemporaneous, though his events may correspond to our own, fact to like fact. "It was," as M.C. Bradbrook asserts, "a general critical requirement that all tragedy should be based on incidents taken from life; and this was one of the main distinctions between it and comedy, where the plots were feigned."[2]

Usually the past events were either lived history, verifiable in the chronicles, or, in the case of comedy, a set of events both familiar and strange (the "wonderful in probable" of my earlier analysis).[3] In Greek tragedy the events were lost in pre-history, codified into religious exemplum, into myth, for the correspondence of pattern to fact as a means of confirming the identification of spectator with protagonist, as well as his difference therefrom, thus reproducing in the reference of the play's statement the split between actors and audience, and also their connection.

Silently to second Cordelia's decorous demureness is to identify with her; to reject flattery with flatterers in the fulsomeness of her sisters. One process of identification, or dissociation, combines with another, and gradually an interaction, between us and the play, provides a ground on which the person we identify with can change: Hamlet can become more resolute, King Lear can become more perceptive, though not only more royal than we but also closer to the threshold of death than we like to think of ourselves as being. He is a *memento mori* long before he actually expires before our eyes.

In the very process of presentation, for any play, a fundamental duality asserts itself through the linguistic conditions and through the process of identification-and-dissociation so dynamically enlisted by Shakespeare.[4]

Achilles, as Shakespeare adapts Ovid's description of him in Reuben Brower's reading, is measured against an ideal of identification with himself, of being *"par sibi."*[5] Hamlet, on the other hand, is more energetically divorced from both an earlier courtier's self and the true nature he will not quite have seen face to face before he dies; and in the light of such movements, Polonius' "This above all, to thine own self be true," is not so much false or vague as uselessly truistic.

Repeating, for wonderment or the mere glorification of order, the doubling of identity between actor and spectator, Shakespeare often doubles or multiplies his persons on stage. In *Love's Labour's Lost* we are given four pairs of noble lovers and almost as many plebeian ones. Twins and their interlocking love affairs are the focus of *Twelfth Night*, where in *Measure for Measure* a chaste sister and a lecherous brother find the safe haven of marriage. Both of the two gentlemen of Verona, the faithful one and the faithless one, find that friendship can subvert as well as sustain, sustain as well as subvert, what look like nearly identical loves.

In *The Winter's Tale* there are two kingdoms, Sicily and Bohemia, distant in place and in association; the daughter of one and the son of the other will find their way to matrimony after the terrible events of the play. And the rulers have been fast boyhood friends, "twinn'd lambs" (I,ii,67).[6] The speech in which they are so designated already posits an achieved identity of pastoral nature, and eventual grace, masking as constant prelapsarian grace: "we should have answer'd heaven/Boldly 'Not Guilty', the imposition clear'd/Hereditary ours" (I,ii,73-75). These two orders of nature and grace will not get together again till the end of the play. Our lulling identification with this charmed courtesy has been putting to sleep the psychosexual substructure that will shortly break out, this boyishly sublimated homosexual overidentification, once a phase and now a nascent obsession, breaking out in the form of a sudden, irrational, and deadly jealousy, effectuating our reactive dissociation from Leontes. The hope that holds us in our spectator's seats will be held in place for four more acts and override a lapse of sixteen years. The figure of Time will be brought in for our sequent and simple identification (allegories are not only simple in structure but allow identification to be simple).

Identification is dangerous unless matched by difference, Ego subsistent as safely distinct from Other through opposition of sex or temperamental discrimination: Horatio and Hamlet are healthy in their friendship, and we are made to feel on the evidence of their teamwork alone that Rosencrantz and Guildenstern are sick; their betrayal of their peers to authority, and their easy alternation of voice with each other, are two aspects of the same defect.

Under too great an identity the saving difference is lost, a magic and primitive horror is called forth. René Girard links the systematic doublings of *A Midsummer Night's Dream*, and its purgative distancing of tragedy into parody, to the deep tendency in society to displace the exchanging identities of self with other, locked in a violence-prone competition to assert self by competing with other.[7] For Girard all social institutions displace and avoid this violence by placing at their heart some kind of one-way sacrifice pattern, in which a man who is both like everyone else and distinguished from everyone else is either actually or in various symbolic forms done to death. This pattern is distinct from, and present as qualifying, all other, two-way patterns; violence shadows love at every turn. Building pairs into the play —*A Midsummer Night's Dream*—serves as a rhetorical method to give this displacement linguistic expression and thereby at once to avoid it and to mirror it.

Even without such metaphysical extensions, the process of identification is a sophisticated one: drama is a product of literate cultures. And it may be seen as holding such forces at bay by giving them voice. As Harold Brooks says of still another Shakespearian tour-de-force of doubling, *The Comedy of Errors*: "The theme of identity is here linked with those of relationship (dislocated or re-established) and of risk. To seek reunion with the lost members of the family Antipholus is risking his identity; yet he must do so, for only if the full relationship is restored can he find content. And then, hints the image of one water drop seeking another, the present individual identity will be lost, or transformed, in another way. It is to claim a sinking of identity in the marriage relation . . . that Adriana [sic] uses the closely similar image in I,ii . . .

> Dark-working sorcerers that change the mind:
> Soul-killing witches that deform the body.

The lines seize the imagination of the audience at the deep level where the ancient dread of losing the self or soul is very much alive."[8]

Identity is dramatized thus as linked to risk, and one's identity is risked, fundamentally, in the very *Geworfenheit* of existence; we are caught, we can only have self-consciousness, in a consciousness of a complicated structure which fundamentally contains the certainty of our own risk. In a tragic play we face the risk of death without risk; it is a make-believe acted out by some like person who is ineradicably other, and he may graze the dark side of identity with real impunity and a resulting significative richness. In comedy, and in *Love's Labour's Lost* in particular, as McFarland puts it: "One of the most important motifs . . . is, indeed, the ridicule of all heroism. Heroism implies the existence of danger; in paradise there can be no real threat of danger, and consequently no need for heroism. As Ovid says of the golden age, 'sine militis usu/mollia securae peragebant otia gentes. . . (*Met.*1.99-100)'."[9] And a dramatic presentation not only envisages risk and affirms security because it is a make-believe. It does so, he also asserts, because it recreates, on the ground of adulthood, the conditions of *homo ludens*. "The security of childhood . . . the defining activity of childhood is play . . . the act of play is always an icon of security."[10]

Furthermore, security, like risk, is linked to the sense of identity, as he goes on to adapt both Freud and Schiller. "What appears to be a renunciation is really the formation of a substitution or surrogate . . . This surrogate, in Schiller's analysis, is art: 'We shall never be wrong in seeking a man's ideal of Beauty along the selfsame path in which he satisfies his play impulse.' "[11]

Self is not other, security is not risk. These opposites are not nullified by a dramatic presentation, but inducted into a transforming sequence in which each qualifies and deepens our sense of the other by having us silently undertake to go through watching what will evoke in us, in alternation and in commingling appropriation, the other in the self and the security in risk, the self in the other and the risk in security.

2

All this dramatic strategy of calling the spectator's identity into question must stir him up as it leads him to ponder the sense of the action he has been watching. The emotion created in the spectator, the force residing in the act of "arousing" and also the effect of "being moved" cannot be distinguished from the larger propositional character of *King Lear* or *Philoctetes* or *Phèdre*.[12] Not only, as in art generally, is the emotion an idea, the effect itself a proposition; but in drama the emotions are patterned, and this pattern constitutes part of the "syntax" of the dramatic statement, all the words and all the actions of a play taken together.

Further, in drama the audience is a live group: it sits there. It is a virtual participant in the communicative act, adhering to the convention that it not respond by words or by any other action than that of signalling its enthusiastic acceptance of the presentation. Where a ritual is involved, as in a Greek dramatic performance, the audience may well signal its participation by silence.

The "uptake" of the auditor is then itself a kind of fiction, since it corresponds only analogously to distinguishable acts such as worshipping, and since pretense is part of the contract. The audience feels sorry for Cordelia with the same emotion that it would feel sorry for the neglected daughter of a neighbor; but the grieving, and all its psychoanalytic substructure, is make-believe; the grieving constitutes not entering a series of acts but only accepting a proposition about such acts in a fuller series. The causal connection between this grief and the relief at the end that someone good is left to steer the kingdom makes the convergence of elements in the total dramatic speech act not only virtual but global: we are made to feel this connection more closely than we are likely to in life between sympathetic grief for a neighbor and relief for a later change of rule in which, after her death, her brother-in-law participates. The risk of making greater connections between events than usual in life is compensated by a heightened sense of security for having made the connections.

The restricted and exemplary set of actions presented for the few hours of a play, just because they are framed, implicitly asserts a sort of *post hoc-propter hoc* causal connection in unity of action. And the shorter time of a show laid over the longer time of events in life already possesses the schematism of foreshortening. It takes only a step to emphasize this in "unity of time," while the delimited space of the stage, however many changes of scene it may admit, comparably foreshortens the varied repertoire of spaces, finite but not felt as delimited, in which people conduct the business of life. Just in the conception of a stage play there is a strong natural tendency, without the Italian and French pietistic classicizing justification, for the unities of time, place, and action. Sophocles, Corneille, the masters of Noh drama, Ibsen, and Beckett, have all made a normative, one may even say an obvious, as well as a classical choice, in exploiting the unities: in pushing the implied syntactic convergence of their presentations towards the high coherence of the unities of time, place, and action.

In such tight plays the future is made to possess the definiteness of the past; potentiality and actuality are made manifest in their interconnections, and celebrated comically or brooded over tragically.[13] In the panoramic theatre as Shakespeare exploits it, this very process is itself inverted. So much so, for one thing, that the comic effect and the tragic effect often accompany and qualify each other. The causality is open, and the double-plot shuttle of causality, used for thematic counterpointing by Jonson and Middleton, is itself enriched by creating many more points of analogy between one plot (Lear) and another (Gloucester), along with causal connections that do not repeat the analogies. (Edgar is analogous to Cordelia but functions quite differently.) Strange, discordant chords are struck at the very moments of resolving tension which would would seem to rule them out. A clown brings the basket of asps to Cleopatra, and then addresses her with a delicacy and lightness that mutes the repartee of the clown into a courtesy that exceeds any of the royal interchanges of the play, touching a quiet sorrow where pity is indistinguishable from mockery, a note found, again, nowhere else in the play, "I wish you joy o' th' worm" (*Antony and Cleopatra*,V,ii, 277). The bawdiness of another nonce-clown is interposed between Iago's statement of purpose and his further insinuation of Cassio's trust (*Othello*, III,i), punning lightly enough to accord courteously with the musical instruments he is punning on, instruments set by Cassio under Othello's window as a kind of peace-offering at once courtly and blind about possible misconstructions of the serenade convention.[14]

As has often been pointed out, in this theatre generally the plots of plays tend to set out their own conditions, and not just to work out conclusions; a Greek play begins at the fourth act of an Elizabethan play. But at the same time, especially in Shakespeare's hands, the plot draws on a rich set of prior conditions. A sense of lateness is thus kept coordinate with the sense of many diverse things about to happen. The shifts of scene, of action groups, of pacing, and the alternations among prose, verse, and song, among dumb show, narration, and presentation, all emphasize this diversity.

Thus the discrepancy between the two or three hours of a play and the length of a life, as well as the correspondence of the play to life, both find coordinated expression, as against the classical practice, French or Greek, in which the discrepancy undergoes maximal simplification so as to serve as an armature for stating some aspect of the correspondence. The ritual telescoping of event is itself ritually fragmented, kaleidoscoped. The strange time out of time, this vacant afternoon of spectatorship, is structured so as to contain in its patternings of connection some residual sense of strangeness. The intercalary hour is not quite ritualized, and it is not firmly divorced from ritual either.[15]

The tendency in this theatre to use large numbers of people, and to group them symbolically on stage in patterns reminiscent of the *tableaux vivants* which had been popular for centuries both retains the ritual element present in such groupings and redirects it symbolically.[16] This symbolism cannot be allegorically interpreted, a symbolism that testifies to some strangeness in calling for explanatory, unfolding, multiple events to fill it out.

3

Sitting in his charmed silence, the spectator is given not just a vision of order in the events enacted before him, and not just a mirthful pleasure at the conclusion of a comedy, a sense of woe or wonder at the end of a tragedy. More than just pity and fear, too, the spectator gains, more fundamentally, a kind of hope which is rendered, ritually as it were, easier of access than the hope which sustains his daily life. He is called on at points of the play to hope that Cordelia will be restored and Kent recognized for loyal, that Thebes will be cured of the plague, that Oswald will shake off his melancholy, that Godot may indeed show up, or at least that one may accommodate to the failure of this expectation. He is also induced to hope that his sense of justice will be affirmed, that Claudius or Iago or Clytemnestra or even Zeus will not prevail. Hopes can be set against hopes: we want Rome to carry the day but also for Coriolanus not to be shaken from his integrity. We want Lear to wake up from his selfishness but for his old frame to be spared so much outrage and suffering. We want Thebes to be cured but Oedipus to stay king. The Aristotelian or pseudo-Aristotelian "flaw," a tool for the analysis of unity of action, can also be seen in the light of its function as a qualifier and transposer over the unity of time: expectations towards the future which are somehow congruent are made, in time, to produce discordancies; and thus a higher congruency. Cordelia is not saved but dies a good death. Lear is not spared but transformed. Iago is found out, but too late. Clytemnestra is brought to justice, but in a way that brings suffering on the son who is also the agent, forcing the gods to redefine what justice is.

When his action is pat, as in *Titus Andronicus*, Shakespeare refers us to a symbolic presence, a mute *tableau vivant*. All the acts of this play are in a sense *tableaux vivants* until the show-down, because Saturninus is totally deaf. Our hope that they will have some effect is dashed. And at the center is an outraged mute, Lavinia. As Emrys Jones says, "At the center of this rhetorically sonorous play is *silence*."[17]

In Marlowe the pattern is set out as an expanded morality, a pattern dependent not on allegorical translations but rather on the blunt sense of an episode, and then the reinforced, similar sense of another. The effect resembles that of Brecht's austerity. Each scene of *Tamburlaine*, of *Faustus*, of *The Jew of Malta*, of *Edward II* reinforces the previous scene. Complexities derive only, and simply, from the one-plus-one derivation of a pointed scene from its predecessor. The order is one of cumulative similarity; the effect, again like Brecht's, is to fix and distance the spectator.

Kyd varies this procedure only by complicating it; Peele, Greene, and Dekker—to run through the list of those from whom the young Shakespeare is likely to have learned plotting, against whom he would have measured himself—remain episodic in their plots without notably focusing their episodes into cumulative effect. Lyly gets the allegorical lightness of masque into *Endimion*, but in ways that assimilate it wholly to a courtly romance transposition of folk festival, "Love is a Lorde of misrule, and keepeth Christmas in my corps" (*Endimion*,V,ii,5-6).

Jonson splits his kinds, relying on verbal and other decoration to do the whole work of sequence, fantasy subsisting on the delight of surprise, in his Masques; and in his plays, he strains, conversely, for a heavy-grained realism (*Every Man In His Humour* being reset from Italy to England in revision). The intentness of one character on money or marriage thrusts through the events to cozen the others. The climax of unmasking closes the circle of a world where motives are relational and the psychology is a faculty psychology removed by an admixture of levitating fantasy. Greed and Lust and Envy and Pride find objects like Alchemy or a Queene of Faerie or a cozened master or a brace of dupes at a fair. On the surface there is a mobile theatricality. But the principle of movement is simple, a sort of theatrical perpetual motion machine. Consequently not just the incidents, but the whole plot, of *The Alchemist* or *Volpone* or *Bartholomew Fair* or even *Catiline* and *Sejanus*, seems no more than an episode, a revision of the Marlovian assertion towards a sophisticated but simple and uniform tentativeness. The substantiality of speeches weighted down with enumerated details is rendered insubstantial in the illusory intent of the speaking character's dramatized alchemy of the word.[18] Gold in the vision of the would-be alchemist is one with gold weighing down the bags of a mortal miser: the concreteness of Sir Francis Drake's spoil and the abstractness of Gresham's calculations are drawn to the line of convergence by the obsessive and prolonged enumeration of Volpone or Sir Epicure Mammon.

Jonson and Marlowe, in their different ways, are simplifiers. They use the broad spectrum of the panoramic stage to make unity of action yield a unified vision of experience. Shakespeare, however, did not, and perhaps could not, avail himself of this art or scope. Instead, he injects the note of mystery, preserving to the end some wonderment in the spectator's sense of risk. He plants an ass's head in Fairyland, and he has the wearer of the ass's head, when everyone returns from Fairyland, take the part of an uncomprehending actor in a clumsy tragic play. *Timon of Athens* has something of a Jonsonian ring; Timon, and those who confront him, are each of them very much in his humor. And a busyness of action works to the end of episodic moral definition— except that, to begin with, the plot concludes with the causally unconnected death of Timon, something Jonson's coherence would never permit. The whole demonstration is interwoven with the execution of a political-military victory. And the gold which is at first an invisible, all-but-inexhaustible purchasing power, and then a glittering metal dug up by a hermit out of the earth, never has the fantasy-dominance of Sir Epicure Mammon's longed-for nonexistent alchemy, the visible and proportional focus of Volpone's "Good morrow to the sun—and next my gold", or the firm allegorical structure of Pecunia in *The Staple of News*.

The Merchant of Venice is a study of cupidity and social interaction in a mercantile community: it too centers on money. But
it overarches and complicates that study with a study of love,
wherein he who easily borrows and needs gold discovers that
slighting gold and silver is the solution to a magic riddle whose
allegory, in itself, is made to suffer connection to events of quite
a different, a more realistic, metaphysical frame.

The impetus of this play seems at once slight and steeped in
longing. The first long scene is a mood piece. The last act, too,
goes on and on. It prolongs the sportiveness over a love-play deceit well beyond the point where all the causal action has been
unravelled. As against delay there is the usual Shakespearian
disproportion of scenes: in Act IV, for example, the first scene
is long, the second short. There is a constant disproportion between the frequency of set pieces, which stall the action, beginning with the long, gratuitous first scene, and the expectations of
the characters and the audience, when the complications of the
plot are so great. In the sphere of money, we are given not just
the normal interactions, as between client and patron and then
debtor and creditor in *Timon*, but an element of risk, of total loss.
These upper-class Venetians are secure beyond loss in the ease of
their functions, which the first scene exemplifies; and at the same
time they are subject, because their wealth is perilously loaded
into ships, to the risk of being stripped of substance wholly. That
material risk is transmuted by the cunning of Shylock, into the
nightmare risk of mortality: flesh, and so life, is to be forfeit if
money is not forthcoming. In the sphere of money, danger, even
such terrifying danger, can only be removed. In that sense money
is felt as a value only in its absence. Once there, it is forgotten,
people go about their business.

Love, too, increases risk. Not only a person's happiness, but the
very possibility of mating at all, is hazarded when Bassanio ventures on Portia's riddle. But that risk, once allayed, brings in
another plenary value. It is most delightfully, most musically felt
as harmonious, in the theory emphasized at the most distracting
moment of delay, when it comes to pass, at the moment of consummation. Being taken for granted in that sphere is not a natu-

ral attribute, but still another threat, and Portia's infidelity-sleight exorcizes that threat. The play's presentational sequence of lending, borrowing, courting, losing ships, judging and being judged, compensating, mocking, and finally consummating, is one which is not explained even by accounting for the balance of risk and fulfillment in the two spheres. Sigurd Burckhardt, indeed, argues that the balance of the two spheres implies both a dramaturgic dexterity and a risk in itself, without regard to the function of risk in each sphere: "What Shakespeare discovers in *The Merchant of Venice* is nothing less than a new principle of order. Symmetry, though easiest to come by, is always dangerous, because it is dichotomous."[19]

A sense of the necessity of disproportion is made to arrive, a measure for the cosmos of mercy, "How far that little candle throws his beams." Justice is redefined through and by love-play as a love-rescue, while Justice has disproportionally delayed the consummation of two weddings. The play produces a sort of religious sense, but the fact of religion in the play is only a qualifying element, not a main integer. What counts of Shylock is mainly his inhumanity, and tangentially his humanity, not whether he happens to be a Jew. A Christian has the charmed advantage, the play would seem to say, of automatic humanity.

There is a disproportion in the equivalences: no interest on his money is too little for Shylock, because he is plotting to take too much. The lack of interest on the loan creates no foreboding in us, or in the Venetians. No connection is made, at the moment, between Shylock's willingness to lend without interest and his blaming this very same trait in his debtor, "I hate him for he is a Christian;/But more for that in low simplicity/He lends out money gratis" (I,iii,37-39). There is also a disproportion in the sphere of love—between the the choice of a modest lead casket and the acquisition of Portia's hand and fortune; and later, too, the ring is too little pay for saving Antonio's life, or else it is too much if the ring is made arbitrarily to stand for Bassanio's entire fidelity. Portia can abrogate that arbitrariness but she sublimely and arbitrarily refuses to do so, in a way that harrows Bassanio with a sense of one angle on disproportionateness.

The request for the ring (V,i) is made parallel to, and dispro-
portionately balanced against *night, bright, love, angels, hush,
candle, good deed*—all brought in for contemplation while the
music is on. The music stops at Portia's entrance. The last words,
given to Gratiano, put the disproportion into finality by a festive
twist. "I'll fear no other thing," he says—after such great risks of
love, life, and fortune!—"So sore as keeping safe Nerissa's ring"
(V,i,306-307).

The changes in pacing and effect are not all ascribable to suspense or to contrast or to dramatic irony, which is only a chief
means to bring about transpositions in audience response. There
is nothing funny in stopping the music as Lorenzo recognizes the
voice of Portia. The silence around her contrasts with the music,
but also continues it: she herself is a sort of walking *musica
mundana;* what she stands for and expresses is coordinate with
what Lorenzo has explained in the music we have been hearing.
We know there is unfinished business because of the dramatic
irony; the identity of the lawyer's clerk and Bassanio's wife must
be brought home to Bassanio, and he must first be put through
the psychodramatic paces of mock jealousy. That grace note of a
conclusion, however, diverges from the two strands of the plot:
it has no necessary connection with either marriage or the deliv-
ering act of judgment, though it derives from both and is made
to unite both. In so much diversity, we are are brought to seek
the thread of unity, as we would not be asked to do in an episodic
play of merely diverting entertainment. The slightness of the di-
version is mockingly hinted at in the last lines, because the ring
they refer to cannot carry, and carries by conventional fiction,
the heavy weight of so much meaning.

It is of course a commonplace that Shakespeare is multivalent.
This is an unusual thing for a playwright to be, in presentation
(where all successful playwrights are multivalent in the sense of
offering a richness of hermeneutic accessibility). Such presentation was offered him, to begin with, by the panoramic character
of his stage convention. We do not "need" Lorenzo and Jessica,
whose active business has been concluded, in the final scene of
The Merchant of Venice. Nor need they open the scene with a

duet running through the complementary pairs of tragic lovers—
Troilus and Cressida, Pyramus and Thisbe, Dido and Aeneas,
Jason and Medea—all of whom are declared to have carried out
some crucial act "in such a night as this." These grace notes come
at us from the side, so to speak, providing us with a sense of the
connectedness of what we are seeing not just because analogies
are drawn, but because the progress of the action admits of their
being drawn. In the third act of *King Lear* there is no need,
though the playwright sets the circumstances up in a way that
creates one, for the huddling group of outcasts to move from the
open storm to the cave, and then to the shelter in an "outhouse"
of Gloucester's castle, and then once more into open flight. Each
area becomes a setting, whose attributes take on the global significance of a given space. But the unity of space is only provisional,
and time undoes that provisionality for a superseding significance,
which, because it is gratuitous (the whole act could have been
played in the storm, or in the cave), comes to seem the more
symbolic.

4

Now the performance of the play is a virtual act in the social
context if it is not explicitly ritualized; it exists during a time left
blank for that purpose in a space given over at least temporarily
to it. The virtuality of the blank lends it the more to being filled
in by what I have called the analogic contagion to other groupings of people in the society,[20] in the England of this time to royal
pageants and folk festivals, the "progression" of a royal entour-
age and the holiday Church procession, schoolboy plays and bear-
baitings and even public executions.[21]

The kind of gathering most similar to plays, lasting about the
same length of time and including both activity up front and
lengthy statements before a silent group, was the church service,
whose semantic function, though it proceeded at the time under
the nearly constant examination of theological debate, was firmly

aimed at sacramental participation. The line between sacred and profane, unclear in a play, was very definite in the church service, to which the parishioners went with dutiful regularity and not on impulse or as part of some celebration or other, as spectators went to a play. The solemnity at least of a tragic play would have been recognizably akin to the solemnity of the church service. And the sequence of prayer, Sermon, general Confession, Consecration, through and to the release of Communion and final Blessing, would correspond more closely to the emotional sequence of experiencing a successful tragedy or even a comedy, than does the imaginable emotional sequence of folk festival, the sequence from boisterousness to inebriation to a jolly fatigue. Moreover, plays were not put on as a direct part of the festival except for those who were not folk, as *Twelfth Night* was acted for courtiers and the court. The plays were urban, put on almost exclusively in London or on tour therefrom: the festivals rural in origin and reference. And in the festival pageants of Misrule, the player was both straight man and butt, the participant both actor and spectator. Shakespearian comedy stands to the folk festivals, Barber continually suggests, as art song stands to folk song. And the songs appearing in these plays are themselves art songs, closer to Rosseter and Dowland than to the Child Ballads,[22] while being kept open, through the mingling of social and cosmological orders, to the rough-and-ready wondering and resigned tonality of the ballad. The folk is attenuated by being refined and transcended by being qualified. And in his handling of song, as in his handling of sequence and of everything else, Shakespeare has a sense of unity mysteriously come through the diversity of elements in his blend.

When the play is put on, we grant it the license of its fictions. Or, in Ohmann's application of Austin, mimesis reverses the usual direction of inference: the "felicity conditions" of "illocutionary" statements are accorded the play at the outset, and its hypothesis is accepted at the beginning, rather than at the end. One among the many consequences of this initial license is the expectation that the series of statements accorded this "felicity" license will be more coherent than in other, more unstructured events held indoors. And at the same time we invest in a play an expectation that this coherence will raise the pitch of response to its events, will produce not simple assent but a state or mood of *alternatively* heightened feeling or an alerted wide-eyed attention, a "woe *or* wonder," in the phrase Cunningham traces back to Donatus from *Hamlet* (V, ii, 335).[23] The alternation, like the pair itself, constitutes a change from Aristotle's pity and fear. And the terms look ahead to Shakespeare's triumphantly multivalent literary vision as well as back to a stock scholastic response.

Keeping the combinatory possibilities among tones and attitudes open allows Shakespeare a richness of presentational freedom unattainable in the orders of a closed dramaturgic coherence. One cannot imagine such a speech as Ulysses' "eulogy of degree" (*Troilus and Cressida*, I,iii,75-137) on the French classical stage. Even less could one imagine such an ideal's being warped to the use of flyting irony—where Ulysses heaps this praise on an Agamemnon so stolidly grandiloquent and so ponderously self-centered that he could not apprehend his own manifest, and just manifested, contradiction of that ideal. The low style of folk burlesque and the high style of courtly effusion are brought forcibly together here by Shakespeare; the popular and the aristocratic are made once again to produce a visionary yield. This effect is intensified through implied contrast to the religion of the audience; the presence of the religious element may be said to be felt in the totality of its exclusion.

This very exclusion in *Troilus and Cressida* permits the losing value of permanent fidelity and the predominating value of mutability and clash to warp against each other. In *A Midsummer Night's Dream* the exclusion from Christian values brings about a different dramatic suspension of divergences. Locating the play's fable in a pre-Christian and legendary Greece keeps open the relation of its view of love—a mystery which bloweth where it listeth—to the Christian scheme. The same strategy takes on extravagant evolution in the final romances, only one of which, *The Tempest*, shows us nominal Christians on stage.

A Midsummer Night's Dream, seen for its maximum of coherence, is enough of an object lesson to seem a little like a morality play; and the play it includes is performed by members of various "mysteries" or guilds, as mystery plays were. Moreover, a muted and sub-Christian chastity is touched on as a negative, and conventional, possibility, when Theseus modifies the ultimatum of Hermia's father by threatening her with confinement in a nunnery. At the same time this nunnery partakes of the fictionalizing which the classical gods always undergo in Renaissance works at the hands of writers who of course cannot believe in them as they might in the Christian God:

> For aye to be in shady cloister mew'd,
> To live a barren sister all your life,
> Chanting faint hymns to the cold fruitless moon.
> Thrice-blessed they that master so their blood
> To undergo such maiden pilgrimage.
>
> (I,i,71-75)

And here near the beginning a faint irony is already present: the Diana of Theseus' praise is served by a chastity quite alien to the moon of this play, which will not be cold and fruitless.

The tragic potentialities inhering in love's illusion are first kept strongly at bay by the sympathetic edict of a ruler; then, through the main dream-action of the play, by the benignly random sorting of Puck's ointment on the eyes of sleepers; and finally by turning festively upside down a story like *Romeo and Juliet*, clumsily performed by the weaver's guild, a performance chosen by Theseus for some decorous appropriateness among other possibilities. Pyramus and Thisbe "die" amid a politely restrained sportive laughter. While the politeness of Theseus in itself embodies a courtly ideal expressed in the kind of high style which Lyly or the sonneteers would represent, a style which notably even for Shakespeare invests the verse of the main body of the play, it is exactly this toned-down Euphuism of which "Pyramus and Thisbe" is deprived. The tragic story itself is here a countercase; the play-within-a-play remains so resolutely fictive that it is made to lack any of the stylized appeal of fiction. The lack of decorum serves to qualify a counterpoised dominance of decorum.

Love, the single subject of the play, functions divergently for each of the four orders of beings it presents; and the play orchestrates the divergences. For Theseus and Hippolyta, legendary beings with something of demigods about them, love has taken place in the past, a foregone conclusion leading to the marriage whose incipient celebration operates as a controlling presence and encouragement for the main persons in the play, the normally nubile members of the polite society of Athens. Love is easy for Demetrius and Helena, Lysander and Hermia; and also it is a mystery, beyond full self-consciousness or self-realization for lovers who have shown in the first place only secondary differentiation from one another. Through the agency of the third order of beings, the fairies, for whom love is a courtly sport and also a mystery in their supernatural keeping, they are brought to resolution. We are meant not to know why Hermia would fall in love with Lysander more than with Demetrius when both love her, and nothing in the enacted events brings us to know. Rather they are enchanted to realign, to celebrate, to wonder, and to accept, whatever is brought by supernatural beings who trail the airiness of theatrical doubt as they bestow amorous certainty. The one instance of crossover among the orders is both temporary and amusing in its incongruousness, Titania's love for Bottom-as-ass. When Bottom himself, as a member of the fourth order, the lower class, becomes himself, he ceases to entertain notions of love other than as the unrealized make-believe of a tragic failure to consummate "Pyramus and Thisbe." These guild members offer a negative image; they are accorded none of the amorous activity granted the lower orders in *Love's Labour's Lost* or *As You Like It.*

Their very exclusion, their ineptness and ironically framed dedication to Theseus, is staged so as to conclude the dream.

Bottom's play offers not the same orders, but the implied significative ridiculousness of ontological distortion: one group of beings, Pyramus and Thisbe along with his father and her mother, repeat the upper-class Athenians of the main plot. But then there is Lion, and Wall, and Moonshine—beings acted by guild members caught in an unperceived impossibility of incommunicable make-believe.

The bungling play-within-a-play, " The most Lamentable Comedy and most Cruel Death of Pyramus and Thisbe," transforms the love tragedy into inarticulateness, and inarticulateness into laughter, distilling a finer laughter and a more exquisite articulateness for the play we are watching itself. Theseus himself chooses the bungling performance among several offered him by his Master of Revels for the respect implied in its very falling short, "For never anything can be amiss/When simpleness and duty tender it" (V,i,82-83). Bottom's failure to become Pyramus in any way articulates his inarticulateness by staging the incapacity to act.

Courtesy-feigning-mysterious arbitrariness of love-aristocracy-success-reality—these are made to reverberate dramatically against bluntness-earnestness-lack of mythic perspective-failure-false illusion.

The metatheatrical strategy here is made to turn the tables on itself. Bottom has already played a role in Puck's magic quasi-masque, the ass's head in fairyland being made to grow upon the very one whose conception of the magic of love, or any magic at all, would be most asinine. And the causality is circular as well as the roles significative: he has come to the wood in the first place so he may rehearse the play, "a marvelous convenient place for our rehearsal. This green plot shall be our stage, this hawthorn brake our tiring-house" (III,i,3-4).

And he is transformed while rehearsing:

PUCK:
> What hempen homespuns have we swagg'ring here,
> So near the cradle of the Fairy Queen?
> What, a play toward! I'll be an auditor;
> An actor too perhaps, if I see cause.

(III,i,68-71)

The first, early sample we are given of Bottom's play exhibits

its counter-significations in the mode of doggerel's failed straining
for articulateness:

> The raging rocks
> And shivering shocks
> Shall break the locks
> Of prison gates;
> And Phibbus' car
> Shall shine from far,
> And make and mar
> The foolish Fates.

(I,ii,25-32)

This counter-asserts the delicacy of connection between the night
of enchantment, a physical condition, and the fated propensity for
love, a spiritual one, by rendering ridiculous in stark assertion
the connection between the deified day and the Fates, who cannot really be called "foolish," though with fond mockery those
who fall in love may be so called, "What fools these mortals be."
"Foolish Fates" is a kind of unachieved metonymy; the attribution would be true within the play as a connection between the
agent and the effect: fated mortals are foolish; "What fools these
mortals be." If Pyramus and Thisbe are subjected to the Fates,
then the Fates would be not foolish but cruel, the intellectual
trait given for the emotional in the mouth of a Bottom who can
be debased-enchanted into the delighted object of love but not a
lover because his failure, demonstrated in the language, to make
delicate discriminations intellectually corresponds to an emotional
failing: he is capable of pride alone, where humbleness draws the
awe of love.

In these lines Bottom refers not to the lovers but to a strong
man, "This is Ercles' vein, a tyrant's vein: a lover is more con-
doling" (I,ii,33-34). But the freedom to choose just any classical
myth exhibits an exclusion of understanding from the discriminations in which they would have meaning.

"How shall we find the concord of this discord?" (V,i,60). So
Theseus asks of the advertised incongruities of "Pyramus and

Thisbe," "Merry and tragical! Tedious and brief!/That is hot ice and wondrous strange snow" (58-59). He is at first intrigued by the contradiction, which he phrases in terms that themselves suggest a polar opposition to Midsummer. The very act of celebration, when the lovers are already "full of joy and mirth" (V,i,28), diverges to encompass an emptiness of erotic fulfillment, via a flatness of language that nullifies the tragedy of unfulfillment by holding it up to the incomprehension of scorn. Beware Shakespeare, someone says, when he uses doggerel. The not-quite-doggerel of the blank verse in the play Bottom finally mounts is indeed "tedious" but is not "brief." The emptiness is one of mere designation, a *flatus vocis* from which the recourse is into a laughter that celebration would not permit to be embarrassed and the incomprehension of the guildsmen would not permit to be embarrassing. To be purged of doggerel is not a gain for Bottom, any more than the ability to sing the harmonious bird-catalogue song which wakened Titania has been able to tune him into the charmed language that is sounding all around him, to which he is deaf. But his deafness must be taken only as a sort of reverse image of their own, of what they are not just satisfied but glad not to be accounting for.

Theseus himself is cheerfully uncomprehending; his "the lunatic, the lover, and the poet" speech is made in order to offer a reason why the events we have just seen could not have happened. The principals, too, are cheerfully uncomprehending on the brink of fulfillment. The retrospective look they take is spoken not from lover to lover but from a now successful suitor to the girl who will wed his former rival.

DEMETRIUS:
These things seem small and undistinguishable,
Like far-off mountains turned into clouds.
HERMIA:
Methinks I see these things with parted eye,
When every thing seems double.

(IV,i,184-187)

The female vision of seeing doubleness in distinct entities caps the male vision of blurring and diminishing all things. There is a disjunction between kinds of the undistinguishable here, and a further disjunction between these kinds on the one hand, which succeed in formulating unsuccess, and on the other hand that of the blurred language offered us by the play-within-a-play, as its transpositions of tragedy into comedy refer us not just simply to the dream but to the disjunctions that the sequence affords, the more clearly for a heightened moment, as in the quotation above when the temporal sequence has been re-imagined as an alternate pair of spatial metaphors.

The insolubility is played down, mocked by Robin Goodfellow in the last words, who asks the audience to "Think ... this weak and idle theme, No more yielding but a dream" (V,i,413-417). And to his main relegation of "all" to the visions of *mere* slumber, he himself counters by concluding with a quasi-religious and judicial category, "restore amends" (427), that subverts the play-reality opposition of this conventional epilogue. Puck's conventional language keeps to a middle distance between the gorgeous poetry of the play and the failed poetry of the play-within-the-play, tuning-down while pretending-to-tune-out. His comparable relegation of the main mystery of the play to simple proverbial wisdom makes sense only indirectly through the roundabout procedure of the dreams in the forest. The pyrotechnic diversities link themselves in by the very act of counting themselves out, and the inadequacy of the summation, at any point and in any style here, includes adequacy as its glimpsed underside, the possibility of an enchantment that does come out all right! This prediction is made, and contradicted, as the active enchanter squeezes juice on the recalcitrant lover's eyes:

> And the country proverb known,
> That every man should take his own,
> In your waking shall be shown.
> Jack shall have Jill;
> Nought shall go ill;
> The man shall have his mare again, and all shall be well

III,ii,458-463

Such splendid counterpointing of divergences requires an implied breadth of signification to carry off.

How smoothly Shakespeare manages his melding may appear by contrasting *A Midsummer Night's Dream* with *The Malcontent* in which Marston has not quite held the discordancies together.

In *The Malcontent* there is an abrupt change of pace at the beginning (I,iii) when Piero intrudes a question upon the amplification of Malevole's satiric flyting and gets a sudden abrupt answer, "You're a cuckold." This particular rhetorical shift mimes the shift presented in the whole play, where a brooding despair, voiced in those speeches and picked up last in the comments of Maquarelle and Bilioso, is countered by an actual success. The elaborate revenge mechanism is suddenly displaced, in Christian charity and courtly scorn, by another of Malevole's odd shorter speeches, "An eagle takes not flies" (V,iv,226).

In his person Malevole fuses six types, the Melancholic, the Satiric, the Vice, the Fool, the Courtier, and the Absent Demiurge (a type to which the Duke in *Measure for Measure* and Prospero in *The Tempest* also belong). The final change in rhythm charges the reassignment of the play's sense from one order of meaning, expressed by the first two or three roles, to another, expressed by the last two or three. The audience of this play cannot be sure whether to laugh or to ponder; satire stands on the border between comedy and tragedy, but here even satire, in the hands of a playwright who is also a satirist, will not stand still to compose its order.

Shakespeare makes divergence in time, a change of pacing, yield signification by not letting the auditor's perceptions relax in a uniform pace. The gradual modification of tempos in *Hamlet* has often been noticed. It goes right to the very end. The last sound in that play is not a speech but the ordnance of Fortinbras, a ceremonial peal referring to an order of dominance. Its ostensible purpose is to honor the dead Hamlet, but it cannot fail to remind the populace, marshalled under a new order in which they will have less say than when in the recent past they could give their voice to Laertes, what the main purpose of those guns was. The double purpose of honor/dominance takes over, and changes the rhythm of all the double purposes and cross-purposes that had been sustained and worked out in the action of the play. The ordnance delicately seals the conquest by asserting in the take-over of rule a continuity that in fact constitutes a full break in continuity. The ordnance burst is a final change of rhythm accompanying a change in order, a sudden capping *stretto*.

Or again, there is a divergence between the distantly glimpsed normal tempos in the Scotland of *Macbeth*, Duncan's ceremonial winding down in relief at the war's conclusion, and the feverishness of activity transposed by Macbeth from the war, where it is decorous, to the normal life where it is not.

Macbeth maintains a headlong pace throughout, partly by the atmospheric device of the witches who, dim in the present, dimly foresee the future, thus compressing time; partly by the hurly-burly of its tone-setting first scene; partly by Macbeth's own predilection for verbalizing his unsteadiness before the abyss. The whole play has the air of Doctor Faustus' last hour. It "imitates a desperate race," as Francis Fergusson shows, even in the Porter scene, "a farcical and terrible version of 'outrunning reason.'" "This is partly a matter of the speed with which the main facts are presented," he says; "partly the effect of simultaneous movements like those of a race: Lady Macbeth is reading the letter at the same moment that her husband and Duncan are rushing toward her."[24] This relatively short play compresses the future into the past till each yawns with the other—an order of evil that is neither open nor closed, a temporality that gets nowhere, like Macbeth's dynasty; and it is also endless, "tomorrow and tomorrow and tomorrow," the way the dynasty of Banquo is to proceed king after king after king.

The varied registers of language and style are brought into powerful harmony, and so are divergences of person and action. Beyond these the action may undergo the perspectival sharpening of a special slant by being framed in what seem to be inappropriate words, as "Pyramus and Thisbe" comes across the stage in a language so inappropriate to tragedy that it interacts with as well as serves a comic vision. In *Cymbeline* the action is elaborated into ironically contrastive patterns, so dominantly that the verse pales before it, or is made at the most intense moments to seem to do so, becoming "awkward" and "wooden" in the face of mechanisms it becomes the business of the language not so much to control as to falter before—a puzzling function for verse in a verse drama.

In *King Lear* the pressure of the end would seem to have exhausted language into formulaic patness, "I have a journey, sir, shortly to go. My master calls me; I must not say no" (V,iii,321-322), or into a taciturnity bordering on inarticulateness before the last things of death, "Pray you undo this button," "Never, never, never, never, never" (309, 308).

Throughout *King Lear*, indeed, the action diverges from the words. An effect of triumph under extreme odds and tragically partial restoration after heavy cataclysm is achieved over, beyond, and against, much that the characters say, as well as over and beyond what they do.

The utterance of the characters, and the guiding ideas around which their words are shaped, express, as William Elton has shown us, some deep bias away from the Christian orthodoxy of the time.[25] One of Shakespeare's main revisions of his source, the old *King Leir*, has been to purge it of its lengthy pious reflections, to change its "God" to the pagan gods, a change not wholly to be explained by adherence to ordinances of James I.[26] Goneril, Regan, and Edmund, as Elton tries to demonstrate, prefigure Hobbes' notion of universal hostility, subscribing to the "chaos of quantity" in their expression of pagan atheism. Gloucester, in his subjection to astrology, voices pagan superstition, while Lear himself, invoking Hecate, the Sun, the Moon, and "Nature . . . dear Goddess" (I,iv,275), speaks of himself as operating under a miscellany of animistic forces. His invocation to the "heavens" suggests the inscrutable Calvinist God, the *Deus Absconditus;* but his declaration to Cordelia, "Nothing will come of nothing. Speak again" (I,i,89), casually comes down on the pagan side of a well-known Christian crux. Generally his remarks, like those of others, accuse providence of either injustice or the kind of unconcern that was associated at the time with Epicurean doctrine. At their most pious, Elton asserts, these characters only show the *prisca theologia* of the "virtuous heathen," and the language even of Cordelia and Edgar has the tinge of non-Christian *sapientia* and *pietas,* a heavy tinge of semi-Stoicism, as in the command to "endure" one's "going hence" which culminates in Edgar's famous aphorism "Ripeness is all," a blend of Stoicism and Christianity. There is at best a submissiveness to an undefined providence in Cordelia's formulation:

> We are not the first
> Who with best meaning have incurr'd the worst.
> For thee, oppressed King, am I cast down;
> Myself could else out-frown false Fortune's frown.
> Shall we not see these daughters and these sisters?
>
> (V,iii,3-7)

As often as not, Elton has shown us, what the characters say pungently rephrases currents of ideas which at the time contraverted the common orthodoxy, or at least did not rise to it. "Fortune" is not the grace of God. Popular superstition about demonic possession, in Edgar's feigning of a man inhabited by devils, is shown to be a fraud: the phrases taken from Harsnett's *A Declaration of Egregious Popish Impostures* (1603) are cast in a light that undermines them.

At the same time, though Harsnett's phrases jibe profoundly with the action of the play. For these devils of Harsnett are said to have induced Edgar, the false serving man become poor Tom, to do the very "work of darkness" that will be the undoing of Edmund, Goneril, and Regan, all three, before it is even achieved. And the hysterical distraction of foolery in Edgar's pretending to be the way his brother—and his father!—really are, finds a more solemn, more desperate echo in the prophetic ring of Lear's excoriations of women's lechery:

> Down from the waist they are centaurs,
> Though women all above;
> But to the girdle do the gods inherit,
> Beneath is all the fiends';
> There's hell, there's darkness, there is the sulphurous pit—
>
> (IV,vi,124-28)

Something diabolical, then, is said to remain to harry human beings, something not distinguished from or at least not in contradiction to Harsnett's subject matter. The reality behind Mad Lear's conviction of diabolical possession qualifies the desperate make-believe of Edgar's.

By and large, then, the ideas these characters express go counter to Christian doctrine, and against any hush before the ways of Providence. And yet the events of the play often narrow them away from the bald statement of a motivating Stoicism or *prisca theologia* or animistic paganism. To the extent of this stir, the events drive them beyond many of the ideas they express: we have to hear their tones to catch the gist of what they are most deeply saying. That, in turn, is more fully assimilable to a Christian climate of feeling, and still more fully because the feeling rising from the events for the characters, and for us, wells up beyond their formulations.[27]

The action and the words, then, do not simply repeat one another. Rather, they work to some extent at cross-purposes, and it is the action, and the feeling arising from the action, that prevails. The widening frame of the spectator's perception must take in a dislocation of the events from the very words of the play.

And yet on the other hand, if we take the events without the characters' responses, the action without the reactions, verbal and other, we will shrink the range of the play in the opposite direction:

> By revealing the intrigue to Cornwall [Edmund] destroys his father and attains his titles and lands. This is the culmination of his original plot.
>
> Gloucester is blinded, Cornwall slain, the French Army landed at Dover, Goneril and Regan vie for Edmund's favor, and Albany comes to the side of the good. Oswald, carrying a letter from Goneril to Edmund, runs across Gloucester, is slain by the disguised Edgar, and the crucial error of the plot occurs—Edgar finds on Oswald's body Goneril's letter. This leads to the unloosing of the knot of the play. . . The death of Gloucester is announced, and then on the repentance of Edmund, who discloses

his plot against Lear and Cordelia, his orders are recalled. But it is too late. Cordelia is dead, and Lear soon dies. This is hardly the story of the psychological development of Lear and Gloucester.[28]

Or it would not be that story, if the characters acted out the events in a dumb show without responding to them. Since they do respond, they do develop psychologically, they are made to plumb tonalities of utterance, and one may take Cunningham's insistent summary of the events as a corrective to the overpreoccupation of a reader (but not of a viewer) with the mere expression of sentiment and idea.

The actions are always stretching the characters into utterances whose disjunctions from what they are trying to voice throws their whole being, momentary words and overall actions, into a fuller dimensionality. As L. C. Knights puts it, "Now if there is one truth that the play brings home with superb force it is that neither man's reason nor his powers of perception function in isolation from the rest of his personality; *quantum sumus, scimus. How* Lear feels, in short, is as important as *what* he feels, for the final 'seeing' is inseparable from what he has come to be."[29] The sum of words, the *"scimus"* of verbalization, is the more forcibly dramatic in its relation to the sum of acts, *"quantum sumus,"* because at no point do the words sum up the acts. The verbal bravura of *Hamlet* has undergone profound distortion, where the words sustain and reaffirm the actions, as much as in Sophocles and Racine, though through a variety of tempos and a plethora of styles rather than in the single uniform style of Racine, the double one (dialogue and choruses) of Sophocles.

As the actor rises to bringing the pith of his utterance to recitative prominence, the events are overtaking him:

EDGAR:
        Tom's a-cold.
GLOUCESTER:
        In, fellow, there, into th' hovel; keep three warm.

                                        (III,iv,169-170)

This plainly stated interchange of words is meshed in a complexity of event comparable to that to which the later, splendid interchanges between Lear and Cordelia are still not fully equal. Son recognizes father, really shivering as he pretends to shiver. Father produces the automatic gesture of charity to the mad stranger which he had selfishly withheld from the son he does not here recognize. They are not ripe for the searing complexities of their recognition; the father still possesses his physical eyes, the son still stands under interdict of death from his father. The momentary small motions of haste, getting shelter from the storm and sanctuary from pursuit, have no predictable causal relation to the resolution, which will move at an even speed to sudden culmination. Now the words of the father, as he gathers Fool and disguised courtier and scorned king and hidden son, merely attest to the piety of prudence which, as we demonstrably see, will fall short and yet somehow be adequate; the disparity between the short range and the long for the characters, and the spectator, is exhibited in the disparity between the words and the action.

Words are all they have, and the best of words will not quite do in the face of these events. The mightiness of the represented struggle produces not just a sense of what is primary in human life, and not just a sense of how persistently formulations will be displaced from the primary, but how life itself, whatever may be said on stage, may yield in the process of asserting, by dumb deed, the primacy of the primary.

The pressure of the events is extreme. Lear makes the initial, as he thinks final, gesture of relinquishing his kingdom so he may "unburden'd crawl toward death" (I,i,40), and he unleashes a sequence of events that makes him live through more in a short space than he has in all his eighty years. The same is true for all the others, as Albany (to follow the Quarto reading) says in the last lines of the play:

> The oldest hath borne most: we that are young
> Shall never see so much nor live so long.
>
> (V,iii,325-326) [30]

It is the death of his daughter that shocks Lear into his own death
—added perhaps to his exertion in killing "the slave that was
a-hanging thee" (V,iii,274). Lear and Gloucester have both died,
in fact, not by being murdered—the common and nearly universal
cause of death in tragedy—but of heartbreak. This does not happen till they have risen to a greater nobility than either had manifested in a lifetime Lear had given over to childish willfulness
and Gloucester to capricious lechery. They die "providentially,"
by reaction to a sequence of events that the play has set before
our eyes. Both have survived the military order for their death.
Both have survived physical disasters mortally dangerous to old
men. Both have gone through the psychodrama of false death,
Gloucester in his false suicide leap from the cliff of Dover, when
he takes his good son to have been something like a fiend come
to carry his soul to hell, and Lear after a curative sleep, who presumes he has died into a hell from which he views a saved Cordelia.

> You do me wrong to take me out o' th' grave.
> Thou art a soul in bliss; but I am bound
> Upon a wheel of fire, that mine own tears
> Do scald like molten lead.
>
> (IV,vii,45-8)

At that point the verse, though still falling short of the action, can
still exhibit a serenity and lustre. The end of the series is so mas-
sively cumulative that it not only reduces the characters to simplicity of utterance but has the effect of hushing the little they do
say by the momentousness of the whole overwhelming past.

The distracted, very last words of Lear take hope from seeming to see life in the dead body: "Look, her lips. Look there, look
there!" At the end he cannot say enough, can say almost nothing.
To start up even so briefly has proved to be fatal. But, with a difference of rhythm that matches the mighty swiftness and central
stress of what he has been through, the words in this same scene
that describe the end of Gloucester are not inappropriate to the
end of Lear:

> But his flaw'd heart—
> Alack, too weak the conflict to support!—
> 'Twixt two extremes of passion,[31] joy and grief,
> Burst smilingly.
>
> (V,iii,196-99)

In this final image, of course, grief preponderates over joy in the language—"woeful" (202), "sorrow" (205), "and top extremity" (207), "grief grew puissant" (216), to go no farther than the description of Gloucester himself.

Lear's response is mortally deep, though silent. He is no longer speaking of his own imminent death. The Shakespearian protagonist, Lear or Othello or Hamlet or Coriolanus, shows characteristically a total and wholehearted response to the immediate action, "Affection! Thy intention stabs the centre" (*The Winter's Tale*, I,ii,138). Pericles speaks of fearing to die from excess of joy:

> O Helicanus, strike me, honour'd sir;
> Give me a gash, put me to present pain,
> Lest this great sea of joys rushing upon me
> O'erbear the shores of my mortality,
> And drown me with their sweetness.
>
> (V,i,189-193)

Edgar's hysteria in the storm scenes derives from his discomfort with his disguise. Lear's prophetic utterances are occasioned by a madness resulting from the unbearable grief of facing his daughters' hostility to him.

We ourselves are responding to the characters' responses.[32] Shakespeare sets a train of events in motion that powerfully shake the spectator. As Pope puts it, "The *Power* over our *Passions* was never possess'd in a more eminent degree, or display'd in so different instances."[33]

What we see on this stage, taken by itself, appeals to our sympathy without further recourse: the image of an old man shut out into the storm by his self-sheltering daughter harrows us with fear and wonder. This primitive sympathy of the audience, while culture-bound, must be assumed as a reaction to the image on stage, not to what the characters say. Any sense we have that Lear is misguided and capricious will not blunt our horror at the treatment his daughters give him, though spectators in a culture like the African tribe that kills an old man every time a baby is born, or the one that kills the king when he reaches a certain age, or the Plains Indian tribe that exposes and abandons the old and the sick, would not so respond. It may be felt that the mythic aura of the play, heightened by its setting in a pre-Christian and pre-Roman Britain, touches in us some memory akin to the callousness of these tribes, some magic of survival and order and deference to mortality connected with the taboo on old age that McFarland strikingly attributes to Lear's situation.[34] And still our sympathy is aroused, our deep aversions are redirected toward attentive pity.

Similarly, in the Renaissance world of dutiful daughters and decorous women, we *must* pity Cordelia as she is refused her share of the kingdom, and we must feel in France a generosity akin to that of the knight rescuing a maiden in distress— a generosity that gains its full dramatic scope when he takes arms against his sisters-in-law. Moreover, we are put in a position of silently backing Kent, who voices our elemental reactions when he begs the king not to shut Cordelia out of the inheritance. Just like the children who shriek to the Guignol to watch out for the man behind him with a club,[35] we are, as it were, tempted to shout "Can't you see that those glib daughters are flatterers who mean you no good? Can't you see the silent daughter really loves you?" This edge-of-the-seat response derives from no cues of language or action, other than such an elemental reaction to a fellow creature's unawareness to danger, beyond our fairy-tale expectation that the youngest of three daughters is the truly saintly one while older sisters conceal a wicked purpose beneath their jostling forcefulness. Other deep echoes may be reverberating in us too, the particular Freudian family patterns, and special evocations bearing on the realm of death that tragedy tends to address. "Freud gives evidence from fairy tales . . . apropos of Cordelia, that dumb-ness is to be understood as representing death . . . a Goddess of Death."[36] On this cue, inarticulateness, or failed articulation, would then be suggesting something that the mood of the play would carry because only the figures in it, neither their words nor their actions, could stand for that.

The sense of these sympathies, prime to the play, must be expanded through the play: our pity for the Fool is intensified by our knowledge of the staunchness of his decision to follow his expelled master, abandoning the very self-serving prudence his aphorisms prove him alertly aware of. So, too, our pity for Kent gains force from his earlier banishment. He does not yet have the satisfaction, since he is technically under sentence of death from the very Lear he is serving, of having his master see him and recognize his devotion. Nor will he ever have that satisfaction; the pattern of our responses will include closing that joy off in disappointment when he begs Cordelia to let him choose the optimum moment for self-revelation, a moment that gets caught up and shuffled past in the cosmic reactions of a preparation for death not only by the master who seems indifferent to the revelation, but by Kent himself ("I have a journey, sir, shortly to go./ My master calls me; I must not say no" V,iii,321-322). With these words he is making the capital gesture of resigning co-rulership in the kingdom. So Edgar arouses our pity by being driven to a still greater succinctness and dark obliquity of utterance in the presence of the father who has wronged him; to whom, later on, he will prove his life-saving, charitably dutiful attention. So our reaction to Gloucester's callousness and foolishness changes once we see the resoluteness with which he brings danger on himself in order to help the outcasts. The same father who impatiently translated his vexation with this very Edgar into a death sentence on him ("Not in this land shall he remain uncaught;/And found—dispatch" II,i,57-58) is brought into the sphere of Edgar's charity, and ours, by risking his life for the king.

The words spoken on stage must be of the present moment. The events that give rise to them, and to which they give rise, must be of both past and future, assuming that there is any kind of coherence to the play. The Fool, visionary beyond the prudence of his earlier allegories, glances at the endless recursiveness of sequence:

> This prophecy Merlin shall make, for I live before his time.
> (III,ii,95)

There is, to begin with, a type of mad fool in the forest wilderness, as Enid Welsford points out.[37] The Arthurian kingdom, with its forest of Broceliande, is a considerably more ordered wilderness than the one Lear inhabits, than the heath on which he roams. And it is also future to the play we are beholding, a fact the Fool prophetically ventures on. In such a pregnant jumble we cannot refer his assertion just to a metatheatrical framing. He triggers an anachronistic series, the real Lear being before the time of the play. The utterance rides a mighty prophetic wind of millennial compass, sailing past the events we see, but not past the meaning they thus touch upon, by suggesting that the sequence will bear a more powerful permutation even than those we behold.

Lear himself reaches for the prophetic note in visualizing an impossible future as a way of outsoaring in serenity, babbling in disjunction from, the command that will be superseded as fully as the fantasy:

EDMUND:
>   Take them away.

LEAR:
> Upon such sacrifices, my Cordelia,
> The gods themselves throw incense. Have I caught thee?
> He that parts us shall bring a brand from heaven
> And fire us hence like foxes. Wipe thine eyes;
> The good years shall devour them, flesh and fell,
> Ere they shall make us weep. We'll see 'em starv'd first.
> (V,iii,19-25)

While Lear is here recapitulating his old cycle from resignation to anger, his *saeva indignatio* is purged by a vision making those who have actively sacrificed (Cordelia having left her kingdom to help her father; he having given up military hope in the stated resignation) into passive sacrifices. In the process he turns the polytheistic gods into something like Christian worshippers; "the gods themselves throw incense" is not far from the iconography of Renaissance paintings in which angels swing censers. He apocalyptically scans Biblical history in proper sequence and item by item, "Jephtha's daughter, who was sacrificed, and of the destruction of Sodom by a brand from heaven, of Samson and the foxes, of Pharaoh's dream of the good and bad years."[38]

He who speaks is the blissfully reunited king being led away prisoner; and his words echo in the context of our quickened, exercised joy and pity at that image, as by its relation to the earlier images of Lear's tribulations and madness, the final one of his all-but-despairing death.

The biblical undertones, for all the firmness and range of their structure, remain triply undertones: to his statements here about the bold officer of the present and future, to his earlier utterances that rage without this vision and control, and to his later bareness of statement, stripped of all these possibilities. The movement from this equipoise of plural reference to the last near-inarticulateness is one of contraction, but after an incredible expansion.

The resurgence of the action, its silent progress, strains the words in other plays too. In *Timon of Athens* the words interlock a sequence generosity-misanthropy with a spectrum sycophancy-honesty. The actions, on the other hand, run a somewhat different course, from lavish giving, to the depletion of a fortune, to death, and from exile to military conquest. So the central figure plays a role in the lives of the somewhat allegorized characters that transcends what the words say, even though the words are especially reflective in their constant attempt to define. The effect is, again, of a simplicity that strangely cannot enter the perceptions of any single character.

In *Troilus and Cressida*, the noble feelings of Troilus, and his sorry fate too, undercut that pervasive cynicism of the Pandarus who has at the same time been guiding his love. In the life of war Hector is the more noble for having Achilles' treachery belie the resigned realism of his willingness to fight, and Achilles is the more debased for the contrast between his braggadocio and his foul play. Here words and actions play back and forth more easily against each other, as they do in *Hamlet*. Hamlet would seem to be saying too much and doing nothing; there is a sense in which all he says is a smokescreen, and also a sense in which it is a delaying mechanism. Meanwhile he does stage the play, trip Rosencrantz and Guildenstern, and strike bluntly through the arras before a soliloquizing appeal to his mother under circumstances when the drift of the words do not suggest the kind of man who will be taking so direct an action. The effect of evil is to isolate everyone in his protestations, to dissociate words from action, to make the most sublime utterances ineffectual, and not just for Hamlet himself, though chiefly for him. Words converge with actions only at the verge of the duel, and then they can do no more than theologize resignation; after the duel they can only point at a future story while the real action that takes over is military, provided with a decorous set of words for this occasion of conquest, as for any.

The voice of command does not ring unchallenged, even in the history plays.

If now and then Shakespeare echoes this or that idea of Montaigne, he may also be said to parallel Montaigne's intellectual procedure in the mastered divergences of his stylistic options, and of his events, and of the interaction between words and events. Montaigne was not so much interested in the testability of ideas, the usual philosopher's preoccupation, as in their suggestiveness. And the effect of Shakespeare's off-glancing words is a powerful suggestiveness. Looked at up close, a statement has a succinct thesis, as do the parts of Montaigne's *Apologie*. Looked at in context, statements iridesce in exemplification of an *esprit ondoyant et divers*, producing in idea something of the openness that Shakespeare manages by keeping his words so fluid in their relation to action that they may not even be said to evidence "disjunction," the words having one kind of order and their center of reference another, as Sylvester reads the *Masque of Blacknesse* and *The Faerie Queene*.[39] Spenser's refined style permits endless fluidities of "mutability" on a fixed base of rhythm and reference. We are at every point stable in granting it the license of its make-believe. Shakespeare bypasses such a contractual certitude between himself and his viewers by keeping his words alive to the quick with the possibility of stretching their contract, a possibility enacted before us.

TWO
The Sounding of the Theme

The staple of the playwright's inherited forms will include both words and actions,[1] not only the language he writes in—Renaissance English for Shakespeare—and not only that special case of speaker-auditor codes we refer to when we say "Jacobean stage." His inherited forms will also include various other conventions or traditions. For example, the playwright's sharing of locale with bear-baiters and cruising prostitutes, the expectation that he will be entertaining, the assimilation of the play-form to other group forms of festival celebration and the increase of plays on the calendar during festivals, the similarity of his status as servant-entertainer for a nobleman to that of the old court fool, the coexistence of such forms as masque and *commedia dell'arte*—all these factors bear on the Renaissance playwright's tendency to put clowns even in tragic plays. There is a clown even in *Othello*, a play whose somber contemplation, of how the noble may be brought low and how the pure may be called on to die heartbreakingly, is unrelieved by any Horatio or Kent, Macduff or Aufidius. Yet this play has room for a clown. A glance at other traditions—at the Noh, or the Greek classical, or the French Renaissance theatre—will provide a tentative historical measure of incongruity for the clown's presence in a tragedy, an incongruity that both historical and thematic interpretation can explain only if they begin by refusing to explain it away.

There are staple figures in this theatre other than the clown. To stay with *Othello,* Iago constitutes an adaptation towards malevolence of the Vice.[2] Emilia is the staple figure of the maid. And many others may be regarded as either types or staple figures depending on whether one locates them in a social repertoire or in a dramatic convention. Cassio is the staple figure of the stage courtier as well as the type young nobleman. In Roderigo's gull,

Bianca's prostitute, Brabantio's outraged father, Gratiano's helpful kinsman, Othello's statesmanly general, and Desdemona's innocent bride, we see staple figures that the playwright has inherited from his theatre as well as types from the society of the time—we find *langue dramatique* as well as *parole*. Scratch further and still other types may be found underlying our characters. Othello is the type Moor in the type situation of noble ally; Reuben Brower convincingly shows him as a function of the type stoic hero and the type corrupted saint.[3] McFarland finds the Pantalone, too, underlying him, the middle-aged husband betrayed in spite of his physical stoutness.[4]

The Pantalone is not only a character. He exists in a plot that is also a staple inherited form, one McFarland professes also to find in *Othello*: the plot of December marrying May. Cross the *commedia dell'arte* with tragedy, which is itself a convention, and the adulterous wife becomes an innocent bride, the jealous cuckold a mighty man ruining himself in self-deception. Still deeper in the play may reside actions still more archetypal—that of the faithless disciple's punishment, of the king's sacrifice, of the sad reconsecration after loss (a pattern to which nearly all Shakespeare's tragedies conform, *Hamlet* and *Macbeth* and *Lear* and *Coriolanus* and even *Timon* as well as *Othello*).

The archetypal element in these plots, their mythic extensibility, remains a substratum in the linguistic and social context of the Renaissance theatre. The Greek dramatist enlists and transposes a charged power by redeploying through structures of statement and reason (*logos*) the force inherent in codified archetypal event (*mythos*). Since the persons in Greek myths held the status of something like public religious figures, and since the events involving them were the manifest content of any play about them, they function in a more transparent modality in Greek plays than do the latent myths in Renaissance plays. This latency, as much as the technical fact that the outcome of the events was not necessarily known to Shakespeare's audience as it was to Sophocles' (unless the playwright chose to show them a Julius Caesar or an Antony and a Cleopatra), gives the movement of mythic patterning a much freer forward thrust on the Renaissance stage. Mythic echoes that Othello wakens he wakens dimly, and what will become of him we cannot know until it happens.

For Sophocles, in other words, the myth permits the superego squarely to purge the monstrosities possible in a sort of undifferentiated id. The myth surfaces into daylight as its known story comes to event after event of the sequential tale. In Shakespeare the myth remains buried in a darkness which may be associated with the unconscious. The Oedipal monstrosities cannot centralize. Their dynamism remains a constant subliminal presence causing the ego to expand towards and shade away from the ego-ideal.

Consequently the Renaissance playwright is free to do anything with the myth but what Sophocles does. The Racine who opts for the Sophoclean coherence locks the manifestness of the myth into a rich fictive dialectic; religion is on a tangent to the play, not at its center, as in Greek plays. Holding it in that position constitutes itself an idea.

Shakespeare, in his convention of free combination, redeploys not only staple characters and plots but also the ideas at his disposal. These ideas were not just in the air of his time; they existed in the virtually codified form of dramatic counters.

The accident that the classical playwright whose works were most accessible to his theatre was also a Stoic philosopher created some expectation that the tragic playwright would exhibit Stoic notions, even if only to filter them. Of course, Stoic ideas were in the air elsewhere than in the plays of Seneca, but not so preponderantly as they appear in the tragedies written in the first decade of the seventeenth century. These ideas may be deformed or contraverted more than some critics allow; but their presence is dominant enough, and conventional enough, to constitute something more fixed in the dramatic vocabulary than a notion the writer happened to pick up. Montaigne provides such bright ideas, whereas Seneca's have already undergone a codification that matches the assimilation of his style, tone, and extravagant procedures.[5]

I exaggerate this distinction somewhat: it would be unprofitable at best, and perhaps impossible, to ascertain exactly at what point a bright idea has hardened into a codified counter, or even to offer a system of Derrida-like deconstructions, in which the distinction would be an inessential one. Yet the way playwrights in this theatre have recourse even to Christian ideas differs from the way they include Senecan Stoicism in their plays.[6] We may say that they are obliged to be Christian all the time but Stoic only on the stage. The codification in a sense frees them to seem Stoic without being so. Machiavelli, too, would seem to have undergone codification so thoroughly that his ideas rarely receive the explicit exposition given them by that author himself in the prologue to *The Jew of Malta.* His postulates dominate the political counters of this stage as much as Freud dominates the sexual counters of our own.

Certainly *The Prince* speaks often of military action and generalship, of managing one's underlings and being careful about reward structures, of employing mercenaries, and of the risk involved in hiring a strong general not of your own city. His illustrations are drawn heavily from the Italian city-states Othello has come to be serving. And in the light of all this, Othello may well be, as McFarland asserts, Shakespeare's most explicitly Machiavellian character.[7] Still, he has lots of competition for that honor, and to say that *Othello* may at the same time be Shakespeare's least Machiavellian tragedy would help throw into relief how pervasively the dramatic counters of Machiavelli are moved on this stage.

Now Shakespeare transforms utterly the staple forms he has received and does so in the interest of at once founding his people on deeper bases and riddling their actions with a more mysterious dynamism. So he does with one large staple form which stands behind *Othello,* a form that comprises characters, and plots, and ideas, all together. This form can best be phrased as an assumption, one so inclusive that it generates *plots* and *characters* while governing the topics on which *ideas* will be brought to bear. This assumption has of course been picked up by critics. It is a commonplace of modern discussion about Renaissance tragedy. But to call this assumption a "revenge" convention, not only confines it to a somewhat smaller group of plays than those it actually informs or governs. The term "revenge" also slants towards males an action that equally, and crucially, involves females, while substituting one point of common response—to seek revenge—for the whole situation in which it occurs. We can get the situation without the response. Revenge is a convention *within* the situation. More importantly, the term "revenge" obscures Shakespeare's transformation of the assumed convention.

The assumption is simply this: Persons who are nobles adhering to a court—the very persons from whom nearly all leading characters in Jacobean plays are drawn—will look and act like courtiers. In addition to being handsome, skilled, polite, and eloquent, they will seek their own ends in the spheres of love and politics. In the sphere of love, attractive people with time on their hands will seek the end of new erotic interests, and their self-interest will be such (perhaps an adapted Machiavellian point) that neither marital loyalty nor the fear of eternal damnation will prevent them from doing so. The conflict of interests will tend to permute: If A loves B, then C, her spouse or prior lover or spurned suitor, will seek vengeance; and this complication complicates still further because it tends to enlist collateral lovers and to permute their complications therein. Moreover, these courtiers will also seek their own interests in politics: the skill and the equality of the participants will be such as to keep any political situation complex and unstable. Furthermore, the erotic complications will permute with the political ones to overdetermine the tendency towards increased complexity. That tendency is assumed to be so dominant that only massive deaths can halt it.

This formula, as phrased, sounds so general as to be trite. But it is specific enough to describe the pattern of a large share of tragedies on the Jacobean stage. It is specific enough also to diverge clearly from Seneca, whose plays, except for *Octavia*,[8] do not center on sexual rivalry; nor do the political actions in his plays exhibit any of the Machiavellian checks and balances.

The most unprincipled character in *The White Devil*, Vittoria's brother Flaminio, describes himself as corrupted by this assumption:

> I visited the court, whence I returned
> More courteous, more lecherous by far...
> We are engaged to mischief, and must on.
> $\qquad$ (*White Devil,* I,ii,312-3; 333)

Here "mischief" is indifferently sexual or political, in this play and elsewhere. In *The Revenger's Tragedy*, outlandish sexual intrigue keeps pace with the cunning contrivances of revenge.

Not only Kyd in *The Spanish Tragedy*, but once the main Jacobean strain has expressed itself, all the playwrights return to this assumption, Middleton and Marston no less than Chapman and Webster and Tourneur, Fletcher and Ford and Massinger and Shirley as well.[9] It is clearly traceable in them, whereas some feats of special pleading are necessary to turn even Chapman into a Stoic. *A Woman Killed with Kindness* and *The Broken Heart* ring changes on it. In *Edward II* it does not stop at the barrier of inversion to produce its complications. It provides a base on which the contrast can rest, as expressed in the title of *'Tis a Pity She's a Whore*. It gives point to the sexual and social aspirations parodied in *Cynthia's Revels* and *The Poetaster*. "Court gallants court, suck amorous dalliance" declares Marston in *What You Will*, who will shortly leave the significantly titled *Insatiate Countess* uncompleted and retire to life as a priest. The staple Jacobean assumption lies behind the action, and perhaps also the odd choice of subject, in Jonson's *Catiline*, where a lecherous-political woman, Fulvia, serves as the hypocritical link between the Conspirators and Cicero, for whom she chooses a strategic moment to reveal a shocking detail about her ambitious lover. Webster and Rowley's *Cure for a Cuckold*, Marston's *The Dutch Courtezan*, and Massinger's *Parliament of Love*, have the common plot of murderous strife set off by a fickle woman among her several lovers.[10] In *The Maid of Honor* two knights of Malta pursue erotic fulfillment, against their vows of chastity, as they engage in political struggle.

The theatre, as an enchanted, open area of social space, tends towards a reversal of the normal conditions of life: the danger of death may operate as constantly on stage as it does infrequently in the life outside the theatre. So the response to the adulteries or amorous intrigues of nobles and ladies-in-waiting at the time indicates by its strength that such sexual activity, while a constant temptation, was something of a deviation, dangerous when it occurred in the actual life of the court.[11] On the stage the danger becomes constant. Spectatorship, with its psychological roots in the sexual curiosity of children, is drawn towards the sensational. The staple assumption of the Jacobean theatre mediates that sensation and philosophizes it by taking an initial knowing stance towards the possibilities of courtly intrigue.

Now Shakespeare is for the most part alone among his contemporaries for going almost always against the grain of this staple assumption. He does present it, more unremittingly than anyone, with no opportunity even on the battlefield for revenge, in *Troilus and Cressida*. And *Titus Andronicus*, which begins with the result of a political-sexual intrigue, not only out-Senecas Seneca in violence but also carries the staple assumption to the implied contradiction of barbaric extremity in the rape and mutilation of Lavinia—as though Laclos had been purged by being rendered as de Sade.

Shakespeare does come to register the incursions of the staple Jacobean assumption almost concurrently with its taking on standardization, about 1600. But always he deforms and reforms it.[12] In *Hamlet* the causal sequence between ambition and adultery has been blurred; we do not know whether Claudius first loved and then aspired, or first aspired and then loved. The single act has brought its chain of connection to a full stop in any case, and the play deforms the assumption by concerning itself entirely with the devastating aftermath in the psyches of the participants. For Hamlet himself the direct erotic interest is pre-marital; both he and Ophelia are eligible. There are no rivals. And that sphere degenerates into hysteria, while the ambitious side of the Jacobean assumption has been separated off in the person of Fortinbras, who knows nothing of all this erotic activity. *Measure for Measure* displaces the assumption downward in a kind of nightmare commonwealth where fornication is punishable by death and yet prostitution flourishes.[13]

Macbeth presents ambition as a function not of adultery but of a sexual psychology in which a forceful military man, surprisingly but accurately, exhibits a submissiveness to his wife, while she cracks in the long run from the rigidity of sustaining her dominance. He feels all the blood he has shed; she only that which it took her unnatural dominance to make flow. Here a sexual pathology which will provide a center of interest for Webster, Middleton, and Tourneur remains an undercurrent, and since Macbeth is married, one divergent from the staple assumption those playwrights embrace.

The consequences of such an assumption are presented almost at the outset of *King Lear*. We hear about Edmund's "breeding" in the second response (I,i,8), before Cordelia and her sisters appear. For Regan and Goneril, ambition brings, in accordance with the assumption, the ambition to adultery—or to lustful remarriage. But they are frustrated by focusing on the same object, Edmund himself. Goneril's amorous assertions have the ring of Vittoria Corambona's, but no act takes place: the discovery of just one love letter of the two transmitted on the battlefield occasions the downfall of all the evil forces, and the Jacobean assumption serves here as the consequence of ambitious evildoing, rather than as its necessary cause, as an extreme of insensitive behavior rather than as a normal, if culpable, index of courtly sensitivity. "Why have my sisters husbands?" (I,i,98), Cordelia asks, and the paradigm of pretended sensitivity masking insensitivity applies first to a parent before it extends to a proposed lover. Her question gathers force through the play on a line that remains only a tangent to the staple Jacobean assumption.

Cordelia's innocence is so energized as to produce a void of horror around the machinations of her sisters, and around their sexuality. When sexuality stands at the center of the play, Shakespeare characteristically energizes the Jacobean assumption about it into a void by setting a serene presence of chastity at the deeper center. In *The Winter's Tale*, in *Cymbeline*, in *Much Ado About Nothing*, as in *Othello*, the false accusation of a single adultery stirs up a whirlwind of action that the calm of chastity stands up against, even though the world is turned upside down and everyone is profoundly harrowed. It is against Troilus', and our own, encompassing disappointment that the ideal of fidelity has gone under, that the grimness of the play's devastating upheavals is set. In the light of that measure does Shakespeare's satiric cynicism differ from Marston's.

Othello—a play with a false adultery, two presumptive ones, the aspiration to another, and a casual amour—deeply redefines this ground of the staple assumption, in the land where sexual-political intrigue had traditionally its most fertile field, Italy.

The result of overpowering amorous attraction begins the play, but the Jacobean assumption is undermined on its own ground by the legitimacy and nobility of the love. Courtly Italy, once the first act has set its conditions, is moved to a void place, to the idleness and concentration of life on an island under delayed threat from the infidel Turk.

In the cast of characters we are not given the normal roster of courtiers which both Venice and the Jacobean tragedy lead us to expect: instead of many handsome, alert, courtly people, there are only two, Desdemona and Cassio. The membership of these two in a society of gracious noblemen, their sharing of a common ground, is demonstrated in the easy familiarity of their interchanges with each other (II,i; III,ii; III,iv). But on inspection the roster of normal courtiers turns out to be a total blank, because Cassio, who contents himself with a casual, somewhat brutal liaison, falls somewhat below the courtly ideal in deigning to take less than a noblewoman as his partner in less than a loving tie. Desdemona, on the other hand, transcends the merely courtly ideal in the profound trust of her devotion to her husband. Only an Iago would see in her the standard Jacobean lady of high manners and ambiguous accessibility, a "super-subtle Venetian." For it is Iago who here phrases the Jacobean assumption:

> She must change for youth ... when she is sated with
> his body, she will find the error of her choice ... If
> sanctimony and a frail vow betwixt an erring barbarian

and a super-subtle Venetian be not too hard for my wits
and all the tribe of hell, thou shalt enjoy her...

(I,iii,348-355)

And again:

When the blood is made dull with the act of sport,
there should be—again to inflame it, and to give
satiety a fresh appetite—loveliness in favour, sympathy
in years, manners, and beauties—all which the
Moor is defective in. Now for want of these requir'd
conveniences, her delicate tenderness will find itself
abus'd, begin to heave the gorge, disrelish and
abhor the Moor; very nature will instruct her in it,
and compel her to some second choice.

(II,i,225-32)

And again:

In Venice they do let God see the pranks
They dare not show their husbands

(III,iii,206-7)

Now these speeches exhibit doubtfulness at the heart of their purposive aim—they are meant to incite Roderigo and Othello; they
may be lies. Here, too, Iago gratuitously mocks as well as entices
Roderigo, since Cassio, not Roderigo himself, is the new partner
guessed. But these nuances only serve to heighten the perversity
of the assumption they voice, an assumption that has already
been debased by being put in the mouth of a resentful underling
rather than that of an ambitious courtier. Iago's temptations of
Roderigo, which frame his temptation of Othello, also mime that
temptation, and the sadistic combination of mockery-enticement,
homosexually structured in the x-ray of Freudian psychology,
renders Iago more desperate in the light of his subjection to the
mechanisms he believes he is controlling, a desperation re-cen-
tered in heterosexual jealousy as he continues to convince himself

of his exaggeration by extending the triangle wherever he looks, much as in *Bussy d'Ambois* or *Women Beware Women*:

> That Cassio loves her, I do well believe it;
> That she loves him, 'tis apt and of great credit.
> The Moor, howbeit that I endure him not,
> Is of a constant, loving, noble nature;
> And I dare think he'll prove to Desdemona
> A most dear husband. Now I do love her too;
> Not out of absolute lust, though peradventure
> I stand accountant for as great a sin,
> But partly led to diet my revenge,
> For that I do suspect the lustful Moor
> Hath leap'd into my seat; the thought whereof
> Doth like a poisonous mineral gnaw my inwards;
> And nothing can nor shall content my soul
> Till I am even'd with him, wife for wife;
>
> (II,i,280-293)

This is the Jacobean assumption full-blown, sounding much like Monsieur's response to Tamyra's repulse in *Bussy d'Ambois* (II, ii,20-48), except that Shakespeare has kept short of his stage the reality by which we might test the truth of Iago's particular suspicion. His closing of the circle by including Cassio among the lovers of Emilia (II,i,301) is either justified by the probabilities of what may tempt a soldier's wife in the superior charm of a young officer and the superior power of a general (and Emilia's later disquisition on adultery does not mitigate that probability). Or else it is a perverted fantasy based on no concrete evidence. Not a shred of detail in the play prejudices either alternative; and the doubt wherein we are suspended at once radicalizes the emotions within the round of adultery ("Jealousy/ ... which doth mock the meat it feeds on" III,iii,169-171) and renders impossible our measuring either the justification of Iago or the extent of his perversion.

The disproportion between his total hostility and the contingency of its basis is matched, in the political sphere, by the restricted situation into which that side of the Jacobean assumption has been displaced. No sovereignty is at issue here, as in the normally staged Machiavellian struggles, but simply one jump in the lower rungs of a military ladder. Unlike the typical Jacobean intriguer, Iago has no positive ambitions. He is purely negative, and passive; he merely wishes to punish someone who passed him over for promotion. And the sordid organizational motive is presented to us in the play before we have any light on the erotic situation at all. Shakespeare gives us a powerful glimpse of the self-willed bureaucratic hell of those who will not accept the priority of competence over time-in-service,[14] a glimpse of a society-to-come more prophetic than anything on Jonson's bourgeois stage, here put at the service of scaling down the political vainglory of standard Jacobean ambition.

Political intrigue having been debased to small-scale resentment, and the large motions setting a Machiavellian stage for international strife having been stopped at the outset by a storm that wrecks the Turkish fleet (II,i,20-24), the stage is clear for the erotic action. But, as we have seen, the "natural" plenum of courteous society is here a vacuum, a sort of psychic emptiness above which a Desdemona has already risen, away from which a Cassio has already been tottering.

The psychic emptiness becomes a field of dynamic forces whose expectations Iago can exploit, largely because the normal, stable courtiers of the Jacobean assumption exist only as a sort of shadow defining Shakespeare's stage. For such handsome persons of stable, predictable attributes Shakespeare has substituted persons so governed by their internal lives and by their whole responses that the field of action is a field of potentiality wherein only the factors are predictable, not the responses.

In *Othello* there is a two-way mirror fluidity between the worlds of action (power, status, society, etc.) and love, each of which has an upward pole of idealism (Othello's ideal "occupation"; his love for Desdemona) and a downward pole of self-interest in action (Iago) and lust in love (black ram-white ewe). There is so much motion stirred up here that the normal aristocratic interaction between these worlds—the "good match" marriage of *Much Ado* or *Taming of the Shrew*, or *All's Well* or *Twelfth Night*—the possible marriage between Roderigo and

Desdemona or the Cassio type and someone—remains unrepresented except as a vacuum center for the stir. Iago, involved both ways (lack of promotion; the suspicions about Emilia), is moving downward from the trust of the honesty to which all attest, and which he uses as a ground for fraud.

Roderigo's motion is downward (selling lands to translate old marriage prospect into new lust), and Othello's runs the whole gamut from ideal to baseness to ideal. Cassio, the nobleman who will be governor of Cyprus at the end, is more vacillating than anyone (in his near-worship of Desdemona and contempt of Bianca; his drinking and self-contempt for drinking). He is especially engaged by anxiety as he shies from the "prudent" wait-till-the-storm-dies-down advice of Othello. His boldness at kissing Emilia, though tentatively challenged in the presence of Iago (II, i), is a part of his new boldness before Desdemona and Emilia (III,i,52-4; III,iii,12-18). The change in Cassio can only be accounted for by a societal and erotic *sprezzatura* of pressing—on the alien ground both he and Desdemona feel—for an engagement of the aristocratic tie between them. To which, in spite of his newly subservient politeness, Desdemona responds not by "he said if you'd wait he'd help you," but with the delight of "*I'll* help you," an appeal to friendship that has an erotic potential, but only a potential, one that would always waver away from Desdemona's unquestioning chastity.

Roderigo, just before the play opens, has been a suitor grudgingly considered eligible by Desdemona's father, and he begins by taking his loss in good enough spirits to stay on confidential terms with Iago, as we learn from his very complaint in the opening lines of the play:

> Tush, never tell me; I take it much unkindly
> That you, Iago, who has had my purse
> As if the strings were thine, shouldst know of this
>
> (I,i,1-3)

The unanswered questions here help set the tone not only of resentment but of the great disproportions in the action, since what causes these emotions is at first hidden; and these questions set the tone for psychic internality as well, since military resentment is confused by, and delays over, sexual union. Worked by Iago through the strong images that are mainly aimed at Brabantio ("an old black ram/Is tupping your white ewe" I,i,90), and spurred on by the plausibility of the Jacobean assumption as he would be presumed to have known it in the conventionally lecherous Venetian society, Roderigo undergoes the progressive degradation of sacrificing his patrimony to a totally frustrating chase. His remoteness from his object shows already at his arrival from the boat (II,i), where time with Desdemona on the high seas leaves him speechless before her, unable to get a word in at the sexual banter. Finally he turns himself into the street bravo stabbed in treachery whose last words are a desperate curse, "O damned Iago! O inhuman dog!" (V,i,62). But even he shows the last vestiges of his nobility in repentance ("O villain that I am!" V,i,28), a repentance shot through almost at once by a self-pity ("Nobody come? Then shall I bleed to death" V,i,45; "O, help me there!" V,i,60) whose sole issue is his final curse.

Such a progressive and internal psychic movement, on a much larger scale, overturns Othello.

It is important, since the play focuses on just such motions of aspiration and obsession, that we see them not only in Emilia, who suddenly rises from humdrum erotic chitchat to the pressure of a self-sacrificing noble action, but also in all the others, and notably in the main engine of temptation, Iago himself. He had gone through a comparable internal transformation, but it largely precedes the play.

There is reason to believe that the trust everyone invests in Iago has been justified by long and faithful service. Trust, to begin with, cannot be the result of a first meeting. It must be built up carefully, and over a long period of time, as it has been for the Macbeth of the first act—even though the Cawdor he supplants has proved that trust may be misplaced. Othello at many turns shows himself to be a pregnant judge of men, and even if he did not exhibit such perspicacity we might attribute it to him as a necessary quality for rising to such a position of trust and responsibility himself. He has associated with Iago for years, and nothing that precedes the play has given him any ground to consider his ancient any less than what he calls him, "honest." Cassio too, though more vain and self-centered, lacking the toughness of the self-made man, still has a keen sense of the interaction in a camp, and he trusts Iago. Emilia would herself seem to be relatively unguarded toward her husband; his request for the handkerchief arouses no more than normal suspicion. And Desdemona, who has travelled as a kind of adoptive daughter or younger friend in the company of this couple aboard ship, lands at Cyprus on terms with Iago so easy-going that she has clearly found no occasion to stand off from the ancient. In a play that deals with profound transformations of character, it is less difficult to imagine such a profound transformation in Iago's own character than it is to go along with the unexamined view that he has remained much the same. For him to have done so would require a deception of some years' duration, an intrinsic improbability. But the truly honest Iago does precede the play. Or as Rymer correctly says—though his conclusions are unjustified—"*Shakespeare* knew his Character of *Iago* was inconsistent. In this very Play he pronounces:

> If . . . thou dost deliver . . . more or less than truth,
> Thou art no Soldier
>
> (II,iii,210-12) [15]

Iago's own proposition, "Knavery's plain face is never seen till us'd" (II,i,306), implies, as its contrary, that if he had been in the habit of knavery, it would have been detected: and so that the use is a new one whose newness he can take advantage of; this indeed is just the point of his proposition. If Iago has not been truly "honest" up to the beginning of the play, the frequent repetitions of that word would be ludicrously exaggerated as well as taunting.

The process of his self-corruption through resentment is already well-advanced in the first act of the play. He would seem to have been helping Roderigo's courtship out of a "hate" for Othello inspired by his being passed over for the lieutenancy. Indeed, his account of prior service contains no hint of deceptiveness:

> And I, of whom his eyes had seen the proof
> At Rhodes, at Cyprus, and on other grounds,
> Christian and heathen, must be be-lee'd and calm'd
>
> (I,i,28-30)

Othello's eyes will search in vain for proof in another sphere, in the selfsame Cyprus, later on. But the ironies about ocular proof are purely prospective, and in this scene it sounds as though Iago's honesty has been founded on a trust that is genuine. So far in this scene, when his first contretemps against Othello—to get Roderigo matched to Desdemona—has been frustrated, Iago shows his rage simply by trying to incite paternal ire through alarm. So far he merely adduces the notion, very possibly new for him, of the contrast between the "knee-crooking knave/That.../ Wears out his time, much like his master's ass" and "Others.../ Who, trimm'd in forms and visages of duty,/Keep yet their hearts attending on themselves" (I,i,45-51). In choosing the second line for himself rather than the first, he would in fact seem to be deciding to part company with the first course, a course that the evidence, including his own "proof" speech above, tends to substantiate for him. In rejecting the first, "Whip me such honest knaves," he is rejecting the very word applied to himself—he is rejecting what we must assume his social role to have been, that of the honest man. The ambiguity loaded into "knave," as between servant and rogue, loads Iago's sneer with a depth-charge of intentional tendentiousness. In preponderating towards the "rogue" sense he is inclining himself towards the self-contradiction of the honest-rogue, both in the destructive inconsistency of the new role, and in the time of separation from an early career of honesty, in which the sense "servant" for "knave" is sneeringly left behind in the global definition of the simple, rejecting role to be subjected to the punishment for being defenseless, "Whip me such honest knaves."

And in the hell of his own making, Iago will turn this very

maxim to the use of complex mockery in pretending to Othello
that he is deciding to abandon the role he abandoned before the
play opened, acting as though the maxim he has firmly adopted
is only a temptation:

> Are you a man? Have you a soul or sense?—
> God buy you; take mine office. O wretched fool,
> That liv'st to make thine honesty a vice!
> O monstrous world! Take note, take note, O world,
> To be direct and honest is not safe.
> I thank you for this profit; and from hence
> I'll love no friend, sith love breeds such offence.
>
> (III,iii,378-84)

Othello himself, in the tortures of his own self-absorbed trans-
mogrification, catches only the surface of these protestations and
can only reply by a perfunctory adjuration, "Nay, stay. Thou
shouldst be honest." [16] To which Iago can add a whine, wherein
self-pity and brazen mockery are versions of one another, "I
should be wise; for honesty's a fool,/And loses that it works for."

Everyone here undergoes his own special rhythm of transformation upwards or downwards: Othello with a massive, well-
nigh cosmic straining before collapse; Roderigo with a wavering
but impetuous yielding; Cassio with a lazy acquiescence held in
check by intermittent resolve; Emilia with a sudden influx of
courageous determination; Desdemona with a quiet, steady, almost breathless intentness on the virtue inherent in love. Iago,
too, embracing odium with headlong delight, exhibits the internal
motions of his psyche as he does so. [17]

But between the first and second acts, on the voyage from
Venice to Cyprus, Iago must have comported himself engagingly
enough to have bred between himself and Desdemona the familiarity his malignity brings him to begin undermining when they
land, enough so that she treats him thereafter with a modified
formality. The temptation scenes in the third and fourth act show
his malignity full-blown, at a pitch of sadistic scorn. In the dis-
embarkation scene he merely plays with denigrating women in
the person of Emilia, idly playing up to Cassio for whom his ad-

miration is revealed in the intensity of a resentment he would seem to be relaxing at the very moment Cassio has kissed Emilia. His turning on Emilia, with overtones of overture towards Cassio, traps him in openly espousing doctrines about the other sex that somewhat alienate a Desdemona still participative enough to jest. And this is no part of his purpose.

Once he has caught Cassio in his trap later in this second act, his success leads him to denigrate the Desdemona whose questions on this score he has earlier evaded ("DESDEMONA: What wouldst write of me if thou shouldst praise me? IAGO: O gentle lady, do not put me to't;/For I am nothing if not critical" II,i,118-119). In the next act he will declare an incidental lust for her; and now he gives rein to a self-delectation in successful evil that performs a huge linguistic distortion upon her:

> And what's he, then, that says I play the villain?
> When this advice is free I give and honest,
> Probal to thinking, and indeed the course
> To win the Moor again? For 'tis most easy
> The inclining Desdemona to subdue
> In any honest suit: she's fram'd as fruitful
> As the free elements. And then for her
> To win the Moor—were't to renounce his baptism,
> All seals and symbols of redeemed sin—
> His soul is so enfetter'd to her love
> That she may make, unmake, do what she list,
> Even as her appetite shall play the god
> With his weak function. How am I, then, a villain
> To counsel Cassio to this parallel course,
> Directly to his good? Divinity of hell!
> When devils will their blackest sins put on,
> They do suggest at first with heavenly shows,
> As I do now; for whiles this honest fool
> Plies Desdemona to repair his fortunes,
> And she for him pleads strongly to the Moor,
> I'll pour this pestilence into his ear—
> That she repeals him for her body's lust;
> And by how much she strives to do him good
> She shall undo her credit with the Moor.
> So will I turn her virtue into pitch;
> And out of her own goodness make the net
> That shall enmesh them all.
>
> (II,iii,325-51)

In this first, clear formulation of the exact means he will use to destroy Othello, Iago here vacillates heavily in his triumph, ending by basing himself on the very "goodness" he had begun by mocking with exultant insinuation. His own exclamation of embrace, encompassing both praise and curse, of the "divinity of hell," leads him from a lustful sadistic falsification of Desdemona into that true picture of her which can serve as the basis for fraud; he proposes to operate upon a truth that generates trust, a "credit" much like what he has himself abandoned. And at the same time, in the internal labyrinth of his soliloquized verbalization, he exhibits a counter-movement of casuistic self-justification which is really the self-congratulation of deceit. The deceit is past; the means for enjoying it here exhibits itself as moving through self-irony from a pretense of fraudulent casuistry to an actuality of fraud. The changing picture of Desdemona measures these motions: from (1) "inclining ... framed as fruitful/As the free elements" through (2) "her appetite shall play the god" and then (3) "her virtue" to (4) "her goodness." The first three constitute a sexual series, seen first in the perspective of physical nature, next in the deification of physical impulse, but finally in the control of impulse out of a fidelity to that deity whose terms are the most consistent language of this speech, the language of sin and redemption, the general Christian process Iago is here blatantly trying to make the engine of its own destruction. The fourth term, "goodness," leaves the sexuality of the first three behind, and the earnestness of Iago's conclusion has turned him away from the enjoyment of fraud to the summary of his intention. His own retrogressive formulations have involved him, in spite of himself, in an ascending series.

2

The kind of psychological motion this speech exemplifies, while too obsessive to allow for introspection, does follow the shifts and contours of an internal dynamism at once restless and purposive, for Iago as for all the other characters. It is not just fanciful to say that the very lack of courtiers to embody standard Jacobean action constitutes the void in which such motion may operate more freely. If there were such courtiers here, they, and their words, would rest somewhat on the assumptions, even were they to struggle against them. It is just such a struggle, in an expected context, that it is the special genius of Chapman to depict, and the energies of the struggle can be traced to the very rhythms of his verse. But the characters in *Othello* are not standard courtiers, and even the two standard courtiers among them are isolated in that void of total testing. The Jacobean assumption is present as the distanced convention that defines the world of Venetian amour and statecraft on the stage for which the particular play was written.

One may "hear" Shakespeare's invented freedom from these assumptions in the very lightness, and deliberateness, of the play's chief character, as he begins the dominant bars of "the Othello music." Othello is caught up, of course, in the trammels of a Herculean self-deception, and every scene in which he appears, through the crescendo of his temptation and crime, dwells on the shifts and contours of his internal psychological motions, within a given speech, and also in the movement from his first speeches to his last, from " 'Tis better as it is" (I,ii,6) and "Keep up your bright swords, for the dew will rust them" (I,ii,59) to "And smote him—thus" (V,ii,359). The qualifying temper of the first lyric utterance, while it contrasts with the blunt directness of the last, shares with it both deliberateness, as the articulation of a decision, and lightness, as involving a kind of trick on the Venetian senate. In both instances, in the peacemaking gesture and in the suicide, Othello is too fast for others, and is, as it were, ponderously too fast, keeping his psyche in tune to the "music" G. Wilson Knight has heard in him, noting the contrast between the fixedness of the "chrysolite" or "marble heaven" of the images he voices, something ponderous, and the shadowy world in which he acts, a place where everything goes very fast. "Killing my self, to die upon a kiss" (V,ii,362), his very last words, gather all this motion up into a sigh as mighty as Antony's, but with none of Antony's consolation.

Remaining much as he is, but at the same time undergoing radical transformation, Othello exemplifies the susceptibility of the Jacobean courtier, without the stated and staple response. The susceptibility is assumed, but the response, in the social differentiation of the characters, finds a universe of freedom to internalize. Every difference—age (Othello), color, class (Iago and Emilia), sex (Desdemona, a "fair warrior" in the man's world of military action)—becomes a vehicle for enlarging the possibilities of each one's response. Yet everyone remains susceptible: Desdemona to love for a middle-aged Moor; Iago to resentment; Roderigo to sexual temptation; Cassio to the treacherous camaraderie of drink; Othello himself to the notion that a dangerous potential instability resides in the very susceptibility of his wife. At moments of strain the standard courtly sexual assumption does get voiced even by Othello, once Iago has got him going, as a trembling barometer needle of his internal storm:

> That we can call these delicate creatures ours
> And not their appetites! . . . Yet 'tis the plague of great ones;
> Prerogativ'd are they less than the base
>
> (III,iii,273-278)

This is the staple assumption, belied perhaps by Othello's possible connection with Emilia. The assumption gets voiced quickly when the handsomeness of the courtier Lodovico is brought up to beguile the sadness of Desdemona:

DESDEMONA:
> This Lodovico is a proper man.

EMILIA:
> A very handsome man.

DESDEMONA:
> He speaks well.

EMILIA:
> I know a lady in Venice would have walk'd barefoot to Palestine for a touch of his nether lip.
>
> (IV,iii,35-38)

And Desdemona counters this forceful fusion of religious pilgrimage and erotic fulfillment by singing the maid's song that "expressed her fortune."[18] The last line of the song, imagined as spoken by someone "prov'd mad," counters the accusation of "false love" with a taunting reference to the equality-in-multiplicity of the staple assumption:

> If I court moe women, you'll couch with moe men ·
>
> (IV,iii,55)

Desdemona cannot be registering the sense of what she is singing. The extremity of her calm distances her from the assumption of the cause underlying the sorrow in which she innocently takes comfort without dreaming that she shares these circumstances at any angle.

The Jacobean assumption, then, serving as a fantasy, a recourse, an expectation, a missing dead center, works as a powerful absence here, a magnetic background. Given the baselessness of Othello's suspicions, there is a disproportion between his natural inclination of "one not easily jealous" and the totality of his acceptance of the assumption once he had been led to do so, ("but, being wrought,/Perplexed in the extreme" V,ii,348-349). This disproportion serves to measure the range of psychic possibility that the play triumphantly sets in sequential form. And it is just at that point of fixed response, at the point of revenge, that Shakespeare parts company for good from a source he has followed at times with remarkable closeness, the *Hecatommithi* of Cinthio. Aside from some time-shuffling, the addition of Roderigo, the interposition of the storm, and the redisposition of characters on the ships to Cyprus (Disdemona sails with the Moor), Shakespeare has provided up to this point of the story only verse, and a tightening interpretation, over and above Cinthio's events. He not only tightens the conclusion, wherein Cinthio the Moor and the Ensign linger till they are discovered at separate times and tortured to confess, but he builds the conclusion around the psychic conditions of the revenge. In Cinthio there is no foregiveness of Disdemona, no confession of Emilia, no revenge of Iago upon her, no suicide of Othello. And the Moor and the Ensign together murder Disdemona, whereas in Shakespeare the smothering of Desdemona is a fantasy of Iago enacted by Othello.[19]

Hamlet, by seeking revenge, activates the whole scheme of projecting upon Claudius that which he cannot face in his identification with his father. The father himself, though dead, is caught not only in the doubt about the modality of his after-life existence but also in his own form of the scheme. As David Willbern points out, the person seeking revenge, in identifying with the aggressor by the overreaction of rejection, triggers a compulsion to repeat the crime by re-staging it, and thereby to control, assimilate and master the past.[20] Hamlet the Father is one of those who faces betrayal in a wife by going first for the lover, whereas Othello attacks in person the wife, the lover only through an intermediary. The emotional involvements, for which Freud provides the analytical framework, carry through the discovery of treachery. When Othello stabs the intermediary, too, there is a disappointed whine as well as a taunt in Iago's reply, "I bleed, sir; but not kill'd" (V,ii,292).

Now private revenge for murder, as Fredson Bowers points out, includes in its complex code not only a clear Christian counter-injunction but customs leading back to the most rudimentary Saxon society.[21] The Renaissance definition of revenge also embraces Danish and Norman law as well as English common law in its Roman-influenced Elizabethan formulation. Revenge for adultery, on the other hand, however fully its mechanisms are woven into the fabric of society, displays more exclusively the internal psychic economy of the individual. Some of the intensity of *Hamlet* derives from its conflating both kinds in a single situation, where the murder is occasioned by adultery and given the added emphasis of a political struggle.

Othello's political mastery is a kind of given; it is part of what his illusory jealousy overturns. Shakespeare magnifies the internal character of the jealousy by founding it on nothing, while keeping his ideal of chastity in triumphant, central focus.

Any jealousy, justified or not, sensitizes all the personal relations that a marriage had solved. In Freudian terms, a person

keeps the sublimation and actuality of his rivalry-identification
with the father in balance when he imitates the father by taking a
wife, whose actual response to him also keeps his ambivalence toward the mother in balance. The interloping lover re-sensitizes
and enormously bends towards distortion every single one of
these relations: the wife becomes the treacherous mother oriented
to another, and the father rebecomes a castrating presence forbid-
ding actuality, at the same time inviting the sublimated homosexuality of identification because the lover has induced a double
identification, between self and the lover who has supplanted the
self, between the lover and the father whose powers he is now
dominant in exercising. The homosexual potential of the double
identification is reinforced by a woman-hate that is triggered by
the wife's enactment of the self's fears and suspicions about the
mother.

The schema may be put in a diagram:

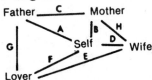

Every axis of relation (A through H) at once activates and para-
lyzes every other, a "green-ey'd monster which doth mock/The
meat it feeds on" (III,iii,166-167). Or in Webster's words, "Jealousy is worser, her fits present to a man, like so many bubles in a
Bason of water, twenty severall crabbed faces" (*The White Devil*,
I,ii,109-111).

The instability of these hate-love responses throws the self into
an imbalance wherein it cannot quite struggle to assert its identity.
The only possible solution, as Othello astutely realizes, would be
the impossible one of not feeling what one feels: "Away at once
with love or jealousy!" (III,iii,196). And he has already declared
this to be impossible:

> Excellent wretch! Perdition catch my soul
> But I do love thee; and when I love thee not
> Chaos is come again.
>
> (III,iii,91-93)

Or else the impossible solution of not knowing what he "knows":

> What sense had I in her stol'n hours of lust?
> I saw't not, thought it not, it harm'd not me.
> I slept the next night well, fed well, was free and merry;
> I found not Cassio's kisses on her lips.
> He that is robb'd, not wanting what is stol'n,
> Let him not know't, and he's not robb'd at all
>
> (III,iii,342-347)

But this too is impossible, and the result of it is to divorce him from his identity:

> Farewell the neighing steed and the shrill trump. . .
> Pride, pomp, and circumstance, of glorious war! . . . .
> Farewell! Othello's occupation's gone.
>
> (III,iii,355-361)

Iago too is "jealous," certain of having been slighted in the emotionally charged area of military preferment, and, as he alleges, in a kind of doubled version of the complex axes around the cuckold "Self" of the diagram above, since there are two "lovers" in Iago's diagram, one of whom is the "self" of Othello's diagram, and one of whom is the false lover, Cassio himself. It is possibly from introspection that he is such a master of intuitive psychology:

> Trifles light as air
> Are to the jealous confirmations strong
> As proofs of holy writ
>
> (III,iii,326-328)

The tremendous ramifications of his sadistic revenge have been constructed on the disproportion of radical doubt (we cannot know or not know that Emilia has been unfaithful) and overresponse (Iago in a decade or so of military service must have wit-

nessed and even suffered other injustices of professional reward).
As such they serve within the play both as a parallel to the disproportion of Othello's response, and as a contrast to Othello's nobility in the very throes of murderous execution.

The battle against the Turks suspended, the displaced Venetians confined on the island awaiting orders, there are no larger
spheres of action to distract them from the momentous and mortal volatilities of these psychic motions.

The play stalls and floats as *Hamlet* does, in Schneiderman's
extension of Jones' Freudian reading. His "sense of his own existence fluctuates in the ether of the aesthetic...The system of kin-
ship fails in its turn since Hamlet's father is now his uncle, his
mother his aunt, and Hamlet is his own cousin. Lacking a single
"true" father, Hamlet cannot sustain any singularity of purpose...
Hamlet is a gap in the play's structure that the character bearing
his name fills to excess. His justification for this over-supplying
is that the gap of the subject has already been perversely filled by
the lecherous Claudius."[22]

Othello does not create such a gap until the deadly diagram has
been activated. And having done so, he must override an all-
embracing sense of this worldly erotic loss no whit inferior to
Antony's by a sense of his own other-worldly damnation: he
must titanically undergo the loss of Romeo, of Antony, and of
Macbeth, all at once, and publicly. He must face the totality of a
monstrous illusion created on the fabric of assumptions whose
basis is real but whose actuality is transcended.

3

Othello's use of speech in his final address as concealment, distraction, and intimation of another reality, is the last in the series
through the play, of which Iago's sadistic manipulations are the
most constant. One mood, suicidal resoluteness, is being overlaid
by another, evocative appeal for retrospective fullness, as Iago

overlays protestations of loyalty by sadistic teasing. So Desdemona at her landing, when she confesses of her banter with Iago, Emilia, and Cassio, "I am not merry; but I do beguile the thing I am by seeming otherwise" (II,i,122-123). So Othello overlays his first suspicions with pretended equanimity. So Desdemona overlays fear with wistful loneliness.

This interpenetration of moods is clear, and constant in the play. It is noteworthy in Othello's first meeting with Desdemona after Iago has planted the suspicion:

Re-enter Desdemona and Emilia

OTHELLO:
>If she be false, O, then heaven mocks itself!
>I'll not believe it.

DESDEMONA:
>   How now, my dear Othello?
>Your dinner, and the generous islanders
>By you invited, do attend your presence.

OTHELLO:
>I am to blame.

DESDEMONA:
>   Why do you speak so faintly?
>Are you not well?

OTHELLO:
>I have a pain upon my forehead here.

DESDEMONA:
>Faith, that's with watching; 'twill away again.
>Let me but bind it hard, within this hour
>It will be well.
>*(He puts the handkerchief from him, and she drops it.)*

OTHELLO:
>   Your napkin is too little.
>Let it alone. Come, I'll go in with you.

DESDEMONA:
>I am very sorry that you are not well.

>   (III,iii,282-292)

Wifely solicitude is here both compassed and invoked by an irony that wavers into appeal. Since Othello never is at rest in the resolution not to suspect her, his whispered self-accusation "I am to blame" subdues the general's voice by including complaint (I to blame when she is suspicious?) as an undertone. "I am to blame" means also "for loving her in the first place," and it hides itself in the pretended self-deprecation of politeness. These possibilities quickly extend and multiply in the headache/budding horns/distracting trifle of his next statement. And by the next, the impatience/tender mockery/minor resignation of "your napkin is too little" brings her so to absorb herself in covering her own growing alarm with routine sympathy that she lets the precious handkerchief drop. This hinge of the entire tragic action is thus occasioned by the double pull of delicate interactions around the nascent instability of jealousy, soon to assume that giant proportion its very emptiness allows.

Here, in the small and "casual" domestic scene at the heart of his causal web, in reinventing the psychological conditions under which the erotic life may aspire to wholeness or shatter the whole man, Shakespeare demonstrates the enacting effect of his thematic invention. He has transformed the Jacobean assumption utterly by the simple and radical strategy of recreating its psychological conditions while rejecting its stable base. The leverage of this strategy will serve him still again, in *The Winter's Tale* and in *Cymbeline,* where the power of fantasy takes on the Protean adaptability it has gained through being free of automatic response.

The overlay of one exhibited emotion upon another thrusts the ground of action tremendously inward. Iago, as he blends a whine with a taunt, not only both invokes dramatic irony and subjects himself to it; he also exemplifies a mysterious, dynamic condition of the soul which is not unlike the upheaval Othello evidences by expressing self-abandonment and self-possession in a single speech. So Richard II, the character for whom Shakespeare invents that great echo-chamber of the inner voice, the soliloquy, blends pride with sorrow and self-exaltation with self-contempt.[23] So Ulysses blends a glorying in his military condition with a satiric contempt for it, a combination that empowers his utterance with a richness unattained by Troilus or Hector. "Honorable murderer," Othello's last characterization of himself, is thus not only an oxymoron, but an attempt, in language necessarily provisional, to put a name upon two titanic motions of the spirit that have run concurrently in him and seem to divide in his confession only to fuse one last time as he honorably dishonors himself by murdering himself.

In the struggle of two moods, through their melding in a single verbal utterance, the taunt cannot reveal just the conscious (or the unconscious), nor can the whine. The combination refers the other to another mechanism; the consciousness of the whine throws the unconscious of the taunt into relief, through the analyzable substructure common to both. The whole melding flow recreates a sort of preconsciousness, just below the level of speech, but pressing to the all-but-realization of utterance, the aspiration forward of the dramatic movement exemplified not in any fixed attitude but rather in the very principle of shift by which one attitude can reveal another, the uncommon depth and mystery of such common responses as jealousy, and love.

4

In the love comedies, and in the tragedies of love, the presence of fulfillment acts as an energized plenum that brings everyone on stage and off to expect that the lovers will wander out of the forest dream into the wakefulness of proper union. Displacing himself from the Jacobean convention allows Shakespeare to base his plenum on a purified love. In *A Midsummer Night's Dream* the very multiplication of orders of creatures and displacements of language and jurisdiction act only to increase the mystery, not to reduce the presence, of the plenum. They are "full of joy and mirth," and the feeling is suffused at every point with *mirth*, a word Shakespeare assigns to love again and again, even in the tragedies. Mirth offers the subliminal sense of a religious joy[24] as well as the contagion of festive jollity. Its plenum feeds the pleasurable transports of the highest and simplest earthly society, a society of two.

The mighty enactment of the simplification into love is worth all the force it holds out against and through. In the split across the stage, the accord between lovers is virtual: what awaits Olivia, Miranda, Viola, and Imogen, what lies behind Juliet, Cleopatra, and Troilus (Cressida having transformed herself into being incapable of remembering) is not a resolving chord but merely a sense that the harmonies need only a chance to be resolvable to be perceived as derivable from the plenum where they would be resolved.

Love in Shakespeare's plays is characteristically pitted against some other force, under the dynamism of which it manifests its own power, whether to succeed or to fail, of raising identity into the fullness of a feeling the play stands to define. In *Romeo and Juliet* this other force is a death-feud; in *The Taming of the Shrew*, the radical recalcitrance of the heroine; in *All's Well that Ends Well*, that of the hero; in *Troilus and Cressida,* a gripping technicality, hostage-bargaining in the overwhelming code of war. In *Antony and Cleopatra* the other force is double: the first a human condition, the mortality-shroud of middle age, pressed by the obsessions of a career; the second force is "the world," to which the ambitious must subject himself. It will not do that Cleopatra is a queen. The world aggrandizes; love apotheosizes. The world is measured and punctual; love is dilatory and also instantaneous. By dramatizing this other force Shakespeare energizes the convention of the love comedy.

Another such force does not impinge on the common convention of courtly love, legitimate or adulterous, though politics may complicate lovemaking. Nor does another force affect the all-absorbing conventions of upper-class matchmaking, the inclusiveness of rules by which the well-bred young are paired off. In courtly love and in matchmaking all other forces are banished or assimilated. The only difficulty known to the wooers who speak in the sonnet sequences is the lingering and ambiguous inaccessibility of the woman whose possible ultimate surrender is the condition of her stated hard-heartedness: it is the condition, too, of the heights of sublimation-assertion to which the verse is driven, by Sidney or Daniel, Spenser or Shakespeare himself. Romeo only encounters the other force after he has broken the hold of the courtly convention, for which Rosaline stands; and Juliet only when she has slipped free of the upper-class matchmaking in accord with which Paris stands on her horizon.

The Faithful Shepherdess, on the other hand, The Shoemaker's Holiday, Bartholomew Fair, and even The Duchess of Malfi, for all the differences among them, are alike in that all their difficulties belong either themselves to the erotic sphere, or are drawn into it by considerations of class.

The enraptured Romeo enters this mystery for the first time as a marvelous release from the yearning immobility of being in love with someone who is strategically or perversely or conventionally holding back. What he has left is precisely the courtly convention:

> her I love now
> Doth grace for grace and love for love allow;
> The other did not so.

> (II,iii,85-87)

Simple as this is, the double terms pose a mystery; it is to a friar that Romeo here speaks of grace and love, the small courtesy linked, in the openness of amorous interchange, to a sign of divine favor.

In entering the mystery, Romeo enlivens alien powers, whereas his love of Rosaline—who is also named as a guest at the Capulet dance—has been wholly contented within the courtly world, for which powers do not exist that are alien.

In a full progress from initial enrapturement through the mutual renunciation of a death chosen instead of life without the other, Romeo and Juliet achieve the quality of their love beyond the shocks of the feud, the mortal power of the other force.

Entirely within the courtly realm of Love's Labour's Lost—itself, however, shadowed at the end by a year-long delay of consummation in piety for a father's death—love operates on the ground of intelligence, in the Renaissance continuation of Dante's premises. "From women's eyes this doctrine I derive," says Berowne. "They are the ground, the books, the academes,/From whence doth spring the true Promethean fire" (*Love's Labour's Lost*, IV,iii,298-300). And it is exactly "wit" that has caused each of the three noble ladies, as each says in her eulogy, to single out her male partner for affectionate notice (II,i,40-76), while the Princess enacts the same values, though not lowering her dignity to express them, by taking the lead in coy witty exchanges with Navarre.

The Romeo enamoured of Rosaline echoes Berowne's doctrine; she "hath Dian's wit" (I,i,207); "She is too fair, too wise, wisely too fair" (219).

Once he has entered the charged atmosphere of truly energized love, however, where self and other, delight and potency, anticipation and fulfillment, oblivion and wakefulness, are mysteriously fused, his expression about Juliet's knowledge ("she doth teach") and illumination (". . . to burn bright the torches") is overborne in a soaring ease of hyperbolic effusion:

> O, speak again, bright angel! for thou art
> As glorious to this night, being o'er my head,
> As is a winged messenger of heaven
> Unto the white-upturned wond'ring eyes
> Of mortals that fall back to gaze on him,
> When he bestrides the lazy-pacing clouds
> And sails upon the bosom of the air.
>
> (II,ii,26-32)

Here there is a sense of liberation from all kinds of gravity, of free uplift, that the whole progress of the play mimes.

Whereas the love is tested against alien powers, its own quality does not undergo qualification. In *All's Well that Ends Well*, Helena's magic healing power and the related magic of her virginity intensify the legendary aura of the play without at all diverting or shaping the special character of its erotic life. In such a play as Fletcher's *The Faithful Shepherdess*, on the other hand, a *shepherdess* in *mourning* who has *healing* talents is *accosted* by a *satyr* and declares the power of *virginity*—and all the under- lined elements are rung in to define the temper of erotic inter- action. The taboo associated with virginity has deep primitive roots; and through religion it generates a peerless intimation of civilization's key procedure, sublimation. Shakespeare enlists all this also in *Pericles, The Winter's Tale, The Tempest, Measure for Measure,* and *The Merchant of Venice.* But Shakespeare tames no unicorns; his virgins are instinct with the promise of wedded chastity, "a pudency so rosy." The quality of feeling in the pregnant Hermione and the married Imogen does not differ from the clarity of Helena and Perdita, Portia and Isabella, nor does the married Cordelia, like Desdemona and Juliet, do other than fulfill her virginal self, though her amorous capacities can only be an inference when the play shows her at another angle. The special erotic tempers of *The Faerie Queene* are left behind; there are virgins in Shakespeare, but no Unas or Britomarts, sacred places but no Bowers of Bliss. Cleopatra's style and situa- tion differ markedly from Juliet's; her temper of feeling is re- markably the same.

The killing of Tybalt intervenes between Romeo's wedding and the wedding night; its fatality is the more ominous for not al- lowing other than a strange congruity between love and death. This congruity, though it dooms the lovers, enters their percep- tions only obliquely. Laments about that situation come after the fact of the love. References to death tend to haunt the transports of the lovers only when they are fearful and separated.[25] This splendid and potent pair move in the tragic sphere uncontami- nated and yet full of foreboding on the enchanted ground that overbears the transports of a Tristan and an Isolde. Only a touch of foreboding, in the blackness of the Ethiop, the "too rich for use, for earth too dear," enters Romeo's eulogy of struck recognition, on the sight of his "jewel"-"dove"-"lady."

They are of course right to feel fear when they are apart, to sense a connection between love and death in the plot. Alien ground does intensify the atmosphere of risk, which in itself is favorable to love, because risk is love's essential condition: the beloved may not respond, and Rosaline has in fact so far not responded to Romeo. Going to the Capulet dance, he visors himself in an incognito which the convention of the time recommends and the feud enforces as a special necessity here for another general aspect of love—its need for privacy and isolation, its first phase of passing through a no-man's-land of anonymity before identity can be celebrated in the flesh.

What normally brings about death for mortal man is time. Love by which he produces his successors, quickens the awareness of time and mortality, a theme Shakespeare dwells on in the Sonnets. In *Romeo and Juliet* the preternaturally rapid and sure-breathed ripening of the love between the rapt pair proceeds at what seems an even, unruffled pace, while the slower events are hurrying behind them. Lightning time, and a perception thereof, must be involved in whatever sense is given to the mysterious phrase in Juliet's expression of haste:

> That runaways' eyes may wink, and Romeo
> Leap to these arms
>
> (III,ii,6-7) [26]

Romeo and Juliet deal in moments, in hours that seem like years, in one long miraculous night of union; Juliet's father hastens—and, by contrast with them, delays—to bring a wedding about in a few days. She has reached the proper time in years—years to be cut off not by her love, but by the disparity in time which preparing for the love entails. The potion she is given should last long enough to put off Paris; it also lasts too long to let her waken at the rapidity of her lover.

She herself fears at first the speed of the *coup de foudre* that awakens her to a fear not easily distinguishable from a heart-in-mouth readiness to love:

> I have no joy of this contract to-night:
> It is too rash, too unadvis'd, too sudden;

> Too like the lightning, which doth cease to be
> Ere one can say 'It lightens.' Sweet, good night!
> This bud of love, by summer's ripening breath,
> May prove a beauteous flow'r when next we meet.
>
> (II,ii,117-122)

Juliet here speeds up her reckoning of what a proper time would be in the very process of recounting how fearfully fast it is. She open-mouthedly belies herself; her "no joy" waxes with a joy she very soon sees as already having taken place—not "sudden," not "ripening," but already given:

> And yet I would it were to give again
>
> (129)

For fast and slow ominously lose their standard of measurement when confronted with the immeasurable:

> My bounty is as boundless as the sea
> My love as deep: the more I give to thee,
> The more I have, for both are infinite.
>
> (133-135)

All this inner progress beyond boundaries happens in the time it takes to utter fifteen lines. Before long she will herself stipulate the lightning definition of love, free in its soaring of the fixed time it must reckon with:

> Love's heralds should be thoughts,
> Which ten times faster glide than the sun's beams
> Driving back shadows over louring hills;
>
> (II,v,4-6)

Time, which governs the progression of alternating scenes, is shifted to produce the sharpness at which these lovers go under: time orchestrates the hastiness of Tybalt, the necessary swiftness of the Duke's merciful commutation of death to exile, the neces-

sary slowness of distant communications, the deep, poetic congruence of the forces causing measurements to overlap with the force
that outlasts them and are also at their mercy—as also in *Othello,*
where jealousy is naturally more rapid in its metamorphoses than
evidential proof in its careful constructions: and in *Antony and
Cleopatra,* where dalliance goes by a different timetable than sea
battles, and the mortally entangled dallier will follow his beloved
away from his most important sea battle of all.

To be young is to be innocent of how time brings all things to
light. Romeo and Juliet are both sublimely innocent in a directness of approach which is unaware that it is not doing justice to
the leisurely, uncertain pace of living complications. Antony and
Cleopatra struggle to hold in equipoise the full, the extensive,
bearing in time, of what it is they are giving up—and how swiftly
it will be borne in upon them. But the youthful lovers cannot include anything but each other in their unfledged perception of the
world's pace. In their fidelity to each other they are faithful to the
motto engraved on the title page of the First Quarto, *Aut nunc
aut numquam,* an "either-or" (*aut . . . aut*) which their miraculously instantaneous self-realization—a more engrossing miracle
than the lightning stroke of just falling in love—turns into a
"both-and," both "now" and "never."[27]

The totality of Juliet's equanimous persistence turns to irony
all the officious bustle of preparation for her marriage with Paris,
and removes the world of matchmaking an infinite distance from
that of amorous union. One main quality of love that these plays
savor is its serene and confident absorption of all temporality into
itself. Romeo and Juliet run their whole course of devotion without giving the fatal intrusion any regard—other than the mortal
and final responses that define the play, "Never was a story of
more woe/Than this of Juliet and her Romeo." Dominating their
lives, those cross-currents have no power to perturb the rhythm
of love's fulfillment, nor does the loss of a whole empire do any
more than step up Antony's final declarations to Cleopatra, and
then hers to him.

Love's Labour's Lost, too, moves on evenly to the fulfillment of dedication, though consummation is deferred for a whole year of mourning, the lovers being heavy with involvement in the public and ceremonial side of their love: the King of Navarre loves the Princess, but it is also a state marriage they are approaching, and their followers are obliged to follow suit. The Princess' devotion to her father tells us nothing psychologically about the character of her affection: the four noble suitors love identically, once they have singled one another out, which they have done before they go through the play's motions of ritual visits, sonnets, dances, masquerades, and gentle mockery.

In *Antony and Cleopatra* the invincible forces against which love supremely asserts itself are not only without but within. The whole course of the play takes its rhythmic contour from Antony's struggles to maintain himself in the Roman world against a love which has none of the powerful drawing power of youth, innocence, and a future lifetime of invested legitimacy. There is no hallowed bond here, though as with the Roman plays generally, Shakespeare presents his forces in a world, across the stage, not bound by the Christian interdict on adultery (the word is used, however), any more than the Stoic conclusions of Eros, Enobarbus, and Antony himself, are bound by the Christian interdict against suicide.

Antony asserts the power of the loyalty he finally evinces by inverting the deep and eternal values of the Christian audience, and the Christian world outside the stage door: instead of complicating or qualifying the Christian element, as Chaucer and Spenser, Boccaccio and Dante do, Shakespeare boldly confronts it with a supreme assertion of a priority it would condemn. And there are no terms which allow us to transpose that Eros into a Christian Agape;[28] it stands, free and sublime and triumphant, but also repeatedly qualified by doubts, fears, and the partners' frailties.

To be only half in the realm of love, when love demands all, spells the psychic distortion of abyssal betrayal, and Cleopatra mirrors that fact at once in the horrid vacillation Antony's abandonment brings upon her:

> Let him for ever go—let him not, Charmian—
> Though he be painted one way like a Gorgon,
> The other way's a Mars.
>
> (II,v,115-117)

In these revealing eyes the beloved Antony's body takes on the tricky divisions of a Renaissance perspectival painting, the side she has not yet seen metamorphosed into a stone-transfixing feminine stare with the split penises of snakes writhing on the head.

But the Mars in him will prevail, when he himself abandons it, when at long last he is abandoned by his tutelary demigod, Hercules. The delay of this process, and the mystery of it, is emphasized in the play by being accorded a whole scene (IV,iii).

Even in the opening scenes, Cleopatra's transports are invested in memory. "Eternity *was* in our lips and eyes," and this love must recreate its present out of what was or else what is never to be, out of remembrances of delight and sheer dedication, "I here importune death awhile, until/Of many thousand kisses the poor last/I lay upon thy lips" (IV,xv,19-21). These kisses are only kisses, leading to no embrace; memory and anticipation become one in a consummation that is forever unconsummated, except in an image that sublimates the whole world, the imperial sway and the top of the organ, into orgasmic fulfillment-obliteration, "The crown o' th' earth doth melt" (IV,xv,63).

These words she speaks as he dies. And Cleopatra's most fulsome delineation of the lover she will soon follow is also given in retrospect, as a eulogy after death, "I dreamt there was an Emperor Antony" (V,ii,76-92), expanding in the might-have-been of remembered aspiration the power which had been what led her to love him originally, "The demi-Atlas of this earth, the arm/And burgonet of men" (I,v,23-24). He died, of course, trying to become that which, had it happened, would have actualized this dream of love; but it could only have happened had he resolutely and totally fixed himself on the hard values of the Roman world that other players in that game are willing to give their all for. She recognizes the illusion and delights in its very illusoriness:

CLEOPATRA:
> Think you there was or might be such a man
> As this I dreamt of?

DOLABELLA:
>   Gentle madam, no.

CLEOPATRA:
> You lie, up to the hearing of the gods.
> But if there be nor ever were one such,
> It's past the size of dreaming. Nature wants stuff
> To vie strange forms with fancy; yet t' imagine
> An Antony were nature's piece 'gainst fancy,
> Condemning shadows quite.

(V,ii,93-100)

So the perspective picture, the Gorgon-Mars, comes true and whole again, but only in the imagination that renders null, "condemning" the whole merely analogic structure of a Platonic universe and its "shadows" of things eternal.

Lovers tend to approach the plenum of a state of divinity, the "Hohe Paar" that Bloch discusses.[29] In particular Antony is referred to as a Hercules, an Atlas, and a demigod, while he decks Cleopatra out in the garb of Isis. The fairies within whose ring love works its enchantment are themselves both lovers and supernatural beings.

This vision of eternity animates, and itself shadows, like a music under the earth, all the fickleness of the lovers, all their trickery towards each other, all jealousy, imperial powers, divine interdicts, and bodily subjections to the passage of time. Its whole sense throws no shadows: it is, in a sense, without value. The play simply envisions its rudimentary, all-etherealizing and time-filling existence.

THREE
Dramatic Irony

Il y a d'ailleurs à chaque fois des rapports internes entre le modèle idéal et son renversement ésotérique, comme entre l'ironie et le fond tragique, au point qu'on ne sait plus du tout de quel côté est le maximum d'ironie. C'est pourquoi il est vain de chercher une formule unique, un concept unique pour tous les langages ésotériques.

Gilles Deleuze
La Logique du sens

The meaningful boundary of signification between the audience group and the players can be enlisted to produce one or another leverage of signification.[1] But the boundary must remain for a performance to be dramatic. In the theatre of Grotowski, as in that of Red Grooms, Allen Kaprow, and Robert Whitman, the boundary can be elided, the audience enlisted as major participants: but a kind of archness derives from the elision of the boundary: it is defined *as* elided. The space of performer and the space of spectator, the time of both, are celebratively mingled by being announced as congruent. Destroy that announcement and the archness is lost with the celebration. A central irony is done in. Drama disappears.

The self-mocking irony of the Happening is a kind of reverse of "dramatic irony," something we tend to define by the norm of Shakespeare's stage. We know who Kent is, but Lear and Gloucester and Edgar do not; we know Desdemona is innocent, as Othello does not; and we know what ails Othello, as Desdemona does not. But in the Happening everyone embraces the same knowledge and the same ignorance; ignorance and knowledge, the spectator's dissociation and the actor's complicity, are functions of one another, and the stage boundary, visible as it is wilfully and playfully blurred, signifies these connections.

In the Greek theatre the personage on the stage moves forward in stage time to round out what the spectator, the other side of the circular orchestra boundary, already knows as permanent in that sequence of the myth. In the plays of Racine and Corneille, which take that classical situation as a pattern to be purified, incidental irony does not last for long: Hippolyte soon learns what Phèdre is aiming at, and Brittanicus' confidence in the duplicitous Narcisse is meant to illustrate the innocence of the one and the slippery treachery of the other. This moral is proportional; it builds to the central resolution in which the one is poisoned by the emperor and the other torn to pieces by the crowd. The irony feeds a revelation in the staged time, which proceeds at the same pace as the audience time, but in a locked step of causality.

On Shakespeare's panoramic stage, where the causality ramifies openly, the dramatic ironies come and go, using the stage boundary as a lever for profundities of perspective. Angelo off-stage is caught in irony when he orders Claudio executed anyway; he believes he has coupled with Isabella, while he has actually fulfilled a delayed marriage contract. Isabella herself, a novice we do not know to be temporary, receiving guidance from a monk we know to be the disguised Duke, is led to the heroic Christian response of passing beyond the desire of revenge:

DUKE:
    His head is off and sent to Angelo.
ISABELLA:
    Nay, but it is not so.
DUKE:
                    It is no other.
    Show your wisdom, daughter, in your close patience.
ISABELLA:
    O, I will to him and pluck out his eyes!
DUKE:
    You shall not be admitted to his sight.

ISABELLA:

> Unhappy Claudio! Wretched Isabel!
> Injurious world! Most damned Angelo!

DUKE:

> This nor hurts him nor profits you a jot;
> Forbear it, therefore; give your cause to heaven.

. . . .

ISABELLA:

>   I am directed by you.
>   (*Measure for Measure,* IV,iii,112-133)

The gestures of language, the ideas, are powerfully direct and concentrated. But they are leavened in all directions by dramatic
irony—over the head (it is not Claudio's), over the forced seduc-
tion (it was not Isabella, as she knows) and over her interlocutor
(who is not a monk). Isabella's whole motion of rising above revenge by way of a mechanism that involves a rejection of both her
own sexuality and her brother's, and a vow not to marry, will
turn out, in fact, to be a step toward sexuality, in a sequence of
her courtship with the very monk whose spiritual counsel, in retrospect, will have been a step along the road to nuptial intimacy.

Not only does the space in this theatre change at the beck of the
actors, asserting by its unlifelike quickness-of-transposition the
bond of communication between audience and stage group, whereas the nineteenth century fourth-wall stage throws its emphasis on the likeness of the stage scene to the actual scene of the
real world. The time also is subjected to those elisions which emphasize the distinctness of the audience's tempo of perceptions; we
have seen Edmund betray his father. The tempo of the actors'
perceptions, too, may be almost identical with that of the audience,
as with Kent's; or not so, as with Gloucester's. But Gloucester, at
another point of perspective, has stood at our own vantage toward
Lear, somewhat undeceived by Goneril and Regan, and yet somewhat deceived by the status quo, as his fresh proportion of deference to Cornwall ("Hail to your Grace!" II,iv,126, etc.) shows.
There is no single major playwright of the time—not Shakespeare, not Jonson, not Marlowe or Kyd or Webster, not Middle-

ton or Chapman, Marston or Ford—who does not take recourse in dramatic irony at important moments. This can be asserted of no other great dramatic tradition.

It is, relevantly, in terms of a philosophical perspective that Bacon defines "The Idols of the Theatre":

> Lastly, there are Idols which have immigrated into men's minds from the various dogmas of philosophies and also from wrong laws of demonstration. These I call Idols of the Theatre, because in my judgment all the received systems are but so many stage plays, representing worlds of their own creation after an unreal and scenic fashion. Nor is it only of the systems now in vogue or only of the ancient sects and philosophies that I speak, for many more plays of the same kind may yet be composed and in like artificial manner set forth, seeing that errors the most widely different have nevertheless causes for the most part alike. Neither again do I mean this only of entire systems, but also of many principles and axioms in science which by tradition, credulity, and negligence have come to be received.[2]

Substitute prior action in a play for "tradition," inference on imperfect information for "credulity," and failure to draw conclusions (as Gloucester fails to deduce how cruel Cornwall may be) for "negligence," and the necessarily partial vantage of characters in a play, their consequent subjection to the irony of our total vantage, does duty for the perspectival exclusions of a philosophic system. Bacon offers this as his last in a series of idols. The Idols of the Tribe ("their foundation in human nature itself"), of the Cave ("of the individual man"), and of the Market Place ("association of men with each other...words plainly force and overrule the understanding, and throw all into confusion"), may likewise be assimilated to the function of dramatic irony in a theatre contemporary with the growth of Montaignian skepticism, the fragmentation of authority between church and state, and the refinement of perspective in easel painting.

Jonson's plays are simple and constant in their irony, constructed almost always on the principle of cozening, where some central character, Volpone or Face or Brainworm, tries to dupe the others, and the sharpness of satiric definition comes alive in the interplay of the shift between what that one person and the audience knows but the rest do not. Even a young demon, in *The Devil Is an Ass*, is no match for the multiple sleights of human-kind. When the cozener is cozened, as Mosca bilks Volpone, a further dramatic irony takes over. Our spectator's time is, once again, caught up short, because it turns out that we could only have inferred the unexceptional universality of cupidity by being eased out of wondering whether Mosca is an exception. We are in on his plot with Volpone, taken in as Volpone himself is taken in, and the *stretto* of this conclusion swiftly patterns what we had wanted to leave unpatterned, our own inclusion in the system. The experiment of the much-admired *Epicene* performs the tour-de-force of joining our ignorance with that of the characters till the very end: we also do not know the bride is really a man. The play centers on a bridegroom who cannot be taken in too much because he cannot hear too much: the silence he orders around him at once magnifies and weakens his suspiciousness. So he knows he is to be taken in; and to that extent he shares what the audience sees happening to him, but not the detail. The audience itself is taken in ultimately by the crucial detail about Epicene's sex.

In *The New Inn* we are given this same disguise—a maid is a man—and others as well; and the unmasking redefines the elapsed time—a whole generation—as coherent rather than haphazard, revealing the presence of a dramatic irony and resolving it at one stroke. *The Magnetic Lady* uses the device of a good cozener, who wins out by enlisting the spectator's vantage, by dramatic irony, over schemes and "practisers."

Shakespeare's deliberate manipulation of gaps in time opens time in all directions of inference. In such an even flow of measured time as, for example, operatic music, it is next to impossible, as Jackson Barry shows, to present dishonesty.[3] An episode of double dramatic irony in Beaumarchais' play comes through as a movingly melodic pledge of mutual love in *Le Nozze di Figaro*. In Shakespeare, where the words preponderate, the direct charm of music refers, ironically or hyperbolically, to a world whose spell cannot be broken by disjunction.

Dramatic irony serves as the copula for the fusion of roles: it is through the interaction between what he does not know and what he does (where we as an audience sit in the position of omniscience) that Lear the madman and Lear the king are brought together in the flow of event. Lear never learns of Goneril's lust —his blast against lechery strikes home by what could be equally ironic coincidence or alerted intuition, and our knowledge of his ignorance, the dramatic irony, operates to suspend both possibilities.

The audience cannot speak, but it hears and it thinks. Thinking, it remembers what it heard, comparing the present with the past. Its silence is compensated for by the totality of its perception: anything that has passed across the stage it knows. Not all characters, in a Renaissance play, are on stage all the time. And comparing the present with the past, the audience is able to perceive the mixing of one mood with another, of Othello's act of rejection with his act of appeal in the same words spoken before Desdemona drops the handkerchief. The leverage of the stage boundary is empowered by the dramatic irony.

Take away the irony, and the force of the overlay, one mood upon another, is also taken away.

If Desdemona knows as much as we know, she is, as we know, sensitive and loving enough to find the means for coping with Othello. The overlay of mood would then become a passing snarl in intercourse and not the supercharging of purpose for the dread outcome.

Without dramatic irony the standard of decorum, already a strong tendency in the role-stereotyping of this theatre, would threaten to take over. There would be no time-fissure into which questions about the decorum could enter, other than by taking in the whole action, and Shakespeare's theatre would be that of Corneille and Racine.

When it moves into the set of revenge, the staple Jacobean assumption, in addition to enlisting a diehard purpose in one character that may link erotic to political desires, aligns the persons through a dramatic irony that can only be broken with the dénouement of the plot itself. Stalking a victim can work only if the victim knows less than the audience that watches the stalking. And the process admits of several turns: in *The Spanish Tragedy*, the slow buildup deceives Horatio's mother, who does not realize the snares her husband Hieronymo is laying for the murderers of their son. Hence she stabs herself in their garden after uprooting the tree where he was hung, providing a further impetus to Hieronymo's purpose. The play-within-a-play cancels a nesting series of dramatic ironies, all contained by the omniscience of the audience: Aragon, Castile, and the Viceroy in the gallery do not know that Bel-Imperia hates the Balthazar who has killed Horatio, nor do they know she loved him for assuming vengeance on behalf of her first lover, whom Balthazar also killed. Her brother Lorenzo and Balthazar have calmed their initial suspicion that Hieronymo knows their guilt, and they have accepted parts in his play. They do not see the silently ironic appropriateness in the fact that Solyman, acted by Balthazar, plans to murder the lover of Perseda, acted by Bel-Imperia. The feigned murders are real, including the suicide of Bel-Imperia, which Hieronymo himself did not expect. The play-within-a-play on stage, and the misapprehensions of their helpless relatives in the gallery, trigger the satisfactions of the Ghost and Revenge, who are watching the whole spectacle-within-a-spectacle. We, in our final turn, watch *them*, and recast their sense of satisfaction by a sense of extravagance which those allegorized characters could not share.

The opening of *Titus Andronicus* wears the air of a conclusion —except for the vengeful purpose of Tamora, whose erotic life serves rather than motivates the vengeance. The formal Triumph of the choice of Saturninus as Emperor, combined with that of conquest, the seeming finality of the sacrifice, the stage marriage of convenience for Lavinia, and the counterbalancing initial Stoicism of Titus—all these are bypassed by the barbaric resoluteness of the Queen. Every grisly twist of event is triggered, and made possible, by the stiff, powerful elisions of a dramatic irony worked far more heavily than Kyd's, if not with such formal elaboration.

The irony keeps the sequence from being episodic: it is governed by a steely purpose, one so Gothic the Romans cannot guess it. Later the Jacobean theatre will develop a pyrotechnic set of ironies, as those that surround the death of Ithocles in *The Broken Heart*, where a throne turns into an execution machine while concealed identities permute with deflected purpose. In *The Revenger's Tragedy* lust and incest crisscross as a son-in-disguise is enlisted by his unwitting victim to pander for his own sister and mother, and it is the mother who succumbs, prevented from consummation by further twists. This victim is himself a stalker, of his own brother; and the father of that family is himself the victim stalked at the beginning of the play. At the climax he tongue-kisses the disguised poisoned skull we had been shown in the opening scene, the skull of the discarded mistress he has killed. Lust and deception keep pace with each other, kept in place by the audience perceptions that control the sequence, permitting the stepping up and redistribution of the dramatic irony in the deadly make-believe of a concluding masque. As in *Women Beware Women*, *The Spanish Tragedy*, and others, the irony spawns a new, complete make-believe on stage—a make-believe that breaks its bounds, as the play-within-a-play of *Hamlet* does not.

Shakespeare opens the abyss of purpose, often, by creating the rift of dramatic irony between his characters. The tempo wherein all does not meet the eye refers itself to the heart. The irony opens perspectives on the interiority of motive in a dramatic tradition that exteriorizes all action into expatiating, recitative words. In the first scene of *Othello*, Iago announces to Roderigo that he intends a concealment: "I would not follow him, then," says Roderigo, still courtly in his decency (I,i,40). "O, sir, content you," Iago replies, "I follow him to serve my turn upon him" (I,i,41-42). And he proceeds to wake Brabantio to hunt down his daughter's bridegroom. In the very next scene Iago turns the tables. In the presence of a new group clustered round Othello, he slanders the very same Brabantio he had "helped," declaring to the Othello he intends to gull that his conscience barely kept him from murdering the father whose ire he had aroused. ("Nine or ten times/I had thought to have yerk'd him here under the ribs" I,ii,4-5). The depths of undermined honesty are measured by the impossibility that anyone who hears the Iago of this second scene could imagine, without sharing the audience's immunity of viewing, what Iago has said in the first scene. A similar ironic succession, where the second scene undercuts the first, opens *Richard III*. After his initial Machiavellian soliloquy, Richard first commiserates with Clarence as he is led to the Tower and then congratulates Hastings on his release. We understand he had a hand in the imprisonment of both. So we are given a demonstration of how far and how fast duplicity can delude; what slowly gathers head in the play is the inferential strength of the other, partially ignorant characters.

In *The Winter's Tale* it is the opening scene, again, which shows duplicity beginning at the same moment as jealousy. The duplicity of Leontes is swiftly revealed by the honesty of Camillo, but duplicity crops up again, malevolently as Perdita is exposed in the crossfire of self-deceptions, benevolently as Hermione is sequestered by Paulina, both malevolently and benevolently as Autolycus' cheating of the peasant foster-parents of Perdita leads to the discovery of who she really is. All these incursions of irony accompany a mystery of motivation: the jealousy of Leontes, the virtue of Camillo, the tergiversations of Antigonus, and the omnivorous cupidity of Autolycus, spring from nowhere, and the characters are consequently at the mercy of them, as the audience is not. But in the long haul, in the romance, the mercy turns out to be merciful, and the breaks in perception occasioned by the dramatic irony serve to veil the mystery.

When Gloucester shares with Edmund his letter from France and his intention to aid Lear, Edmund abruptly performs the shift of irony the instant his unwitting father leaves: "This courtesy forbid thee shall the Duke/Instantly know, and of that letter too" (*King Lear* III,iii,21-22). The closure of the irony comes after Gloucester is blinded, to crown the mockery he must endure:

GLOUCESTER:
    Edmund, enkindle all the sparks of nature
    To quit this horrid act.
REGAN:
                    Out, treacherous villain!

Thou call'st on him that hates thee. It was he
That made the overture of thy treasons to us;
Who is too good to pity thee.

(III,vii,85-9)

The irony, as it is resolved, leaves in its wake the contradiction, as between the perceptions of the audience and the assertions of the characters, in "nature," "villain," "treason," "good," and "pity." Four of these terms are simply inverted, but "nature" nests several contradictions, as between the lustful boast of the bastard-fathering Gloucester and this appeal to the tie of blood; as between the Nature which is Edmund's "my goddess and my law" and the cold-bloodedness implicit therein; as between Gloucester's astrology and the self-subsistence of Edmund's selfishness; as between Gloucester's reliance on the family tie and these "unnatural" daughters.

The short-range contrast in the characters' expectations quickens the contrast of our own, longer-ranged but circumscribed. By the blinding scene we measure how loaded with prospective irony were Gloucester's words at the conclusion of the scene where Edmund had "exposed" his elder brother's treachery:

Loyal and natural boy, I'll work the means
To make thee capable.

(II,i,84-85)

"Natural" is here, too, subject to dramatic irony the way the "bond" of Cordelia is. Already it is made to mean both "bastard" and "dutiful to your real father." Dramatic irony is the mechanism by which we are enabled to bring the contrastive elements into focus, whether or not our expectations are confirmed (we knew all along the elder sisters were evil) or surpassed (we had not expected them to do themselves in over Edmund, or to see him utter a deathbed confession "in spite of mine own nature").

Dramatic irony modulates the flow of action so it may enlist a causal intricacy beyond what is perceptible from just one set of events. In *The Witch of Edmonton* Frank pledges a secret marriage to his fellow-servant Winnifred, whom he has seduced. In the next scene their master Arthur reveals, unexpectedly, that Winnifred has been his mistress too. But she refuses, unexpectedly, as a married woman to continue the connection. Her new loyalty does not prevent Frank, who is concealing her in hope of inheritance, from saving the inheritance by bigamously marrying the daughter of his father's creditor, showing the man the letter which he had wheedled out of Arthur declaring him to be unmarried. At every turn a fresh facet of knowledge leaves a new character at a different angle of ignorance. Every turn of irony complicates the events. So in Ford's *Perkin Warbeck*, Katherine, Perkin's wife, as she confronts him on his way to execution, feels both loyal sorrow for her loss and shame at his easy capitulation. At the same time she exhibits a filial duty to her father, a gratitude to the faithful rejected suitor who has been attending her, and something like submission to her own king, the Scotch James IV, who has himself abandoned her husband in the effort to patch up his alliances. The fact that no one of these recipients of her feeling can fully know her response to the others acts to sort her feelings out, to make of them an orderly array undisturbed by further action at this last moment of the play.

It is the dramatic irony in which the Gadshill prank has been carried off that provides the ideological armature for Falstaff's self-parody in the battle scene where he plays dead. Because of the earlier scene, the vulnerability of the buffoon cannot be dissociated from the selfishness, and the tempo of the night-exploit harmonizes somewhat with the tempo of the earnest battle.

The title of *The Comedy of Errors* announces that the operation of dramatic irony will be constant; it will be the only constancy in a situation where the identity of name and birth poses the riddle of true identity. The mistakes take place in a day, but in a magic day with mortality tied to it as a legal condition: the father, if he does not find ransom, "Dies ere the weary sun set in the west" (I,ii,7). He has come to Ephesus in the first place searching for his lost sons. In the last act he speaks of himself as perhaps unrecognizable because of his advanced age—introducing another criterion than the physical likeness of one Antipholus to another by which the recognition of identity might be blurred in the mortal span of time. The trick, applied with a consistency beyond Plautus, throws shadows of quite un-Plautine seriousness. The intimations released in the romantic conclusion already glimpse the sphere of the late comedies, where dramatic irony plays a role subtler than the identity concealment of these twins.

The identity concealments turn the dramatic irony back on the dramatic condition in *Twelfth Night, As You Like It, Two Gentlemen of Verona, All's Well that Ends Well*, and *Cymbeline*, by having boy actors act a girl pretending to be a boy. Love lends itself easily to such illusion, as in the trick of multiple eavesdropping on Malvolio or the false assignation in *The Merry Wives of Windsor*.

Love is caught in another illusion, that of time: there is a season for mating and a potential lightning in every encounter between the sexes. The dramatic irony of the sex-disguise reins that temporary mystery into a willful progression.

A merely contrastive irony of event can be very powerful. When Troilus swears vengeance on Diomedes and then we are given the cruel stroke of the courteous lecher's victory,

> Go, go, my servant, take thou Troilus' horse;
> Present the fair steed to my lady Cressid.
> *(Troilus and Cressida,* V,v,1-2)

we have reached a moment that matches in intensity the unveiling of Cressida's dalliance with Diomede by the Ulysses who heaps this coal on the head of his enemy guest (V,ii); eavesdropping brings him the pressure of knowing what we know. All the irony is brought to bear on the one moment: we are privy to no special knowledge, and the general knowledge itself, the dramatic moment itself, suffices to make us enter the grim mood of Thersites and Pandarus. So earlier in that play, the horror of Cressida's arrival in the Grecian camp is sexualized when one by one, mute fear mingling with desperate coquetry, she distributes kisses to the throng of bullies who receive her—to all but the

Ulysses who cannot stomach the scene, though he sees only the coquetry. Our knowledge of him, the Greeks' ignorance of Troilus, is of little moment here. The dramatic irony is not brought heavily to bear. The pressure of the present operates not only with the dramatic irony that the Greeks do not know about Troilus; it offers also a thematic irony, as between pretended courtesy and real exploitation, in the world envisioned where such actions kill the heart (lechery) and take the life (war), proving the aptness of Thersites' shriek, "War and lechery confound all!" (II,iii,71).

Dramatic irony, however, connects present with present, and also, cumulatively, present with past: Its contrasts are always double, and its significative doors open and close at the same time. When Orlando, faint from hunger as we have just been shown, bursts in on the feasting forest community of the Duke (*As You Like It*, II,vii), whose courtesy we have just seen, their ignorance of each other refers to an order of gentle irony the grimness of his situation and the managed lightness of theirs. They do not know of his desperation, and he does not know of their courtesy: the actions immediately preceding have shown us both, and put us in the position neither can enjoy of contrasting his present with theirs.

But we are also contrasting Orlando's past with this present, nor is that contrast a simple one. He has declined from the humbled but well-fed nobleman consigned to the farmyard. But he has already risen, to the extent of his aspirations, whatever their low point. The decline and the aspirations quickly find issue, as the Duke takes charge:

ORLANDO:
> He dies that touches any of this fruit
> Till I and my affairs are answered.

JAQUES:
> An you will not be answer'd with reason, I must die.

DUKE SENIOR:
> What would you have? Your gentleness shall force,
> More than your force move us to gentleness.

ORLANDO:
 I almost die for food, and let me have it.
DUKE SENIOR:
 Sit down and feed, and welcome to our table.
ORLANDO:
 Speak you so gently? Pardon me, I pray you;
 I thought that all things had been savage here

                                        (II,vii,98-107)

Orlando, himself nature's nobleman driven back to nature, has yet to learn that wilder nature can produce noblemen withdrawn to their own Utopia. But being nature's nobleman, he learns it quickly, and against such checks, with all their contrasts focused through the dramatic irony, the courteous state of affairs is made to prevail here that will prevail also at the end of the play. Jaques' song in his previous scene touched, without knowing how prophetic its simple aphorisms should be, on a situation where extremity of difficulty and ease of control throw mutual light on one another through the division between stage and audience:

> Who doth ambition shun,
> And loves to live i' th' sun,
> Seeking the food he eats,
> And pleas'd with what he gets,
> Come hither, come hither, come hither!
> Here shall he see
> No enemy
> But winter and rough weather.

                                        (II,v,34-41)

—which is true so far as we have seen, but not through the play. Orlando, as if to answer the call he did not hear, has "come hither." He gets the food he seeks. But Oliver will meet an enemy other than winter and rough weather, a lion who almost kills him. The natural savagery, potentially worse than that of the civilized enemies in court to whom Jaques' song refers by contrast, turns out benignly to reconcile. The prospective, prophetic ironies of the song, however, are a descant on the ground which the dramatic ironies manipulate, turning division into union and the ignorance of disguise systematically into the fullest knowledge of sexual union.

The contrasts brought into expression by dramatic irony may be still wider in divergence than those we find in *As You Like It,* seriousness from flirtation, hunger from plenty, indifference from love, selfishness from courteous sharing. "The quality of mercy is not strain'd; It droppeth as the gentle rain from heaven," Portia says, disguised as the lawyer Balthazar (*The Merchant of Venice,* IV,i,184-185). Lawyers are not theologians, but this bride is not really a lawyer. That she puts on the act of being one sets out for the audience, privy to the disguise, contrasts among theology, law, and married love. The mercy will extend to the erotic play in the mockery of infidelity with which she later tests her bridegroom, safe in her disguise. The contrast between Bassanio's relief at Antonio's not losing his life and his jealous bewilderment is redirected, through the irony we perceive, into a moment of gentle afterplay at the hands of the bride whom he had already magically risked his marriageability to win in the same suburb where they are headed. "How far that little candle throws his beams!/So shines a good deed in a naughty world" (V,i,90-91). In little Portia's formulation, the testing after a good deed also throws its beams into the naughty world. The dramatic irony centers her to carry off the contrastive sequence of her gestures, to bring commercial risk and mortal usury into relation somehow with amorous attraction and marital equilibrium. The man whose recklessness has him risk a friend's life to borrow gold turns out to be the only one penetrating enough to pass over gold and silver caskets, to choose the leaden one of the marriage test that also saves the friend's life. The quick shifts of the irony keep our perceptions dispassionate enough, detached enough, to yoke these incongruities without violence together.

In *Cymbeline,* the king himself, to begin with, rules his kingdom courteously and decisively, qualities he shows in his handling of the Roman ambassador Lucius. Yet from first till nearly last, like the Saturninus of *Titus Andronicus*, his ignorance of his queen's hostility to him gives her free rein to act, before our eyes, the Wicked Stepmother to his daughter. The Lear buried in him, who had banished the Kent-like Belarius on the witness of "two villains" and would not listen to his Cordelia-like daughter, is never given a chance to indulge in the pyrotechnics of inner upheaval, so complex and so removed from his perception is the action the audience is privileged to witness. Dramatic irony compounds starkness with delicacy and cushions the shock of death with the joy of reunion.

The audience, while it takes in the whole action, listens on a plane of mystery to which the characters themselves, for all their alert responsiveness, do not have access. The gallery of the capable—Imogen, Belarius, Guiderius, Arviragus, Posthumus, Pisanio, Cornelius, Philario, Lucius, and in some ways ultimately Cymbeline himself—is fuller than in any other play of Shakespeare. And yet in no other play are the characters so much at the mercy of what is at once beyond their control and within our perception. Iachimo, more adept than Iago, and far more malevolent, since he holds no grudge against Posthumus and would seduce as well as mortally slander his victim, is not hunted out; rather, he confesses, caught in the process of an action other than the seduction-trap he baited, the military contest between Rome and Britain.

No one in this play at any given time, till the end, has all the requisite pieces of information. Characteristically the capable characters exhibit courtesy in the face of this "accidental" incapacity; the most ignorant, the king himself, displaying courtesy most frequently. Courtesy may frame the bitterest exchange:

POSTHUMUS:

                         I hope you know that we
  Must not continue friends.

IACHIMO:

                         Good sir, we must,
  If you keep covenant.

                                  (*Cymbeline*, II,iv,48-50)

And yet at the same time Cymbeline gives way to an impulsiveness which is the other side of his response to the ignorance he cannot breach, threatening Pisanio with torture to elicit information (IV,iii,11-12), and in a prior action banishing the loyal Belarius, for a mere imputation of the very act, being "confederate with the Romans" (III,iii,65-70), which the pressure of events will force him to pass over as incidental, and actually as unperceived, in the Posthumus he has also impulsively banished and is correspondingly obliged to reinstate.

Cymbeline, who knows next to nothing but what he must know as a king, is mated to a Queen who knows everything but whose manipulations others will perceive. The alertness of her stepdaughter nips in the bud her vicious motions, even before our ironic distance has been activated to measure her. We have been given nothing to make us suspect the courtesy of her first speech till Imogen's immediate response removes the Queen behind the glass walls of our irony:

> Dissembling courtesy! How fine this tyrant
> Can tickle where she wounds!
>
> (I,i,84-85)

But Imogen herself cannot imagine the limitations to this tyranny, as daughter to a parent of the opposite sex whose deficiencies she has been forced to make up, becoming a paragon in the process. Her opposite number would seem to be Cloten, who is son to a parent of the opposite sex. But his parent, the Queen, pretends to have no deficiencies of knowledge. He, consequently, has been unable to develop in her protective shadow. He is monstrously cut off from understanding any trifles that transpire; it takes next to no dramatic irony to cut him off. He is defined, without irony, as an unwitting buffoon, who cannot perceive the decorum of what everybody sees—much like what the Queen has turned her husband into, except that Cymbeline possesses reserves of strength. Imogen's true opposite number is one whose name defines him as having outlived the parents of both sexes, Posthumus.

The test which the plot activates for the capacious love of both is to overcome the slander of adultery, something neither Imogen nor Posthumus is able to do by any other than the circuitous route of passing through many events half-perceived by them and wholly perceived by us.

Before this main communicative strategy of dividing what crosses the stage barrier ironically from the action on stage, the steady flow of language on stage can itself be thrown into the relief of deficiency, when the poetry goes simple before the rapid changes of revelation. Or else the language can be thrown into the relief of excess, when part of the irony consists in the launching of poetry far too rich for those giving it utterance. This is notably the case for the songs in the play. The first song is given to Cloten, who shows an ignorance greater than ours by breaking decorum to sing a serenade in the morning (rather than the evening) to a woman who is both unreceptive and, as a wife, technically unavailable. Moreover, he sings at a point in the play which induces a further, contrastive irony, since the song scene comes just after Imogen's bedroom has been penetrated by Iachimo. That intruder has spent most of the prior scene noting the contents of her room in a rich poetry that describes not only the "mole cinque-spotted" beneath her breast but the tale of Philomel she has been reading, her appearance in the bed, and the loveliness of her eyes, "now canopied/Under these windows white and azure, lac'd/With blue of heaven's own tinct" (II,2,21-3).

All this night, till the "dawning/May bare the raven's eye" (48-49), Cloten has been stupidly playing cards, distracting himself even from such perception of his own inequity as that on which Iachimo clicks with a rhyme ("I lodge in fear;/Though this a heavenly angel, hell is here" 49-50). The next rhyme, coming soon after the prose of the card game's aftermath, occurs in Cloten's song:

> Hark, hark! the lark at heaven's gate sings,
>   And Phoebus 'gins arise,
> His steeds to water at those springs
>   On chalic'd flow'rs that lies;

> And winking Mary-buds begin
>   To ope their golden eyes.
> With everything that pretty bin,
>   My lady sweet, arise;
>   Arise, arise!

(II,iii,19-27)

Cloten's literary appreciation is adequate to this song; he calls it "a very excellent good-conceited thing; after, a wonderful sweet air, with admirable rich words to it" (II,iii,15-18). But there is a disproportion between his sense of the song and his blunted perception of the use to which he would put it—"—and then let her consider," he goes on, something Imogen obviously will not do. The misfired perlocutionary force, under these failed illocutionary conditions, will wrench away from the richness of the locution, and that disproportion dissociates the ineffable verses from the strange and discordant act that immediately occasions it. In this way we are given an auditory foretaste of the blest world toward which the crooked smokes are enjoined to climb from altars at the end of the play, the heaven which both the verses of Iachimo and the song of Cloten do actually name, to an effect that the irony delays in time and displaces firmly from these speakers.

By the time we hear a song sung again, Cloten is really dead and Imogen supposedly so. The song links them, since it is sung in obsequies, just after we have heard a mysterious, "solemn music" over her false corpse and his headless body. It is sung by false rustics who are caught in several dramatic ironies—over a girl they imagine to be a boy, a princess they imagine to be a corpse, a sister they imagine to be a stranger, unconnected so far as they know with the Cloten who has been pursuing her in order to rape her. The song speaks also of a noon sun, not a dawn, enjoining not an alerted attention ("hark, hark, the lark") but a permanent inattention:

GUIDERIUS:
>   Fear no more the heat o'th'sun,
>   Nor the furious winter's rages;

Thou thy worldly task hast done,
   Home art gone, and ta'en thy wages.
Golden lads and girls all must,
   As chimney-sweepers, come to dust.
ARVIRAGUS:
   Fear no more the frown o'th'great;
      Thou art past the tyrant's stroke.
   Care no more to clothe and eat;
      To thee the reed is as the oak.
   The sceptre, learning, physic, must
   All follow this and come to dust.
GUIDERIUS:
   Fear no more the lightning-flash,
ARVIRAGUS:
      Nor th'll-dreaded thunder-stone;
GUIDERIUS:
   Fear not slander, censure rash;
ARVIRAGUS:
      Thou has finish'd joy and moan.
BOTH:
   All lovers young, all lovers must
   Consign to thee and come to dust.
GUIDERIUS:
   No exorciser harm thee!
ARVIRAGUS:
   Nor no witchcraft charm thee!
GUIDERIUS:
   Ghost unlaid forbear thee!
ARVIRAGUS:
   Nothing ill come near thee!
BOTH:
   Quiet consummation have,
   And renowned be thy grave!

(IV,ii,259-282)

So deflected by the multiple dramatic ironies, the song not only misses its aim, since this is no funeral for Imogen; but most of its points are lost, except as, in a still further irony, they happen quite accidentally to strike their mark: so in fact she need fear no more "the frown o' th' great," being great herself, which they, unwittingly great themselves, cannot know. The "tyrant's stroke" has laid her low, because the "physic" she has taken was aimed for her by her tyrant, the Queen who believes it to be a poison and so has delivered it to Pisanio, who presumes it to be a cordial and passes it on to Imogen, as the Queen had guessed might happen, not knowing that her tutor-physician Cornelius would not trust her with a poison and has given her a soporific instead. The actual drug strays harmlessly through this maze of misconceptions, which the soliloquy of Cornelius has briefed us on at the moment of initial transmission. The song weaves its rich, ironic strands over all this.

In the final scene, which begins as a marshalling and disposition of battle captives and ends as a restoration in family, throne, and kingdom, everyone is marshalled on stage, come to the long end of wanderings and imperceptions—everyone but the Queen, who "despairing, died" (V,v,61). Everyone else is visible to us, standing to register complexly, often with a final twist, the resolution of the involuted ironies.

The first is the king himself, who in sustaining blows far more severe than any given to Lear, responds with a quiet charity so heroic that it seems to have the effect of lifting the cloud of ignorance under which he has operated throughout. In learning that the queen "abhorr'd his person," saw his daughter as a "scorpion," poisoned her, and plotted to see Cloten crowned, his response is to look for the fault in himself, and to clear himself:

> Mine eyes
> Were not in fault, for she was beautiful;
> Mine ears, that heard her flattery; nor my heart,
> That thought her like her seeming. It had been vicious
> To have mistrusted her; yet, O my daughter!
> That it was folly in me thou mayst say,
> And prove it in thy feeling. Heaven mend all!
> (V,v,63-8)

It is at this point of humility, grief, and supplication that Lucius, Iachimo, the Soothsayer, Posthumus, and Imogen enter, just too late to hear the death of the Queen, and so undeflected each from his own compacted expectancy, each possessing pieces of real information and pieces of false information that the real information of others will reveal. Pisania is present to register what the medicine "really was," in the Queen's report, which he transmitted to the disguised Imogen, while Belarius, Guiderius, and Arviragus must hear in this account what they imagine to be the prelude to their reckoning for the murder of Cloten.

There are so many multiple revelations that even the scholars count them differently. They come on at a pace, and in a complication, even greater than the "unconscious" undercurrent revealed when the play is read as a dream, its sexual latencies made manifest. If, as Murray Schwartz skillfully reads out that emotional rebus,[4] Imogen's sexual object must be displaced into a castration—the decapitation of a Cloten who embodies a rough phallic energy—before she can join it in the person of a Posthumus, who has himself shied clear of genital union by exaggerated fear-desire responses to the attack on her honor; then the play shows an ego-management of "heaven's" charitable ego-ideal. And of course it is force, not inner disposition, which separates Posthumus from Imogen. But the key interaction is not between conscious and unconscious—a dynamic present in any play, or indeed in any literary tale whatever, to say nothing of any narrative; but rather the interaction between knowledge and ignorance which the play pyrotechnically deploys, saving its most concentrated effects for the extended bravura of the final scene. Surface is surface, known or not; mystery is mysterious beyond any tango of unconscious with unconscious, and eros is blessed by courtesy, not by roughness.

At the point of vision and reconciliation it is piety towards some unexpressed principle of order that Cymbeline most notably exhibits, as though doing homage to the mystery of coherence in events which the partial blindnesses of all had abundantly demonstrated. Though he is victorious, he promises to pay the tribute, blaming his earlier hesitation on "our wicked Queen" (V,v,461), this revision into vassalage of his earlier courtesy a final, but benign, touch of his own persistent imperception.

What Schwartz says of this play may set the keynote for the modality of its vision of action: "We feel that latent ideas shape manifest events, but our sense of the relationship between manifest event and thematic continuity becomes hazy and precarious." —Except that the play, through its manipulation of ironies, accepts haziness as a kind of necessary concomitant of mortal existence and celebrates precariousness by steering all its risks to the safe haven of fulfillment, so long as those risks are undertaken with a charity that at times will have to assume heroic proportions. Without that matching arousal in all the characters, the poetic justice would be merely jejune. Without the mystery of cause it is the central function of the dramatic ironies to lay out, it would be sanctimonious. Shakespeare's manipulation of that stage resource saves *Cymbeline* from the automatic piety of most romances, and from their arbitrariness of event, by erecting arbitrariness into a principle of human perception.

Here, finally, the psychoanalytic possibilities are themselves short-circuited into mere character, where the mystery that progresses is one of plot. The moment of the grotesque marriage-primal scene traced by Schwartz—a dead, headless Cloten-as-Posthumus beside a drugged "phallic woman" Imogene-as-Fidele—is linked to the subsequent moments that supersede it.

The dramatic irony, when it so omnipresently draws the veil, or rather the one-way mirror, over the character's perceptions, suggests the possibility of a further veil, the play becoming this life, in which we see "as in a glass, darkly." The veil operating between the stage group and the audience, which blinds the characters, induces, by a simple step of logic, an intimation that a far more impenetrable one may exist between what is seen by the spectator—the stage events—and the still more complex order of events in the real world outside the theatre, events for which the play stands as a formula whose dramatic ironies announce the deceptiveness and simplicity of the finality celebrated in the foreshortened space of an immobile, wide-eyed afternoon.

FOUR
Play

1

Dramatic irony flexes the dependence of its own significance upon the fact that a charged line divides what is said on stage from the listening audience. No folk pageant can avail itself of such a linguistic resource; though it may ironically turn a fool into a king, it dwells in the pure present of its performance, and its sweep is inclusive. Dramatic irony, on the other hand, checks the present by a recent past, and its sweep is always quizzical, inclusive or exclusive as the event may happen to be. The activation of this resource metatheatricalizes the action by so raising the question of how far the action applies, on stage and hence in reality.[1]

In this theatre, dramatic irony is only one among a large repertoire of metatheatrical postures. Hamlet raises the question later explored by Diderot, the paradox of the uninvolved actor's ability to simulate emotions:

> Is it not monstrous that this player here,
> But in a fiction, in a dream of passion
> Could force his soul so . . .
> What's Hecuba to him or he to Hecuba,
> That he should weep for her? What would he do,
> Had he the motive and the cue for passion
> That I have?
>
> (II,ii,544-555)

Hamlet here links the actor's relation with Hecuba to his own relation with the mother for whom he himself is putting on the act of madness. Hamlet has a "motive and a cue for passion"; the actor reacts "but in a fiction, in a dream of passion," and the first term, "fiction," is meant to be contrastive, its opposite being, as for us, something like "reality"; the Latin "make-believe" of "*fictio*" is still fresh in the word. At the same time, while "dream" "of passion" taken together are a mere amplification of simile for "fiction," taken separately each is coded for identification with Hamlet himself, who "peak[s]/Like John-a-Dreams, unpregnant of my cause" (II,ii,562)—a phrase that shades him into the fool-figure he has been miming by the way of "dream." This phrase, in turn, states his indecision by means of an "unpregnant," that admits of analogic assimilation both to Hecuba of the "o'er-teemed loins" (II,ii,502) and the mother whose birth of Hamlet himself is touched on in the graveyard scene (V,i,143).

Here, as he meditates on the actors who have been summoned at his order and are rehearsing offstage to fulfill it, his crescendo of cause-effect separation from the over-reactive actor crosses over by way of identification, since it sees the actor in Hamlet's position—and, resting on the word *stage*—Hamlet in the actor's. To define "stage" here, we must first identify "stage" with reality and then divest it thereof; we must put the very word through its metatheatrical paces, since if the actor were Hamlet he would no longer be an actor and his realm no longer the stage, unless he were in a play called *Hamlet* like the one we are seeing:

> What would he do,
> Had he the motive and the cue for passion
> That I have? He would drown the stage with tears,
> And cleave the general ear with horrid speech;
> Make mad the guilty, and appal the free,
> Confound the ignorant, and amaze indeed
> The very faculties of eyes and ears.
>
> (II,ii,553-9)

A sense of make-believe, comparable though ultimately simpler, animates Jonson's plays. From the point of view of presentation, these plays centralize dramatic irony by situating cozeners at the key point of the plot. From the point of view of conception, they riddle with doubt the very verve they exhibit, in an ambivalence towards the animation of theatricality which Barish[2] locates in the quick of Jonson's moral system. His simultaneous stress on the imagination and distrust of it heightens the illusion[3] of the play, which may in itself be built on incredibilities, as Leech[4] points out: *The Alchemist* celebrates unusual activity and merriment at the time of a plague, while *Volpone* would seem to teeter on the brink of breaking dramatic irony at every moment. The Masques themselves are incredible in their very conception, mockeries in which the audience is invited to participate, confections whose very falsity is part of their conception.

Now Shakespeare, though he may well have been invited to write one, seems never for all his wit to have written an out-and-out masque. Though *A Midsummer Night's Dream* draws on playful supernatural beings and metamorphoses in a comparable celebration of artifice, it relates them to a human order. The same may be said for the masque that opens *The Two Noble Kinsmen*, the one that diverts the action of *The Tempest*, and the masque-like elements in *Cymbeline*, *Pericles*, and *The Winter's Tale*.

Shakespeare, especially in his comedies, keeps the Renaissance self-mockery of artifice, of which the masque is an especially airy confection, well within hailing distance; and yet he never summons it to do the entire work of the play. The strange partial uses to which he puts metatheatricality keep that aspect of the stage open for strange deformations of signification inaccessible to those contemporaries of his who were willing to sleep or nod in contentment with the magic platform put at their disposal.

The stage area, to begin with, is at once especially free and especially fixed. In relation to all other areas of social behavior, it is free, unmarked with the particular significations that are assigned to home and church, field and barn, city gate and cemetery. With respect to the mapping of social functions, the stage is a free area, a wilderness or no-man's land. And it assimilates itself powerfully to being used as such: the heath of Lear makes it into what it is open to, a danger-ridden area where strange terrors and physical perils beset a man. The plain of *Macbeth* and the midnight battlement of *Hamlet* draw on something of the awe surrounding such wilderness areas.

Taken by itself, however, the stage is the ground not just for the free presentation of arbitrary events but for the ordering of events into a tonal harmony and causal tightness not possessed by the events of life outside the stage door. As Duvignaud puts it: "That which Panofsky has called the passage from 'collective space' (*Agretatraum*) to 'systematic space' (*Systemraum*)—that corresponds, as a whole, to the construction of a privileged space in which there is projected an image of the human person which will soon become 'Man'."[5] The stage is fixed in conception; to donate three hours and one's silence to the theatre raises the expectation that a vision of some orderliness greater than the miscellany of everyday events will be exhibited. Even the Happening raises this expectation: its message, that order is as random as the everyday, constitutes an invocation to celebrate randomness. That invocation, as such, is a vision of order that renounces the notion of expecting any vision of greater order.

Shakespeare, who surrounds his persons in mystery, plays fast and loose between the special freedom and the special fixity of the stage. The area which is a "system," if space is taken as space, uses up the total stage, assigns named significations in the "wooden O" plenum of a present, the space-as-space. At the same time the area is taken as a "wilderness" where these significations can change in a twinkling, from palace to heath, from street to closet. The space is a space-in-time: "the dark backward and abysm of time" (*The Tempest*, I,ii,50); for the events presented are conceived as past and then projected forward—the reminiscing Prospero will be conjuring up persons from the past and of the tempest which may whirl as an image of the same chaos that an abysm yawns for.

The two-sided nature of the stage space lends itself to a duality of role. The doubling of identities, common in Shakespearian comedy, will lead into, or play against, two loaded areas: households or kingdoms, castle or forest, city or suburb, double cities. The riddle of identity seeks its magical solution in the doubling or contrasting of locales.

On a stage whose actors had some of the profanity of outlaws and yet were liveried servants of a nobleman or even "The King's Men," the criminal king is a recurrent subject.[6] The King is a principle of order and the madman, without being a criminal (though Poor Tom must evoke the Elizabethan Poor Laws), is a principle of chaos. As Lear changes from one to another he moves from one kind of space to another—except that the cave where he crouches out of the storm, in the age-old primitive Britain, is a kind of rudimentary kingdom where he holds sway. His real madness is set in the metatheatrical perspective of Poor Tom-Edgar's feigned madness and the Fool's convention of mad talk. The dramatic irony with which Kent compasses them turns them into something not far from the play-within-a-play. The mad are those in society who are, otherwise, classified as unclassifiable. Prison, as Foucault points out, was not used for the function of

confining the mad in the Renaissance, but rather for confining exalted persons like Richard II or later Lear himself.[7]

The order of the stage, like the order of the play, does not
confine Lear to a space defined simply as a wilderness. As the
play comes to a close, Lear and Gloucester are not killed but escape the condemnation on them both. Each survives to die of a
broken heart: thereby they align themselves with the spectators
of their own tragedy. By including them in the effect, it includes
us reflexively, and realigns both their bitterness and their quiet
along a metatheatrical axis. Something similar happens in
Othello. He cannot bear his sense of his own guilt—the soldier in
himself does away with the murderer in himself, and he stages
his suicide in such a way as to catch his auditors off guard enough
so that those on stage will not prevent him, nor those in the audience anticipate him. His elaboration of motive, his seeming reminiscence, are made to serve this purpose, and Eliot's view of his last
speech as unduly histrionic and posed has lost sight of the delicate
metatheatrical balance in which self-transcendence and self-dramatization are a single act.[8]

The play-within-a-play offers the most explicit version of the use
of the stage to perform a transformation on what the stage events
are supposed to mean. The stage boundary, which had not yet
developed into a full proscenium, was recent enough to permit
of the transposition that would metatheatricalize it. " In the Elizabethan theatre," as Anne Righter emphasizes, "the line dividing
a world of shadows from reality came to separate the actors from
their audience. Medieval drama, on the other hand, drew its
boundaries between a fragmentary, secular environment and the
cosmos of the play."[9] When that striking line is moved inside the
play, so that on stage there is reproduced over again the contrast
between audience and actors, living reality and stage illusion,
then the question about a pattern in reality, which the play an-
swers, refers itself further on: by contrast with the play-within-a-
play, the play we see seems more real; but its metatheatrical dis-
posability is once again called into question if the whole process,
play and play-within-play, are taken as commenting mutually on

each other. The significative structure does remain firm, just because the actor creates his universe by speaking it. On the proscenium stage of bourgeois realism, however, it is not the actor's words that create the illusion but the stage itself, the replica-room with the fourth wall knocked down. In the metatheatre of Pirandello the significative structure is not firm. The status of the six characters, or the past of Enrico Quattro, flows ambiguously through the stage area. "The Murder of Gonzago" in *Hamlet* stays firmly in place.

Lionel Abel has shown how thoroughly, even aside from the play-within-a-play, the self-dramatization of the characters in *Hamlet* pervades the play.[10] Each is not only putting on a show for the benefit of the others, but projecting a special plot of his own upon the others, much like a dramatist.

> You that look pale and tremble at this chance,
> That are but mutes or audience to this act,

Hamlet says (V,ii,326-7), and the word "act" comprises both the reality of the mortal actions he is caught in and the presentation of them on stage for the contemplation of a dramatic audience whose bodies register their reaction.[11] Hamlet tries to utilize his own histrionic teetering on the brink of identity to quiz and nonplus the other characters, and his evocation of the play to try the wound of the king ("I'll tent him to the quick" II,ii,593) will measure that effect by the king's disposition of responsiveness in ways that are similar to himself ("A dull and muddy-mettl'd rascal" II,ii,561) and to the audience ("You that look pale" V,ii,326; "If'a do blench, I know my course" II,ii,593-4). The play-within-a-play constitutes a partial mirror image of the events preceding the play we are watching, except that the murderer of Gonzago is "one Lucianus, nephew to the king," not the Claudius figure, but the Hamlet figure himself! The story, then, in Hamlet's interpretation at least—and we have no other—reasserts the displacement of complication it is meant to solve. It offers not only the disturbance to the profoundly disturbed king, but also a lesson too fast, and too disconnected and explicit, for the preoccupied Hamlet himself to grasp.

The play that Hamlet chooses to have the actor-characters warm up on, nests comparable analogies, but more comfortably: instead of the identical murder of a good king by usurpers, we have the murder of a good king, Priam, by bold, deceitful invaders. His wife Hecuba does not share in the spoils, as Gertrude does, but stands on horrified. Priam and Hecuba are not middle-aged lechers but aged parents. Troy is an exemplary ancient kingdom, not the seat of lust and intrigue, modern Italy. The young man who commits the murder has all the resolution before which Hamlet has shown himself to be wavering. There is such a young man in the play, Fortinbras, who enters Denmark with a deceptive transit-permit, just as Pyrrhus has entered Troy in the deceptive wooden horse (though from there on the parallel does not hold). The point of doubling in this play-within-a-play also centers on the murderer, but here Hamlet doubles with a partial ideal, Fortinbras, whereas in his correspondence to Lucianus he doubles with his nemesis, the murderer Claudius.

The play-within-a-play has its intended effect of throwing the king into alarm. It disrupts the scene. Its point is to act, and act upon people on stage, where usually, as in *The Spanish Tragedy* and in *Women Beware Women*, the play-within-a-play culminates the action, occurring in the fifth act and not the third, and its point is as much to disguise as to illustrate: not to reveal, but to conceal until murders have been effectuated.

Hamlet grazes the stage once again: complementing the fustian of "Dido and Aeneas" and the couplet-artifice of "The Murder of Gonzago" is a silent comedian whose skull is thrown up out of the ground, the jester Yorick. Uncovering the skull, the grave-diggers indulge in a gallows humor much like that which Hamlet has himself used on Rosencrantz and Guildenstern, but Hamlet's response is to turn the tables on gallows humor for nostalgic reminiscence. The jester induces him not to mime them, as these clown-gravediggers themselves have been doing, but rather to capitulate his childhood:

> Alas, poor Yorick! I knew him, Horatio: a fellow
> of infinite jest, of most excellent fancy; he hath
> borne me on his back a thousand times. And now how
> abhorred in my imagination it is! My gorge rises
> at it. Here hung those lips that I have kiss'd I
> know not how oft. Where be your gibes now, your
> gambols, your songs, your flashes of merriment
> that were wont to set the table on a roar?
>
> (V,i,178-85)

Hamlet at once resumes the note of mockery. But this pause of *Memento mori* and *Ubi sunt* puts him back in touch with feelings that will swell with purposiveness in the resolute formulations of his last speeches. The fusion of roles, of parts, clown with gravedigger, and the contemplation of a histrionic activity that has found its final end, moves Hamlet out of the fusion of roles that has been his resource and his entangling limitation from the start. Hamlet's recourse to metatheatrical staging, actual in "The Murder of Gonzago" or imagined in the remembered antics of Yorick, splits into one form of external formulation a process he is sustaining all the while by overlaying one mood upon another, the way Othello does. But Hamlet is self-conscious as well as histrionic. His self-consciousness at once victimizes him to his staginess and liberates him for the kind of mentalism that can readapt to his intolerable conditions: "I could be bounded in a nutshell and count myself a king of infinite space"—but not quite—"were it not that I have bad dreams" (II,ii,253-5). The histrionic potentiality in his self-consciousness, the awareness in the histrionic presence, permits him to mediate among all the pressures on his mind, or at least to attempt mediation, between the bewilderment of oncoming madness and the imperative to set his father right, between the dictates of vendetta and those of God, between an agonizing courtship and a courtly obligation, between the concerns of the philosophy student and those of the military courtier, between the threatened stepson and the obliged son of a murdered king. No one of these concerns does not bear on the others: all lie beyond the statesmanly prudence that Polonius exhibits and enjoins upon his daughter and his own son, the son whose speedy resumption of familial and political imperatives is asked to face none of Hamlet's overwhelming questions. Hamlet does not face them so much as enact them, and the strange, expansive inner shifts in his role are brought about through his staged and theatricalizing manipulation. His coping capacity appears splendidly in the attitudes he so adaptively puts on for an occasion that includes our own.

In the Utopia-Arcadia of Duke Senior's Forest of Arden, the exiled group are putting on the act of their ideality, in accord, as it were, with the title of the play itself, *As You Like It.* Their speeches of praise announce the necessity of recreating ideality at every moment. It is sustained by their acts, by the words that virtually suspend them in self-congratulation as in self-exhibition, since for them the only business of living would seem to reside in voicing their delight with their condition—except to assimilate newcomers to the ideality. One wandering group (Celia, Rosalind, and Touchstone) contains a clown, and Jaques' encounter with that man makes him wish to assimilate that role himself, to act it out in the make-believe court of the Duke :

JAQUES:
    A fool, a fool! I met a fool i' th' forest,
    A motley fool. A miserable world . . .
    And in his brain
    Which is as dry as the remainder biscuit ·
    After a voyage, he hath strange places cramm'd
    With observation, the which he vents
    In mangled forms. O that I were a fool!
    I am ambitious for a motley coat.
DUKE SENIOR:
    Thou shalt have one.

                    (II,vii,12-43)

Jaques defines the enviableness of the fool in terms of his ability to be merry before a miserable world by venting his observation in "mangled forms." To ask is to receive in the enchanted forest, and the Duke so assures him. The scene of granting Jaques' wish is itself interrupted by the incursion of another disturber of paradise, the hungry Orlando, demanding food for himself and the aged Adam. That wish, too, is granted, and the incursion is at once assimilated to a conspectus of meaning whose observations distance and theatricalize that hunger too. At the same time there is a tonal abruptness; Orlando's hunger is desperate, whereas their banquetting is light and leisurely.

"All the world's a stage," spoken by Jaques in the role he has been granted, would seem to apply to Arden insofar as everyone is acting there, and not to apply insofar as the forest group have freed themselves from the preoccupations of embattled society. They have, indeed, freed themselves from blind acting by total acting, from the mortality of the seven ages of man by "merriment."

The seven-ages Topos begins with a double uncertainty: we do not know exactly how a hungry Orlando fits into the series, since his incursion evades congruence with the series; and we do not know at which of the younger roles of the seven to locate him, though soon the lover will be appropriate. But the conclusion of the series is suddenly clear, since the description of old age is immediately followed by the entrance of the eighty-year-old Adam.

DUKE:
> Go find him out . . .

ORLANDO:
> I thank ye; and be blest for your good comfort! (*Exit.*)

DUKE:
> Thou seest we are not all alone unhappy:
> This wide and universal theatre
> Presents more woeful pageants than the scene
> Wherein we play in.

JAQUES:
>   All the world's a stage
> And all the men and women merely players;

They have their exits and their entrances;
And one man in his time plays many parts,
His acts being seven ages. At first the infant,
Mewling and puking in the nurse's arms;
Then the whining school-boy, with his satchel
And shining morning face, creeping like snail
Unwillingly to school. And then the lover,
Sighing like furnace, with a woeful ballad
Made to his mistress' eyebrow. Then a soldier,
Full of strange oaths, and bearded like the pard,
Jealous in honour, sudden and quick in quarrel,
Seeking the bubble reputation
Even in the cannon's mouth. And then the justice,
In fair round belly with good capon lin'd,
With eyes severe and beard of formal cut,
Full of wise saws and modern instances;
And so he plays his part. The sixth age shifts
Into the lean and slipper'd pantaloon,
With spectacles on nose and pouch on side,
His youthful hose, well-sav'd, a world too wide
For his shrunk shank; and his big manly voice
Turning again toward childish treble, pipes
And whistles in his sound. Last scene of all
That ends this strange eventful history,
Is second childishness and mere oblivion;
Sans teeth, sans eyes, sans taste, sans every thing.

                                        (II,vii,133-166)

                  Re-enter Orlando with Adam.

The function of this speech has been to serve as a meditative
pause, reading the book of nature, here a theatre, at every turn
("This our life, exempt from public haunt,/Finds tongues in
trees, books in the running brooks,/Sermons in stones, and good
in everything." II,i,15-17). It is inserted while Orlando fetches
Adam, and their dual entrance serves as a silent epitome of the
speech, a youth leading an old man, as well as a sort of contradic-

tion of it, since their concerns of the moment are not phraseable in any of these classical commonplaces. The initial opposition of Jaques, "merry-miserable," was between the clown and the world, but not the make-believe/real world of Arden, only the distant stagey world which he later describes. The Duke sees it not as a sort of morality play, with seven ages substituting for seven sins, but rather as a "pageant," that procession where royalty and commoner found a common, transient function. He rephrases Jaques' earlier terms not as a contrast but as a comparison of a common quality, "we are not all alone unhappy ... more woeful pageants than the scene/Wherein we play in." The "wide and universal theatre" is seen as "more woeful" than Arden, but at the same time, "*this* wide and universal theatre" includes Arden. And joy is touched on in the other meaning of the "play"; the metaphor has it "act our part," but another opposite of "play," "work," will also bear upon his meaning, since they are idle in the forest; and the opposite of "occupy oneself as a solemn adult" as well, since those who play all the time, children, are characteristically joyful—though not the woetrammelled children of the seven ages, where the infant is absorbed in functions of nurture and the school-boy in the functions of learning, towards which both his mouth and his feet are objecting ("whining," "creeping like snail/Unwillingly"). Most of the items in the series involve sadness, or at least an absence of the joy evidenced by the lovers later on in the play. To that extent the illustrations are not only more formulaic than the lives we see before us, absorbed in romance-like typified roles though they may be; but they are also narrower, since life offers the range of merriness-woe that the Duke's abstractions do, while his and Jaques' theatrical metaphors do not.

The only point of correspondence between the seven ages and the plot of *As You Like It* is the lover, and that is also the point at which Orlando and Rosalind in their Arcadia will re-enact their own psychodramatic play-within-a-play, in terms that are not contemplative but energetically active, serving for courtship and not just for contemplation, and aiding, by the contagion of their doubling boy with girl and shepherd with nobility, a realignment into possible linkages of the courtships surrounding them.

The seven ages flash like a distorted mirror of the themes of the play.[12] Life is fuller than they suggest, not only because they over-typify, but because all their persons exist in a kind of soporific village life, whereas it is wandering that permits a larger discovery to all these principals, not least to Duke Senior himself, whose own access to a different area of space, and a different kind of space, a forest different from his Dukedom, has allowed him to indulge in these meditations.

The purpose of the Masque in *The Tempest*, put on at Prospero's behest by mysterious figures of supernatural origin, is to delay the fruition of the very fertility it at once celebrates and plays down by locating human mating in a vision of harvest. We are shown Iris, Ceres, and Juno, and then nymphs and reapers, describing a confrontation with, but not confronting, the "Deity" Venus, "her blind boy's scandal's company," and "Hymen's torch" (IV,i,92-97). Prospero's attention to one plot, the marriage of his daughter, so absorbs him here that he has momentarily forgotten the other which his own management of the tempest's aftermath has split off from it, the plot of the shipwrecked wanderers. So the reality of politics collides with the reality of the marital ceremony—an inversion of what had happened to Antonio and his company, since they have come within his sphere in the first place on their way to celebrate the marriage of Claribel in Tunis.

"I had forgot that foul conspiracy," Prospero says, "Of the beast Caliban and his confederates/Against my life; the minute of their plot/Is almost come. [*To the Spirits*] Well done; avoid; no more!" (IV,i,139-142). The demon who would have raped his daughter is leading a debased version of the ancient plot against Prospero, aided by the servants of the usurping rulers. It comes as a moment of recall that interrupts rounding out the play-within-a-play, redirecting its easy, muted analogies to the necessity of gathering one's forces. Prospero describes the spirits' play in terms which fuse the magic of their spirituality, the make-believe of their performance, and the illusionism of life on this earth—the whole not a mere contemplative definition, like Jaques'

quasi-fool's speech, but an inducement towards the redirecting of
cheer in both the future bridegroom and himself, "be cheerful,
sir."

PROSPERO:
> You do look, my son, in a mov'd sort,
> As if you were dismay'd; be cheerful, sir.
> Our revels now are ended. These our actors,
> As I foretold you, were all spirits, and
> Are melted into air, into thin air;
> And, like the baseless fabric of this vision,
> The cloud-capp'd towers, the gorgeous palaces,
> The solemn temples, the great globe itself,
> Yea, all which it inherit, shall dissolve,
> And, like this insubstantial pageant faded,
> Leave not a rack behind. We are such stuff
> As dreams are made on; and our little life
> Is rounded with a sleep. Sir, I am vex'd;
> Bear with my weakness, my old brain is troubled;
> Be not disturb'd with my infirmity.
> If you be pleas'd, retire into my cell
> And there repose; a turn or two I'll walk
> To still my beating mind.

FERDINAND
  AND
MIRANDA:
> We wish your peace.

(IV,i,146-163)

Prospero's initial lesson is that Ferdinand should match in mood
what he has just seen, be "cheerful" now that the "revels" are
ended. Prospero next refers to an earlier lesson, reminding his
captive pupil that the actors belong to another world and are
therefore imperceptible once they are finished, the repetition of
their disappearance "into air, into thin air" a gentle mockery of
his limits. Next though, those limits are universalized, first in a
phrase that makes the substance of what has just been seen, or

what is ever seen, or what is imagined, a "vision" without foundation, "baseless," and an allegation that in its concentration disposes of all medieval epistemology along with its nominalist restrictions ("baseless" being a more sweeping definition-by-negation of substance than that allowed by any system). Indeed, what has happened to the spirits will happen to all on earth, and to "the great globe"; the spirits "are melted"; they "shall dissolve." What disappears disappears totally, being a transient dramatic display, a "pageant" which is "insubstantial." The further lesson from this is that the substance that makes up the possessors of a vision, their "stuff," is also baseless and insubstantial, "such stuff/as dreams are made on," and the conclusion is a *memento mori* occasioned not by the wisdom, Prospero gently suggests, but rather by the age ("old brain"), the physical infirmity ("weakness") and the disturbance ("vex'd") of the speaker. His definition metatheatricalizes all the events which are a result of his conjuring, and all other events, on stage and off, by analogy to them.

The key juncture is not between make-believe and reality, or acting and earnest, but rather between spiritual and terrestrial, "stuff" and "baseless": it is the blending of *these* terms that the metatheatrical metaphor serves, and the whole itself is made to serve an especially rich, but also an abrupt and transient, moment of dramatic interaction. Prospero's culminative act of staging will be the pang-inducing circle wherein his natural rivals from time past will purge their iniquities. That play to come will feed directly and not tangentially into the action, with a bluntness foreign to the delectations of the Masque, and with a desperation quite the opposite of its easy playfulness, superseding the splendid definition after the Masque as the silent return to the mainland supersedes the powers of the book drowned on the way home from the island.

In *Pericles* we are given three distinct ways of presenting action—in the normal mode of dramatic utterances on stage, in dumb show, and in the narrative summaries of Gower. The change-off in stage presentation forces a wider split than the usual rhythmic changes, from prose to blank verse, and from these to song. The re-staging in other terms, even more than prose or song would, displaces the blank verse dialogue from our given assumption that this is the form which action across the stage barrier will naturally take: we have three natures, not one, and they metatheatricalize each other.

Dumb show is a conventional resource for a play; *Gorboduc* introduces each of its acts with a dumb show. But these dumb shows are recapitulative, as in *Hamlet,* or else allegorical. In *Pericles* the dumb show conveys action all by itself, and completely in itself, a rounded scene. This Renaissance dumb show is unlike the dance-mimes of the Noh theatre, which present a choral commentary on what has already happened, remaining in the same sphere as the past-recited and -presented action, as though to spell out the potency lurking beneath the very same words, rather than transposing them. The Miracle, the Mystery, the Pageant, and the Masque work themselves up to the point of needing words: words are their fulfillment. The dumb show quintessentializes the fulfillment, without recourse to words. Our mimes, too, are different from these, either expressing the simple emotion of one Pierrot-figure, a lyricizing of the dramatic—he can be inarticulate over just his one deep feeling of exalted nostalgia—or else presenting a kind of riddle, a mimetic show of butterfly-catching or rope-tugging by dispositions of the body: a dance.

Gower's narrative, in rhymed tetrameters, is at once quicker and more ordered than blank verse, neat and fast and thus conveying by voice alone some of the breathless propulsion forward that fast dramatic action by itself may bring about, casting the spell of a contrastive dream-like slowness over the main action of the play. Since a tale from his own works is being dramatized, the author-as-actor obviates, or rather metatheatrically pretends to obviate, the possibility of dramatic irony, simplifying the relationship across the stage barrier between stage group and audience group into that simply of speaker and listener, at the same time interposing himself between audience and actors, thereby distancing the actors, through the wrong end of a time-telescope. He speaks in the meter that tells this tale in the *Confessio Amantis.* And time is his preoccupation.

As Jaques does for the village of the seven ages of man, Gower also offers a window on a world unlike the play:

> Now sleep yslaked hath the rout;
> No din but snores the house about,
> Made louder by the o'er fed breast
> Of this most pompous marriage feast.
> The cat, with eyne of burning coal,
> Now couches for the mouse's hole;
> And crickets sing at the oven's mouth,
> Aye the blither for their drouth.
> Hymen hath brought the bride to bed,
> Where, by the loss of maidenhead,
> A babe is moulded.
>
> (III,i,1-11)

Pericles himself is never seen sleeping after any rout, though these couplets have him do so after his own wedding, the rout here described but not presented. Neither he nor the Marina whose conception is here recounted can rest in the peace of such a Flemish interior. Theirs is the world of a cat and mouse that are not immobilized as here into mere decorative vividness; they must wander the seas, before and after, until the resolution. Pericles has neither seen nor resembled the cricket who can sing at the oven's mouth, nor is the notion of being "blither for their drouth," anything but antithetical to what has been presented in the action, where people caught in famine are shown to be first desperate and then treacherous: "blither for their drouth" is an emblem which their unforeseen sufferings cancel out.

Already, by moving between dumb show *and* narrator, Shakespeare carries off the distancing of stage event and the displacement of audience response, the suspension-by-contradiction, which Brecht enjoins for his *Verfremdungseffekt*. And indeed Gower and the dumb show carry out Brecht's three conditions for achieving *Verfremdung*.[13] They transpose the events into the third person, they throw them into the past, and they accompany them with a commentary.

2

How, indeed, are we to take a play of Shakespeare's? This fundamental question hovers in the metatheatricalized universe the play keeps alive. *Pericles* is a sort of fairy-tale, and the mechanisms of its staging keep us from assigning it full, sober credibility. How far and in what way we should believe is an open question, and the only closure on this question is a metatheatrical one, referring us back to the play itself.

"Words above action, matter above words," Jonson says, in the Prologue to an entertainment (*Cynthia's Revels*, 20), as he prepares to work an enchantment simpler than Shakespeare's, though in the same theatrical convention, on the matter that lies beyond the relation between the words and the action (unless "matter" be taken to mean only designata). It would seem that words and action were all, and assigning priority to words ("words above action") would solve the question—but there remains the question of "matter," which can only involve the relation between words and action.

As I have said elsewhere, the words in the recitative convention of this Renaissance theatre relate to the action as manifest content to manifest content.[14] There is a kind of objectification here that seems more simple by having the verse insist on its own manifest amplification and forthright explicitness, rather than exploiting its necessary latencies by keeping the language at the humdrum level of leaving much unsaid (Ibsen's practice, where words are to action as latent to manifest), or rather than really suspending the coordinates by which the manifest and the latent could be discriminated by effectuating the virtual erasure of the distinction across the stage barrier (Pirandello, who serves as the model for the different adaptations of radical illusionism in Beckett and Ionesco). In Shakespeare the latencies, not only the underlying mythic patterns but the significance that is invested in them, are kept at a sort of wondering distance for which Prospero's famous "cloud-capp'd towers" speech will stand as an elusive formulation.

These plays, unlike the Moralities and Mysteries more closely attached to folk or religious celebrations, were attended voluntarily, and for a fee, by individuals who chose to do so, not by the collective population of a town but by a random group of inhabitants in a city. The voluntariness of the commitment in the audience-addressee, freshly perceived as a new convention, might have given an impetus to keep the significative structure open until the exit effected a kind of closure on it. Make-believe, and the significative mystery inhering in it, can be almost heard in the breathless progression of the verses, the untiring forward thrust of the Marlovian "mighty line" and all its later adaptations. When Hamlet, speaking of the actor, says:

> What's Hecuba to him or he to Hecuba
>
> (II,ii,552)

the second clause is either superfluous or nonsensical, really, if we pause to look at it. "What's Hecuba to him" is all he means to say, "he to Hecuba" does not really round out but teeters on meaninglessness. Hecuba, who exists only as a character in a play, cannot have an attitude towards someone not in the play, towards the actor, who may at some point act the role "Priam," but is not the same "he" as the one to whom Hecuba is nothing (since within the play, of course, Hecuba is something to Priam). This verse, in its impetus, opens up the quick arbitrariness of the inventive speaker who here "free-associates" in his soliloquy, pretending to balance the clause out by performing a sleight-of-word on the metatheatrical distinction it undercuts. The possibility entertained here pretends to round out but actually sets up a mutual exclusivity which is not exclusive because it draws our transient awareness to the possibility rather than to the contradiction.

Even in so straightforward a play as *Doctor Faustus*, no way is given us to resolve, on the one hand, its presentation of damnation for seeking forbidden knowledge through a pact with the devil ("Nothing so sweet as magic is to him,/Which he prefers before his chiefest bliss" Prologue, 25-26), a Christian morality-exemplum, and, on the other hand, our virtual certainty that Marlowe was an atheist. Beyond the delight shown in the scene of hoodwinking the Pope (III,ii) and the spurring vigor of Mephistopholis, it is impossible to get from what Marlowe seems to have believed to what the play clearly says. The whole cannot be ironic, nor is it easy to conceive of an impious poet turning his great gifts to the taunting production of a pietistic play. The clarity in the play's meaning is shadowed by the riddle of its credibility in the whole context of the writer's conviction.

In *Cymbeline*, as elsewhere, Shakespeare has recourse to the artifice-delighting and metatheatrical presentation of "gods" through the veil of the classical deities who had the status of fictions or allegories or euphemisms, as "Jove" would mean "God," even in Marlowe; "Be thou on earth as Jove is in the sky" (*Doctor Faustus*, I,i,77), the bad angel says, forced to the classicized circumlocution by a prohibition on his using the divine name.

The Jupiter of *Cymbeline* is something more than an artifice. He leaves a real paper in Posthumus' hand, on which is written an oracle that a Roman Soothsayer can correctly interpret, when he has wrongly predicted a Roman victory. It has taken a dream-vision of his parents, and further information imparted by them, to bring the imprisoned Posthumus to see Jupiter. His head is cleared, and also everybody's. The supernatural scene, whose fictive status also cannot be resolved when an artificial deity hands over real objects, is followed by acts of alert intelligence on the part of a king who has seemed, though courteous, half-asleep through the whole play. *Post hoc* but not *propter hoc*, since there is no reason to assign a direct causal operation of Jupiter upon Cymbeline, except that, in the sequential responses of an audience, who start with the assumption that the play is as coherent in time as its events are ordered in space, *post hoc* is felt somehow to be *propter hoc*, especially in a magical atmosphere that has some of the striking coincidental resolution of a fairy tale. The clouds that Jupiter clears are felt to include the clouds in the head of Cymbeline.

A Midsummer Night's Dream, before it culminates in a metatheatrical relegation of tragedy to inarticulateness, presents on the same plane, treading same boards before our eyes, two different kinds of creatures, men and fairies, with three subclasses of men; Theseus and Hippolyta are legendary beings with something of demigods about them; the lovers are normal members of the polite society of Athens. The third group, the guildsmen, put on a play-within-a-play that also offers still another variety of kinds of being: Pyramus and Thisbe along with his father and her mother, but also an animal, the Lion, and two inanimate characters, Wall and Moonshine. This ontological mixture is felt to be ridiculous; what then of putting fairies on a plane with men?

The fairies for the most part are confined only to night, and to the no-man's-land of the forest. And their activities rarify into fictiveness under the aegis of the play's title, a "dream." Even on their own ground, the midsummer night forest, their roles draw on folk mischief and erotic imagination, Ovidian courtesy and Irish bedevilment, as C. L. Barber says;[15] Shakespeare's fairies are more courtly and benign than those of British folklore. "The humor of the play relates superstition, magic and passionate delusion as 'fancy images.' The actual title emphasizes a skeptical attitude by calling the comedy a 'dream.' The humor keeps *recognizing* that the person is a personification, that the magic is imagination." But also the imagination is magic, and the spirit of love, by being transposed to the agency of the most mischievous of the fairies, is dramatized as beyond any self-consciousness or self-realization in lovers who had shown in the first place only secondary differentiation from one another. So we are meant not to know why Hermia would fall in love with Lysander more than with Demetrius, when both love her—nor does any set of events bring them to know. The set of events enchants them to realign, to celebrate, to wonder, and to accept whatever is brought by the quasi-supernatural beings, who trail the airiness of theatrical doubt with them as they bestow amorous certainty.

Witches, like ghosts, possessed a more awful certitude of relation to the supernatural than the "immortal" fairies or the classical gods.[16] So they are shown generally in the period as human beings given over to the devil. Doubt did not hang over them except for a select few in a country ruled by a king who had written on witchcraft. As Williams puts it of the "creed" that women could become witches by making a pact with the devil "[Francis Bacon was] not able to get rid of the principles upon which the creed was based. Sir Edward Coke, his contemporary, the most acute lawyer of the age, ventured even to define the devil's agents in witchcraft. Sir Thomas Browne and Sir Matthew Hale, in 1664, proved their faith, the one by his solemn testimony in open court, the other by his still more solemn sentence."[17]

In the subplot of *The Witch of Edmonton*, an old woman translates resentment into subjugation to a familiar whom we see on stage in the person of a talking dog. In Jonson's *The Sad Shepherd*, though the genre of pastoral admittedly advertises its own fictiveness, Mother Maudlin turns into a raven and imprisons Erline in a tree as Sycorax had imprisoned Ariel. And in *Henry VI, Part One*, at the demise of the witch Joan of Arc, actual devils are brought on stage at her invocation ("Enter Fiends," V,iii,7).

The existence of Macbeth's witches, on their lonely northern plain, cannot be doubted, within the play. But their mode of existence is mysterious, shading beyond crones into Norns and demons. Their intimations, their enticing declarations, possess the same mystery as does the theological doctrine of predestination, since the congruity of what they foretell to what happens is not subjected to neutrality, but rather to a pattern in which Macbeth's acceptance and Banquo's rejection are both caught up in the human alteration that is the deep concern of the very plot we see. And Macbeth overrides Banquo quite soon, so that even Banquo's rejection of them cannot be taken by itself as defining, or submitting to, the Witches' predictions.

The white magic of Prospero is as effective as the black magic of Faustus, and while it dominates the play, it is theatrical enough not only to cause its events but to be appropriate only for an island where supernatural beings, good and evil, are found to be dwelling. At the beginning of the play the magic serves as a desperate political recourse on the part of one who has resigned himself to needing none. At the end it is the occasion for a moral renunciation.

So the magic is secretly subject not only to a fictiveness which Prospero states to be like that of the world—it is a magically induced spectacle out of "thin air" that occasions the comparison. Time is a character in *The Winter's Tale*, and he equates female beauty ("grace") to what the beholder sees ("wond'ring"), in words that also identify God's favor with the occasion for marvelling:

> and with speed so pace
> To speak of Perdita, now grown in grace
> Equal with wond'ring.
>
> (IV,i,23-25)

"Speed" is part of the make-believe in *The Winter's Tale*: The death of Mamillius, the death of Antigonus, the false death of Hermione, the suspicion of Leontes, the restoration of Hermione, the alerting of Polixenes all happen so fast (and so successfully— the other meaning of "speed") that they trail the air of make-believe. And at the same time the play allows for a feeling of endless immobility, especially in the prolonged time-stalling of the pastoral enactment in Act Four.

As though to keep make-believe alive, we are shown satyrs, (presumably rustics in disguise) diverting these pastoral festivities, the more purely fictive for being mute. Perdita, who crosses the roles of courteous shepherd's daughter and aspiring Princess, discourses on art and nature, a fictiveness that is illustrated in the dances she leads. As though to heighten the make-believe, we are given music with them, in a play which for Shakespeare is relatively unscored. The reality that bursts in on this time-stalling gives not a make-believe, for Hermione was never a statue; she is a mockery, and thereby replaces a miming of loss with a restoration as unhoped for as forgiveness had seemed inaccessible to the king.

Recovery is already posited, however, in the formal expectations of romance: like the *Marchen* of which it is a more artificial variant, romance expects the closure of "happily ever after" as much as a Latin sentence awaits a concluding verb. The futurity sensed as thus automatically blissful has something of the Edenic about it, and Shakespeare's light touch on these expectations elevates the mood as it suspends the make-believe of these enacted progressions.[18]

In *Pericles* the self-cancelling recursive riddle that opens the play is something magically darker than romance or fairy-tale, since in them the riddle tends to be solved and the solver to get the girl. But the incest riddle offers "heads I win, tails you loose": if Pericles does not solve it, he forfeits his life; but if he does solve it, he reveals in the very solution a scandal that would lead the king to take his life. And of course he loses the girl either way, whereas in the usual mythic motif even seemingly impossible conditions are met by the hero. Pericles' only solution is to slip away into the Machiavellian deduction of a series of political steps quite foreign to romance and fairy tale, leaving the unmanageable threats of enchantment for the more manageable threats of enlightened political self-interest, into a future which will gradually induce him back to the sphere of enchantment, which hangs unpredictably and inescapably over the dispersed cities of this Mediterranean.

Cymbeline fuses history and fairy-tale romance, the concerns of political subsistence from the history plays extended back to include the king of Britain at the time of Christ, and the familiar romantic concerns of familial restoration and sexual justification. These are also the concerns of *The Tempest*, where the politics is muted but conclusive, the end being not just the marriage that has been guaranteed by Act Four, but the return to the mainland and the restoration into political balance that the nearness of Prospero to death (V,i,305-6), his final resolution out of his dim past ("the dark backward and abysm of time" I,ii,50), and the "insubstantial pageant" throw into mysterious relief.

In *The Merchant of Venice* we are given one kind of fairytale in the subplot and a linked one in the main plot, where a young girl, still retaining her virginity as the bride of a man called away, invokes the magic of that state and poses as a legal prodigy in a Renaissance Venice that would surely not admit of such itinerant judgment in its model city government—of which the more realistic *Othello* offers a dramatized example. This Venice is shrunk to a medieval popular stereotype in which Jews demand a pound of flesh, ships sink and then mysteriously come in. Its ruler is a simple, benevolent presence and not the sad, sophisticated counsellors Othello serves. Silver and gold, in the tests that Aragon and Morocco do not meet, and Bassanio's feckless prodigality, link one theme to the other. The ring trick is robbed of its suspense by the theatrical trick of dramatic irony, distancing the sequence by make-believe as the plot has already been distanced by the air of make-believe every romance radiates.

The relegation of adultery and transvestism to mimicry allows the complexities they stand for to be managed by being laughed away. The ring trick is echoed in the subplot, where Jessica and Lorenzo trade the ring Shylock's wife gave him for a monkey—an image that in the metaphoric sphere performs a comparable transformation by making bestiality an extension of the caprice of marriage through the inversion of exchanging what is the symbol of marriage for the beast who stands, among other things, for blind lust ("As hot as monkeys" *Othello*, III,iii,407). It is Jessica and Lorenzo who subsume the tragic tonality into celebration by rehearsing the names of the protagonists who would be tragic lovers without the resolution of fairytale—if Bassanio had not solved the riddle there would have been no Portia to deliver the releasing judgment, but if he had not wanted to court Portia he would not have needed this particular loan. And Bassanio, while preparing to answer the riddle, runs through his conjectures while a song about the source and accessibility of imagination ("fancy") is being sung:

> Tell me where is fancy bred,
> Or in the heart or in the head,
> How begot, how nourished?
> Reply, reply.
> It is engend'red in the eyes,
> With gazing fed; and fancy dies
> In the cradle where it lies.
> Let us all ring fancy's knell

(III,ii,63-70)

But the knell of fancy is a distant make-believe, as the later melancholy of Lorenzo and Jessica is only a qualification. Lorenzo, too, talks about a music he hears. The stage induces the music both to carry this sort of message and to throw the message melodically beyond a meaning that can only be its own.

Music helps to sustain the fairy-tale atmosphere of dream-like calm and wish-fulfillment, as Paulina commands the music to immobilize the wonderment of Leontes in *The Winter's Tale* while he sees the statue turning to the mobility of life. But our perception of the dividing line between us and the actors does not cease to "frame" the stage, to use Gregory Bateson's term. "From within that frame the producers and actors may attempt to involve the audience in an illusion of reality as seemingly direct as the experience of dream. And, as in dream, the play has metaphoric reference to the outside world. But in dream, unless sleeper be partly conscious of the fact of sleep, there is no curtain and no framing of the action. The partial negative—'this is *only* metaphor'—is absent."[19] Now what Shakespeare does at times is to heighten the "metaphor" by approaching as closely as a coherent plot allows to the inner logic of a dream: sudden feelings, unnatural powers, causeless rapprochements, are central to these last plays, as well as a "musical" luck or a "tempestuous" misfortune independent of the character's own actions. In a dream, Bateson also points out, the figures only set up *relations* among themselves. It is for the waked dreamer to put the labels "Father," "Mother," "Superior," "Lover," and so on, upon the mysterious figures in the dream, whose *relations* reveal their identity. To emphasize fairytale is to deemphasize character, and thereby to emphasize relations without according plot, a causal interaction, more than the provisional status that refers it back, again, not to the before-and-after syntax of the dramatic statements so much as to the metatheatricalizing agency of the stage boundary.

The drama on stage appropriates the participative play of festival, which is not yet theatrical and so cannot be metatheatrical. Yet the festival is a special heightening that, set on stage, invests staginess with an emphasis of something more than make-believe.

The newness of this process, in Barber's interpretation, quickened Marlowe's sense of the possibilities inherent in recasting what amounts to the Mass in what amounts to the blasphemous framework of make-believe, as Faustus through his orality of gluttony, mouth-sexuality, and verbalization, short-circuits redemption into a perversion of Communion.[20] The play does not have to signify this latent pattern—*Doctor Faustus* is actually, in structure, a moderately straightforward Morality exemplum—in order to harness the power latent in the subversion of earnest religious participation into theatricality.

Shakespeare quickly harnessed the implications of the new vehicle, subtilizing his conception well beyond the simple demonism of Faustus. The devil called up to prophesy in *Henry VI, Part Two* has no parallel in Shakespeare's later works, and only occasionally does he underscore the make-believe, as in the induction of *The Taming of the Shrew*, where the spectacle is shown to someone who is himself an actor, Christopher Sly, the captive groundling, "waked" from a "dream" that is in fact a reality. The Page mocks him by pretending to be a "wife" he has forgotten, and he turns away as an English "nobleman" to contemplate the exemplum of matchmaking for well-born Italians.

In a play the special reality of events on stage more orderly than those in life contradicts the special suspension of reality that allows pretending actors to say that which they do not mean, and even to perform gestures which they do not mean (where the function of kinesics and paralinguistic coding, Bateson acutely shows, is to give an unconscious guarantee of sincerity).[21] This contradiction, which puzzled Diderot, is manipulated by Shakespeare through the process of calling attention to the make-believe, to the special suspension of reality, by means of bringing it to bear on the special reality, of defining it. So we are given not just a causal sequence in which Portia saves her new husband's friend, but a fairy-tale for the engagement and a fairy-tale for the judgment, with the subordinate choral comment that theorizes the music whose pure make-believe (it is only the artifice of its sounds) and pure signification (whatever it means, it must mean without the intermediation of words, and must call forth not assent or dissent but response or deafness) restate the conjunction of the theatre in total auditory terms.

Shakespeare thus makes likeness (of stage event to life in the world outside the stage door) and difference (of the stage make-believe from reality) comment on the outside world, a kind of positive and superabundant presentation of meaning-capping-meaning while meaning-subverts-meaning. A negative counterpart of this would be the Mallarméan interpretation of *Pierrot le Fou* as Derrida reads it.[22] Shakespeare's soliloquies, of course, are not mute, and even his dumb shows offer something other than the Mallarméan act of sealing in muteness the doubled identification of the silent representation. The dumbshow in Shakespeare alters, repeats, comments on, invades, concentrates, but always interacts with, the events accompanied by metered or unmetered words that at moments may also have music playing alongside them or in tune with them. The plaiting together of conventions of discourse (fairy-tale and history) or universes of discourse (words, music, bare mime) leaves open till the conclusion just which of the elements will be dominant. The opening of *Lear* has the ritualized pageantry of enacted history.[23] And it also has the fairy-tale abruptness of quick decisions, of two evil elder sisters and a good younger, which induces the expectation that the younger will triumph, an expectation both fulfilled (Cordelia and Lear enjoy the bliss of reunion) and shattered (she dies; and does not live happily ever after, on this earth at least). So the expectations of history—that the forceful will prevail (*Henry IV, Richard II, Antony and Cleopatra*, and generally all histories)—are subverted by the expectation of moral fable, that the good will prevail.[24]

By at once doubling the addresser from his addressee (others, or in soliloquy the self on stage/the listening audience) and sealing them from one another (the main addressee, the audience, cannot respond), the axis of signification in a play is at once strengthened and questioned. In Greece and Japan something like a ritual concentration keeps that axis stiff. In classical France, a pluralistic medieval background of folk festival and religious allegory similar to England's is deliberately abjured and the Greek practice is adopted as a formalizing and normalizing element in the code of presentation. In the bourgeois theatre, the fourth wall convention proceeds by pretending that the axis is not there; the strengthening and the questioning are levelled in a skillfully managed neutrality. Shakespeare and his contemporaries, however, press that axis to make it yield intimations of how arbitrary it really is, thereby engendering the wonder that make-believe can be so full of meaning, and the delight that it is so. The fixed and focused perspective that in Renaissance painting allows for the simultaneous presentation of close and distant objects in firm relation to each other, is imported into this theatre not in the *coulisse*-tunnel of the French or Italian stage, but on a bare stage, by the energetic structuring of speeches whose expansiveness seems to reach out into undefined distances.

Pirandello works differently though his message can be harmonized with one Shakespeare occasionally delivers. In his meta-theatre, reality recedes into the past, which he dramatizes to recover reality.[25] The persons on stage, making the impossible attempt at recovery, are caught up in the partiality of the observers, or else, in *Six Characters*, in the necessary insubstantiality and possible vividness of invented persons. The attempt is also caught up in the double-edged character of language. It is words that must be used to separate illusion from reality: the past that could determine who the woman is in *As You Desire Me* cannot be resurrected, but only spoken about; and words are arbitrary formulations that reflect the angle of the speaker and his own displacement from events. To advance, then, must be to recede. In Shakespeare, however, reality is not a past, or a present, that resists apprehensions; it is a pattern of past and present and future that transcends and is transcended by the moment, which the flash of metatheatrical doubling calls into play, celebrates, and assists in making to surge forward.

The film has not even a fourth wall: the audience in the blackened room is not conceived, by the film, to be there. We cannot tell whether the images on the screen are meant to be past or present; when Resnais and Robbe-Grillet make the characters themselves focus on that fact, the views their words state and the views of them the camera presents converge in a statement of the limit between illusion and reality that a lover cannot cross, within the pattern. Metatheatrical postulates give no guidance where the limit itself is subject to the principle. Film cannot be subject to this doubt because it can only incidentally "quote" film or "quote" still photography in sequence. The quotation cannot form a total qualification, though it can sustain a delicate irony, like the stills in Fassbinder's *Effie Briest*. *L'Année Dernière à Marienbad* presents a total meta-illusion without a trace of the dramatic irony which always comes into play in Shakespeare's metatheatricalizing. Film absolutizes the flashback, which a Hitchcock will use (blurring whether what we see is past or present) with a momentary dramatic irony similar to that in a detective novel, a deliberate obfuscation whose sole function is to trigger surprise rather than a penetration of the exhibited events with intimations about the very nature of illusion.

What is seen on a screen is taken for real (there being no stage boundary), while what is seen on stage is taken for make-believe. If, as one thinks about it, therefore, the film relies on this assumption and becomes a kind of documentary and does deal with real people, then that reality will either be obviously propagandized, *Der Triumph des Willens*; or newsworthy; or else it will be adjudged flaccid and unnewsworthy. *Cinéma verité*, as in *Chronique d'une été* or the films of the Maysles and Wiseman, exploits either the sensational or the newsworthy, assimilating easily to the newsreel as a form. Warhol, on the the other hand, in *The Kiss* and *Chelsea Girls*, lets the camera dwell on the played-down unnewsworthiness of an experience flowing with such deliberate slowness that it raises questions in the viewer's mind about the relation between the visible on the screen and psychological motive—a necessary relation, not a metatheatricalized one, since the camera, in its conception, cannot find a way of saying that it pretends to take a picture when it has taken one: it begins with a reality. *The Loud Family*, notably including a devotee of Warhol, illustrates sensation and boredom in deliberate alternation.

The camera can call attention to itself, can act like the frame on a painting, by shifting its single frames quickly, offering them multiple, changing angles, blacking out, offering sequences of slow motion or rapid motion. Its repertory of devices are all means for presenting the flow of what is offered as having been picked up by a lens and so available to sight—as real.

However they may be wrought, however abruptly cut or elaborately mounted, the images of the cinema are dwelt on in an even flow of time, a time that cannot permit the figures any extensive verbalization without the sense that one is dwelling on a visual picture for a long time. The figures act in something akin to a deliberate dumb show, punctuated by the laconic rubrics of speech, foredoomed to a final solemnity that invests even the dwindling figures of a Chaplin, even the suspension of the clowns with which Antonioni terminates *Blow-Up*.

The clowns of Shakespeare are as bound as they are free in their make-believe. And when those other than clowns—Perdita, or Portia, or Prospero, or Edgar, or Hamlet—call attention to the sportiveness or the urgency of their make-believe, they are, as it were, not simply bound in a frame: their very frame, in fact, has them conceived of as creating from some silence far within a splendid flight of formulation that will plumb the depths of the silence out into which the audience will walk when the play is over.

FIVE
Style

La vertu allusive du style n'est pas un phénomène de vitesse, comme dans la parole, où ce qui n'est pas dit reste tout de même un interim du langage, mais un phénomène de densité, car ce qui se tient droit et profond sous le style, rassemblé durement ou tendrement dans ses figures, ce sont les fragments d'une réalité absolument étrangère au langage. Le miracle de cette transmutation fait du style une sorte d'opération supra-littéraire, qui emporte l'homme au seuil de la puissance et de la magie. Par son origine biologique, le style se situe hors de l'art, c'est-à-dire hors du pacte qui lie l'écrivain à la société.

Roland Barthes
Le Degré zéro de L'ecriture

Les grandes images ont à la fois une histoire et une préhistoire. Elles sont toujours à la fois souvenir et légende. On ne vit jamais l'image en première instance. Toute grande image a un fond onirique insondable et c'est sur ce fond onirique que le passé personnel met des couleurs particulières . . . . Il y a un sens à dire qu'on "lit une maison," qu'on "lit une chambre," puisque chambre et maison sont des diagrammes de psychologie qui guident les écrivains et les poètes dans l'analyse de l'intimité.

Gaston Bachelard
La Poétique de l'espace

1

Music, which counterpoints, intrudes on, echoes, and transports the words in Shakespeare's plays, differs from this other, main mode of auditory communication. Music is direct, where words, loaded with association and locked in syntactic patterns, are indirect; music cannot lie.[1] The directness of music involves its being associationless to anything other than the secret of the feelings its rhythmic progressions evoke and embody. It is "the food of love," framed, in language, by the query of wonderment that music itself cannot render in any explicit way, not "music is the food of love," but "*if* music be the food of love. ." ; and it charms to the pure continuance of itself ". . . play on" (*Twelfth Night*, I,i, 1), rather than subjecting itself, like the interacting words and actions it may accompany, to implicit qualification.

Purely stylized, the entry of music in a play of Shakespeare's is random, whereas in Greece the music was further coded for a fixed stylization of relation to a kind of speaker, the choral group, and to the rule of structural alternation, that it be broken by dialogue.

Why music for the play? The Greek would give a ritual answer to this question. In Shakespeare's world the music has a private, intimate side; Bacon "would many times have music in the next room where he meditated."[2] In Greece the modes were themselves key signatures of signification. In Renaissance music, modal or not, these significations do not exist by themselves[3] but refer to the words they accompany, paramount and resplendent as they pick up and throw off the elusive and enchanting melodies that enter them.

Music reminds the audience of an order not mitigated by the interaction of purposiveness, which directs every speech in a play.

This purposiveness defines the speech of a play as distinct from the kind of lyric that will be fully rounded in itself, the words of a song by Dowland or a song by Shakespeare qualifying the play the same way music does. Every lyric poem closes round its defined subject proportionally. Shakespeare's poems, as distinct from his plays, overdetermine that closure by choosing not only the rhyme which was mandated for lyric poetry at the time but kinds of rhyme that emphasize closure—the box-clicking couplet of the Shakespearian sonnet, the interwoven rhymes of the Italian stanzas in *Venus and Adonis* and *The Rape of Lucrece*, and the rounded-out quatrain (abba) of *The Phoenix and the Turtle*, which offers a closure more definite than that of some other contributions to *Love's Martyr*, where it first appeared.[4]

In these poems the images tend to be either coherent (*The Phoenix and the Turtle*), a single metaphor presented as inclusive; or else they are neatly successive, the anaphoric stages of an *amplificatio*. In plays, on the other hand, on this stage as on the Greek, there may be a deep, overall subliminal pattern of imagery areas, as Spurgeon and Clemen demonstrate. But in an individual speech the figures come up almost randomly, as though thrust upon the mind of the speaker, as he presses his intentional words into their purposive framework.[5] Unlike a poem, a speech demands an answer. Or if it is a soliloquy, it declares some relation to a plan, if only hesitancy before the thicket of possible plans. The speech is not closed but open, reaching out intentionally to the future of other, qualifying speeches.

In an early play like *Gorboduc* the speeches seem endless, trapped in their rhetorical present, summations of political position rather than incitements to further action. They are not yet harnessed to interact powerfully with the plot. But the blank verse line, if properly balanced, becomes a "mighty line," in Kyd almost as much as in Marlowe; its lack of rhyme[6] keeps its conclusion uncertain and therefore its purposiveness strong. The speaker can seem to be urging himself to carry on, out of some energy that presents the illusion of seeming inward, because outward circumstances, the styled markings of the language, do not require him to carry on. So Tamburlaine is not so much eloquent as he is purposive: his expression is the chief trenchant exemplification of a force of motive that will attempt to take over the entire world: it is in this energy alone that he surpasses Mycetes and Cosroe, Theridamas and Bajazeth, all of whom show the usual matter-of-fact mastery of Machiavellian principle. And it is in his speeches alone, as a sign of what is within him rather than as an effective force on his auditors, that this energy manifests itself. (Theridamas is struck with wonderment before Tamburlaine begins to speak, and Zenocrate is proof to his words, while she gradually succumbs in the train of his successes.) The blank verse line, each line, serves as a springboard for the "vaulting ambition" which will not rest, since even the "sweet fruition of an earthly crown" presents only a moment of delectation in endless conquest, a transient dominance for a man whose mortality will ultimately have to manifest itself.

Macbeth is wrought up, being in a position of rebellion against the leader who has just rewarded him with a title, much as Tamburlaine is ambitiously rebelling against the Cosroe who has just made him general of armies. Macbeth, of course, exemplifies not just the vaulting ambition of energy but something deeper that makes him falter before it, as he did not when winning Cawdor's title by reasserting the military force of the Scottish power. The dramatized purposiveness, the present gathering of past forces into a futurity, is transposed to a new dimension as the witches reshuffle the natural order of time by a prophecy that thereby invokes the ultimates of good and evil.

The mighty line undergirds his hesitation-soliloquy, at which I would like to take a long look. Every single line of it is a springboard for the next, the enjambments producing the effect of leaping still more propulsively ahead:

> If it were done when 'tis done, then 'twere well
> It were done quickly. If th' assassination
> Could trammel up the consequence, and catch,
> With his surcease, success; that but this blow
> Might be the be-all and the end-all here—
> But here upon this bank and shoal of time—
> We'd jump the life to come. But in these cases
> We still have judgment here, that we but teach
> Bloody instructions, which being taught return
> To plague th' inventor. This even-handed justice
> Commends th' ingredience of our poison'd chalice
> To our own lips. He's here in double trust:
> First, as I am his kinsman and his subject—
> Strong both against the deed; then, as his host,
> Who should against his murderer shut the door,
> Not bear the knife myself. Besides, this Duncan

> Hath borne his faculties so meek, hath been
> So clear in his great office, that his virtues
> Will plead like angels, trumpet-tongu'd, against
> The deep damnation of his taking-off;
> And pity, like a naked new-born babe,
> Striding the blast, or heaven's cherubim hors'd
> Upon the sightless couriers of the air,
> Shall blow the horrid deed in every eye,
> That tears shall drown the wind. I have no spur
> To prick the sides of my intent, but only
> Vaulting ambition, which o'er-leaps itself
> And falls on th'other.
>
>   (I,vii,1-28)

The packed language, the great conflating images of his last lines, are signs of an internal turmoil as much as they are splendid descriptions of it. The vastness of the spiritual struggle is exemplified in having a speaker seem to force these words out of himself in the pressure of his amazement, an effect that would be lost completely if this were presented as a rhetorical set-piece without a definite speaker, as a poem and not a dramatic speech.

But at the same time Macbeth's speech has a rhetorical compactness which makes its structure classifiable as partaking, all at once, of *division*, "a severing of the whole into parts," *expedition*, "reckoning upon divers parts," *prosapodosis*, "that overthroweth no part of the division but returneth some reason to each member," *dilemma* "which proposeth two sides and overthrows both," *periphrasis*, and *paraphrasis*.[7]

The revelation of a private darkness, the tortuousness, of this speech, dispels at once the soft sounds, festive lights, and calm preparations for welcome that immediately precede it, *"Hautboys, torches. Enter a Sewer, and divers Servants with dishes and service over the stage. Then enter Macbeth."*

The infant whom Macbeth forces to undergo the challenge of the elements, the "naked new-born babe,/striding the blast," set in a dramatic context, refers not only to some mannerist vision of *putti* (which it would in a poem) but further (which a poem without a set speaker could not so incidentally signify) to his own spirit, exposed in trials for which it is too tender (the "blasts" are reminiscent of the Witch's heath), and also to Duncan, naturally horsed though left behind by Macbeth ("Where's the Thane of Cawdor?/We cours'd him at the heels and had a purpose/To be his purveyor; but he rides well,/And his great love, sharp as his spur, hath holp him/To his home before us" I,vi,19-24).

Macbeth's horsemanship is here blinded, projected onto heavenly avengers, merged with the wind that the "babe" is striding (*blasts/sightless couriers of the air*) in a montage of adulthood with infancy, and itself, as his personal spiritual condition, left stalled ("I have no spur"), the moment he would stall, "trammel up" the horses of action. What the babe stands for, "pity," is an emotion he contemplates himself as the awful instigator of, and his tenderness of visualization is contrasted with that of the cruel mother his wife declares herself to be in the very next speech, "I would, while it was smiling in my face,/Have pluck'd my nipple from his boneless gums,/And dash'd the brains out" (I,vii,56-58). Since it is her own child Lady Macbeth unequivocally speaks of— "I have given suck, and know/How tender 'tis to love the babe that milks me" (54-55)—she is willing to expose to torment the child of the husband who imagines a child exposed to torment: their fantasies lock in identity as well as in opposition, and there is a psychoanalytic dimension of inadequate personal realization for a woman who projects a post-partum hostility backwards and for a man who alternates between childish and adult images in figuring his feelings.[8] These motions are part of the objectified stirring of evil, a tempestuousness dramatized in the vividness and uncertain progression of the recitative speeches as they are set one against the other, and everything poeticized into them, images and rhetoric and rhythm, is at the service of that larger dramatic motion, as being in the mouth of a person we see subjected to the forces which his words are at once coming to terms with and creating.

The images of Macbeth's conclusion (19-28) have hallucinated into a pitch of garbled visualization, returning to the quickening and foreshortening syntax of his opening (1-7), after he has made an attempt, ultimately vain but momentarily successful as evidenced by the balancing clausulae and moderate progression of his words (7-19), to weigh the considerations "against the deed." Here, as often in Shakespeare, virtue is pellucid ("so clear in his great office") and evil turbid. The dramatic movement of this soliloquy is spoken in the interval before his wife's arrival while servants are seen busily setting the table in the torch-lit room, quickening the turbidity into vivid actualization.

2

Even when close to its simplest and most seemingly colloquial expression, the blank verse of drama is still ordered. Its light and normative pattern quietly asserts the formality of an utterance that a live speaker brings more forcibly into fusion with colloquial expression than a sonnet, say, would suggest, set on the page or, as the origin of the term "sonnet" suggests, set to music. And yet the formality is there. The diction, the syntax, and the structure of idea, as well as the rhythm, do not just produce random deviation from the spoken language, in dramatic verse any more than 'in lyric. Rather, they offer a proportionateness, a tendency towards normative terms in the diction, balance of clausulae in the syntax, and a neatness in the consequent structure of idea, within a short compass, that exemplifies what I have elsewhere called "The Refined Style."[9]

This style, the norm in Western verse from shortly after Homer right to our own time, having been domesticated into English from French, Italian, and Latin practice at least since Chaucer, serves Shakespeare as a ground base. Indeed, the founding of his staple rhythm, the blank verse line that had ironed itself out[10] at just about the time Shakespeare's career was on the rise, may be conceived of as proceeding by giant steps because it had not to invent anew but to acclimate to a slight change in rhythm a proportionateness already attained for English style. Wyatt's triumph is deft but not new:

> They fle from me who sometime did me seeke

offers a disyllabic, nearly spondaic word, at the center of an otherwise monosyllabic[11] line balanced around a simple chiasmus (*fle from me; did me seeke*) with the two verbs themselves in simple antithesis (flee-seek).

Shakespeare begins Macbeth's speech here on a recognizably similar patterning:

> If *it were* done/when *'tis done,*/Then *'twere* well

The three clauses, each rhetorically marked (*if, when, then*), are varied with repetition in the simple auxiliary on an A B A frame (*it were, 'tis, 'twere*) to the same verb—with the capping variation that the return to A, "'twere well," varies the identical main verb "done" by delaying it across an enjambment. (A—*done*/B—*done*/A—). The presence of the three clauses themselves, in a binary measure, strains against the natural rhythmic and syntactic division of the line, and that strain is built into the sound of the line as an instanced variation from the design, the discrepancy reaching its maximum on each instance of "done."[12]

Already present in this heavy manipulation of the refined base, here dexterously kept to normative and monosyllabic diction, is an indication of something stirring[13] inside the speaker beyond and beneath his "refined" formulations, the mighty tremor of hesitation that runs away with the verse here into a modulation and a repetition more than mere refinement would afford. The refined style, for instance, is too controlled to permit the seemingly random repetition of pronouns and demonstratives: *it, 'tis, 'twere, it, this, here, here, this, this, these*—all in eight lines.

The voice of a speaker engaged in dramatic action, as it invests with purposiveness the utterances it brings forth, strains away from this refined base as it attains a liveliness greater than the set speeches of *Gorboduc* or *Cambises*. Marlowe raises this accessible dramatic afflatus to a constant hyperbolic ring that suggests, by its elevation above refinement, the aspirations it is embodying as well as defining. Shakespeare characteristically swoops and veers from the refined base, not maintaining except as a special effect the constant elevation that Marlowe had achieved; and in this whole speech there are only a few lines that, taken together, stay at the Marlovian pitch, though even they enjamb too freely to sound entirely like Marlowe's:

> Will plead like angels, trumpet-tongu'd, against
> The deep damnation of his taking-off;
> And pity, like a naked new-born babe
> Striding the blast, or heaven's cherubim hors'd
> Upon the sightless couriers of the air

... It is not only the images and the subject matter that remind one of Marlowe here, of *Doctor Faustus*.

Poetry, Jakobson tells us,[14] projects from the axis of selection (along which one word is chosen for a function instead of another, "done" instead of "performed"; "trumpet-tongued" instead of "loud") onto the axis of combination (along which words are added to one another in a syntactic pattern, *if* plus *it* plus *were* plus *done*, to form a clause in accord with the rules of English). So, in the first line, the words selected are projected onto an axis of combination beyond the one governed by the syntax by being ordered into a line of binary rising meter; a further arbitrary rule of combination for their selection in this line is that they all have only a single syllable.

These lines, in a form that will occasionally use rhyme, have the further "regular" combinatory feature of *not* rhyming, a special effect for dramatic verse of the norm for non-dramatic verse that the arbitrary combinatory feature of rhyme be superadded. Two couplets did occur barely thirty lines before (I,vi,66-69), and a whole series of shorter-lined couplets in the Witches' scene (I,iii, 8-36).

Words in poetry tend to be more interreferential than in normal discourse because they are thus more complexly combined, the two axes of speech having the third feature in verse of projecting the first axis upon the second. Hence their relation to phenomena, as individual lexical items and as combined in syntactic patterns, is felt to have a kind of freedom and arbitrariness about it—an effect which the refined style tries to iron out into a total order, but which the lyric will itself harness, as in Shakespeare's last lines here, or as in his songs.

Linguists have noted how certain syntactical patterns tend to call for certain related ones, how certain verbs attract certain nouns. This subtle determinant of speech, the predictability of "valences" and "substitutes" as Hockett calls them,[15] seems to lose its hold on poetry; so much so that poetry can give the impression of leaping somewhat freer, as one may say, of speech's laws of gravity:

> When that I was and a little tiny boy,
> With a hey, ho, the wind and the rain,
> A foolish thing was but a toy,
> For the rain it raineth every day.
> > (*Twelfth Night*, V,i,375-378)

The expression "when that" for "when," an archaism in Shakespeare's time, does not expect "and," an almost nonsensical grace note balancing "when that." In such an economical poem we do not expect the redundancy of "little tiny." We do not expect the near exclamation of "With a hey ho, the wind and the rain" to precede the main clause which we are waiting for after the "when that" clause. We do not expect "wind and rain" after "hey ho." We do not expect, for our main statement, the mere truistic identification of the near synonyms "foolish thing" and "toy," nor the qualification "but." We do not expect "every day" after "the rain it raineth," for the article with "the wind and the rain" in the second line implies natural rain, and it is not natural rain that rains every day; rather it is some metaphorical rain in a metaphorical world this lyric is gaily confusing us into.

This passage illustrates quite strikingly the associative freedom of poetic syntax, but such associative freedom resides in the very conception of poetry, and we do unconsciously expect of a poem that it will dance off in some such way and not simply walk the measured space of our everyday speech. As Arnold Stein says, Yeats exhibits the boldness, the "sprezzatura" of a Renaissance courtier, in his movement of words in a line like "Reel shadows of the indignant desert birds," where "reel" does not anticipate "shadows," nor "shadows," "indignant."[16] Nor does "striding" anticipate "blast," "heaven's cherubim" anticipate "horsed," or "sightless" or "couriers," or "air."

Poetry, further, on the axis of selection, vivifies the whole range of sense in the word it may choose, including its history in its own and in other languages. The word "ruin," Owen Barfield shows us in making this point, retains in poetry some of the land-slide-collapse force of the Latin *"ruina,"* and hints at a process as well as designating the result of the process.[17] "Surcease" not only signifies both "stop legal proceedings" and "die"; it also suggests excess through the Latin-French prefix it retains (sur- super-; *sursis, supersedent*). "Die" in the poetry of Donne often implies two central events in life, and a connection between them; this almost never occurs in the prose of the period. In Marvell's lines:

> The Mind, that Ocean where each kind
> Does streight its own resemblance find

the capitalization of Ocean permits us to refer the word back to the classical Oceanus, which girded the globe. If we follow Milton Klonsky in finding that the poem's central reference is to Plotinus' world of forms,[18] then Ocean is also the neo-Platonic Ocean of Being—the "sea of time and space" as Blake and Porphyry called it. "Kind" is at once colloquial and scientific. "Resemblance" does not mean exactly likeness; the prefix *re-* here has been revived from its etymology and gives the word "resemblance" a very special meaning which the whole poem is defining. What is meant

by "resemblance" is a very complex idea which not the dictionary
but the rational idea of the poem, along lines Empson traces in his
comments on this passage,[19] may explain. "Resemblance" carries
all the ambiguity of:

> Annihilating all that's made
> To a green thought in a green shade.

The mind's resemblance, in Marvell's use of the word, makes resemblance mean: (1) a parallel in the mind for things created
(all that's made); (2) an identity in the mind with things created;
(3) a classificatory system in the mind where "each kind" can
only "streight its own resemblance find" after it has been regis-
tered in the mind. The only true semblance then would be a resemblance, and Marvell has, in the demonstrable thought of the
poem, carried the meaning of the word "resemblance" far beyond
its common meaning, largely by leaning on something underlying
its common meaning, that is, its derivation through French from
Latin. By leaning on *re*, he has used the history of the word to do
what Valéry tells us all poets do, to create a new meaning for the
word itself by virtue of the word's syntactic conjunctions in the
new coherent world of the poem.[20] Something of the sort may be
happening with "ingredience" in Macbeth's "th' ingredience of
our poison'd chalice/To our own lips."

The special sense a poem may give to an individual word may
be connected with another particularity of words in poetry, the
tendency for a given poet to rope off certain words from poetic
use. In theory the whole dictionary is available to the poet, but
like any other user of a language, once he has chosen a subject,
there are large areas of diction he is almost certain to leave un-
touched. Yet beyond the limits of tone and subject there is the
tendency for a poet to confine himself to some special narrower
group of words which we call a poetic diction, and to avoid the
other words in the dictionary. Marvell, for instance, speaks of the
earth here; but he could not use the word "globe" the way Wordsworth or Shakespeare do, as a near synonym for "earth," nor
does tone or subject prevent him from using "globe." Wordsworth

could not use "kind" in Marvell's sense. Neither poet could use the word "hotel" in a poem as T. S. Eliot does. And none of the three would be likely to use the epithet "rosy-fingered," except ironically. The breadth of Shakespeare's vocabulary, which this speech exemplifies, takes on a hyperbolic ring as it regains for high utterance a range beyond the formal range of "poetic diction" in the nondramatic conventional verse of his time.

Not only does every individual poet tend to build up a particular poetic diction, but, as Elizabeth Sewell tells us, poetry in general seems to favor certain kinds of words.[21] Since I am taking the point from her, it will be simplest to see this through her own classification of words. She orders words by the criteria of whether the word is stable and whether the reference is stable. The word is unstable only in her last class, which the "nonsense" of Lewis Carroll verges on. Her first class, *stable word plus stability of reference*, includes numbers, scientific terms, the invented language of the logician, and so on. In her second class *the word is stable and it has an unstablized diversity of reference*. Here belong names of animals, birds, plants, and so on, so long as the reference remains somewhat diverse. "Dog" belongs in this class but "Pomeranian" in the first class as having a stable reference. It is in this class that Miss Sewell claims, correctly, most of the terms in poetry fall. Poetry, all poetry, tends to follow Dr. Johnson's too exclusive dictum—when he censured Dryden's use of the word "diapason" as technical—that poetic diction be general. One runs into the word "dog" in poetry much more often than one runs into "Pomeranian," "eohippus," and so on; and in Miss Sewell's division of this class into words by nature diverse such as "sea," "cloud," and "sky," into semi-abstract words like "room" and "street," and into class words like "tree" and "animal," we encounter the substance of almost every poetic diction. Her third classification, *stable word plus unstablized diversity of reference*, includes abstract words, and poetry tends to use these too. Her fourth class exhibits an *absence of reference*: dead words, and the like. "Trammel," "surcease," "ingredience," "be-all," "end-all," "taking-off," strain these norms, which the rest of the speech may be seen to follow.

Most modern theorists of semiology, from Peirce and Saussure to Quine and Lacan, have insisted on the mediate, and hence on the plural, character of the linguistic sign: the letters *horse* do not refer to an equine quadruped; rather they notate the signs for certain sounds which quite arbitrarily correspond to the image of the equine quadruped—giving, with reference just to the word, at least three terms (sign, sound, image) and not two (sign, image); then two again if sign plus sound becomes a *signifiant*, the image a *signifié*. All this has to do just with a word; the relations between word and object are even more complex. In Shakespeare there is, as Gustav René Hocke asserts, a rhetorical ambivalence, a tendency at once to complicate in artificiality and to simplify in forthright naming the relation between word and object, thereby creating what he calls mannerist *"sprachliche Illusionsperspektive."*[22]

Poetry, by enriching the word while confining it arbitrarily to the somewhat narrower lexicon of poetic diction, emphasizes, as it were, the possibility of making all these complexities serve in a more complete order than the lexicon or even than the order of syntax would allow in natural language.

And then, having done this, the poetry spoken by a dramatic character, in such a Renaissance play as *Macbeth*, plays fast and loose with all these structures, making mediation itself as arbitrary a process as the semiological coding of phonetic into phonemic elements is implicitly felt to be. For *horse* we get *couriers*, a description (horses *run*, the French force of *courir* made live in the word) as well as a metaphorical identification (these *couriers*, while "sightless," carry messages as other couriers do: the cherubim riding them embody their own messages, in a heavenly language free of the mediations of earthly speech); and *horse* itself is displaced from the common noun, out of the common diction of poetry, to figure as a rare verb, emphatic rhythmically in its terminal position, *horsed*. This process is further heightened by the seemingly improvisatory force of word play. As M.M. Mahood points out, *sightless* means both *invisible* and *blind*;[23] the Folio reading of *Schoole* for *shoal* produces the complication of "bank and schoole," a classroom in phantasmagoria with a sea strand, the very confusion providing an atmosphere where one might "teach bloody instructions."

The two aspects of "axes" of language in Jakobson's system, substitution or (roughly) diction, and combination or (roughly) syntax produce, in figurative analysis, two poles of designation: metaphor, where one term (*babe*) substitutes for another (*pity*), directly or by implication ("prick the sides of my intent" implies substituting a concrete *horse* for an abstract *intent*); and metonymy, wherein a combination is produced by one form or another of contiguity (couriers do not replace cherubim; they are the carrier for the thing carried, since it is really the cherubim who are couriers of the heavenly message, not the wind on which they are "horsed"). *Couriers* are metonymically contiguous to *cherubim* as well as metaphorically substitutive for *wind*.

So, in the figures, the process is repeated by duplication which has also happened in the rhythm, the projection of the axis of selection or substitution upon the axis of combination. Or as Jakobson puts it, glossing Goethe's *"Alles Vergangliche ist nur ein Gleichnis."* "Said more technically, anything sequent is a simile. In poetry where similarity is superinduced upon contiguity, any metonymy is slightly metaphorical and any metaphor has a metonymical tint."[24] Something of this inclusive possibility must have been felt by Abraham Fraunce, who begins *The Arcadian Rhetoric* (1558) with the distinction between metaphor and metonymy. Lacan links dream analysis with semiotic theory, making the process one of choosing either to elide the distinction between signifier (*shoal*) and signified (*imminence*) in metaphoric substitution, or to maintain the distinction (*couriers* remain along with *cherubim*) in metonymic combination.[25]

These processes constitute, for Lacan, the chief index and mechanism of linkage between unconscious and conscious as the person frames his words in a context which, with the fact of utterance itself, it is felt must exemplify both. The secondary process of language always shows signs of its origin in the necessary structure of unconscious mechanisms maintained, most notably by language, between speaker and auditor (a relation that the patient-analyst framework abstracts by fixing it). And certainly our feeling is not only that Shakespeare is a great poet in this passage, but that the speaker in whose mouth he has placed it is unusually stirred up, manifesting the profundity of his stir by the great figurative leaps of his language.

Now it may be said, in elementary semiotic analysis, that metaphor *also* evidences a combinatory power, the relation of signifier to signifier, since we are given one signifier (*babe*) for another (*pity*) by a kind of combination, before they are referred to reality. The vulnerability of an emotion is compared to the vulnerability of an infant; but also in the supernatural world the babe that seems vulnerable is really not so; he will "stride the blast" and "blow the horrid deed in every eye" as an *alternative* (*or*), either actual or logical, to powerful cherubim. So that one act of combining signifiers (*babe* with *pity*) itself combines with another (vulnerability with something like its opposite). The substitution of metaphor, it may then be said, itself acts by a kind of combination, since both the signifier and the thing signified, the reference and its referent, make sense only with relation to the double signifier, babe plus pity. And this is by no means to metonymize metaphor. For metonymy itself, in elementary semiotic analysis, may be seen to involve if not the selection process (rather than combination), then a more direct reference between signifier and thing signified, since only a part of the reference, the courier-horse, is needed to suggest the referent in reality, the message carried by cherubim.

Putting so much semiotic action in the mouth of a supposed speaker, the imaginary person embodied across the stage boundary, activates to uniformity a device of language to which the rhetoricians of the period gave considerable attention, the "figure" of *prosopopeia*.[26] This conceived of the speaker's first-person address as a transformation of an impersonal rhetorical base, a feigning in the conception of the utterance itself. "The perfect *Prosopopeia*," Fraunce says, "is when the whole speach of anie person is fully and lively represented; wherein we must make both a fit and orderly accesse too, and regresse from the same *Prosopopeia*." In a play, the line of "regress" is cut off.[27] The only movement is forward, and there is a thrust towards that other element of rhetorical structure for Fraunce, the *climax*.

The purposiveness of Macbeth's speech here undergirds its

elaboration higher and higher on the ladder of climax, the points of transition being located rhythmically within the line to mime his "fall o' th' other," rather than end-stopping, as do the majestic climaxes of *Tamburlaine* and *Richard II*. Moreover, the tendency towards tight logical balance, which Barish notices as a peculiar feature of Shakespeare's prose in contradistinction to Jonson's [28] —a refinement of Euphuism toward the bare but abstract armature of colloquial speech—is constantly present in the stages of the thrust forward. Macbeth's speech could not only be outlined as a logical argument, in more steps than the A-B-A movement, from disturbance to balanced assessment to disturbance; at each stage, in each enjambing sentence, the logical balance is intricate, and prior to the upthrust of the metaphors that subserve it:

> But in these cases
> We still have judgment here, that we but teach
> Bloody instructions, which being taught return
> To plague the inventor.

Here are many antitheses: implicitly between "these cases" and others, explicitly between "still have" and "done quickly"; "judgment here" and "be-all and end-all here"; "here" and "the life to come"; "judgment" and "teach"; "teach" and "being taught"; "bloody" and "judgment"; "instructions" and "assassination"; "instructions" and "inventor"; "still have" and "return"; "plague" and "jump" (in so far as jump means to leap free and escape the consequence of being plagued). As Bertram Joseph puts it, "in each case contrasting ideas are joined together to make an expressive and compressed statement. The arranging of words in this kind of pattern of equivalence or of opposition makes it possible for the playwright to ensure that the individual ideas can be distinguishable within comparatively complex, and yet succinct, statements:

> And let my *liver* (1) rather *heat* (2) with *wine* (3)
> Than my *heart* (1) *cool* (2) with mortifying *groans* (3)
> (*The Merchant of Venice*, I,i,81-2) [29]

Joseph emphasizes the necessity for indicating antitheses, and
producing climax, in the process of speaking lines; and he finds
the feature a common or indeed constant one in the style, as:

> That which *hath made* (1) *them* (2) *drunk* (3)
> *hath made* (1) *me* (2) *bold* (3).

or:

> Be Kent unmannerly
> When Lear is mad. What wouldst thou do, old man?
> Think'st thou that duty shall dread to speak
> When power to flattery bows? To plainness honour's bound
> When majesty falls to folly.

King Lear, I,i,144-148

The equivalents are as follows: "be"-"is"; "Kent"-"Lear"; "unmannerly"-"mad"; "duty"-"power"; "shall dread to speak"-"to
flattery"; "to plainness"-"to folly"; "honour"-"majesty"; "'s
bound"-"falls."

The pressure forward of the purposive utterance is made to com-
press these logical nestings, and so the complexity of antithesis
suggests the thrust of the flight upward of climax. The sense of
eloquence, of staying above the normative speech of usual interchange outside the theatre, is magnificently sustained, in the effect
of orotundity that may owe something both to the expansive
preaching in this oral society (that also ate much) and to the improvisatory copiousness with which the well-educated courtier
would supposedly be endowed.

At the same time, the speeches, however copious, have a
mother-wit of succinctness beyond rhetorical amplification, suggesting the limit of the very language they are pressing, a sense
that Indo-European poetry has tended to have of itself, not only
since the "inexpressibility trope" of Dante and medieval poets
generally, but since the time of the Vedas.[30] At one limit of verbal invention, Shakespeare qualifies the hyperbole with mockery,
Berown's "taffeta phrases, silken terms precise,/three-pil'd hyperbole, spruce affection,/Figures pedantical" (*Love's Labour's*

Lost ,V,ii,406-8) , echoed in the bombastic euphuism of Holofernes. At the other limit, he holds to the simplest words and most elementary predications of the language, Cordelia's "And so I am, I am!" (*King Lear,* IV,vii,70) which is an entire speech, and Lear's "never, never, never, never, never," the conclusion of one, a climax that is a kind of descent.

3

Fortunately, since there is no existing theory of signs which can account for the base of that high form of linguistic behavior to which we accord the designation "style," one may notice features of signification, or even of style, without accounting fully for the base or bases on which they have been formed, and without necessarily either producing or subscribing to a special theory of the relation of style to other forms of linguistic behavior that it may wholly or partially include.

So we may simply notice that Shakespeare, or another, does not so much stay within a poetic diction, as Racine and Corneille, or even through prose Ibsen and Chekhov, may be said to do; rather, he offers conjunctions or areas that may or may not stretch the "valences" expected in the linear string of a statement.

> Or memorize another Golgotha
>
> (*Macbeth,* I,ii,41)

which does not especially stretch valences, rises above the refined style and strikes both the auditors in the audience and the auditors on stage with its elevation, not only because it evokes an ultimate analogy, of Macbeth's first battlefield to the Christian sacrifice; but also because it combines, in an expected way with a figure that is metaphoric if taken as a comparison and metonymic if taken as analogy, words that each posit a different selection-set. "Or" declares the category of alternation, while "another" that of reproduction, of the series in time which, once a second is produced, may be extended endlessly, much like the seed of Banquo who are paraded one after another before Macbeth's eyes—a procession of Golgotha's, where the first had been thought unique. "Memorize" belongs to a category of social acts (the private sense, "commit to memory," does not occur till the nineteenth century), to which "celebrate," "consecrate," "confer," "anathematize," and many more may be said to belong. "Golgotha" is a *place*, not an act (though the locus of an act), one which, until Christ's victory over death, suggests oblivion and not memorialization, "the place of skulls." It belongs to a category of fields or hills. Its act belongs to a category of religious events, a category of sufferings—a category which relates it to the battle it is describing. For Christ it is a triumphant suffering, as this battle has been.

The line itself is presented not as a fact but a supposition in the mouth of a bleeding captain whose last fainting utterance it turns out to be, since at that point he stops himself and pleads his own incapacity, analogous himself to the Christ on the cross because he is ignoring his wounds in order to bring this gasping message to the Scots.

The register in which Shakespeare writes activates a large, permitted set of linguistic coherences wherein the areas from which words are drawn are smaller sets brought into play when the words move in temporal sequence towards the unknown future of the drama. *Memorize* comes together with *another*, *another* with *Golgotha* in what are already implied partial antitheses—since their selection sources are different—that are already partially resolved—since they come together without a strain being put upon the valence-strings expected in an English sentence. The smaller intralinear antitheses are wrapped together rhythmically by the strong unitary marking of the single line, and concatenated with the larger interlinear ones, the still larger ones from speech to speech. The order is headlong, unpredictable, changing—in a word, dynamic—whereas one may see a stasis, of whatever magnificence, in the speeches of Sophocles or Racine.

In its language, the overall play produces constant mediation, and for Shakespeare it dynamizes the mediation, of contradictions among the terms of antitheses, of binary opposites. This function of mediating between the antitheses of binary opposites Lévi-Strauss assigns to the translinguistic act of myth, wherein the stories, independently of the temporal sequence in which language would necessarily cast them, reveal set upon transformed set of binary oppositions. While Shakespeare draws on the resonance of myths subliminally for his plots (a subject beyond Levi-Strauss' analysis, which deals with signification-patterns and not resonances), and while he will often conclude a sonnet with a proverb that sounds like a myth, he performs, by manipulating language itself, the operation of mediation.[31] The concluding aphorism-couplet of the sonnet seals a myth by virtue of relying on the attributes of its registers, wherein the Poet is performing Poetic Composition-Attention-Persuasion-Wooing of a Mistress whose attributes ultimately refer to an idea not dissociable from either the myth of Venus or the myth of the Queen of Heaven:

> So, till the judgment that yourself arise,
> You live in this, and dwell in lovers' eyes.
>
> (Sonnet 55)

This combines those two myths, as well as that of the Last Judgment, by asserting the survival-value of poetic artifacts over the fleshly mortality of human bodies, a commonplace that finds a place in the same register.

The act of conflating several registers of discourse in his rhetorical set, like the act of making implied predications in the running flow of statement, presents not so much a mediation as the result of a series of mediations. That is, in myth the set of terms, say *earth* and *sky*, are not joined but preserved in their distinctness by the term *water*, which can be seen indifferently as a middle term between both or as half of a binary pair with either. No act of identification, of predication, has taken place.

In language, however, predications set out partial identifications, "multitudinous seas incarnadine/making the green one red," runs one liquid into another, one color into another, so that all the liquids lose their very character of proliferation (*multitudinous*), or at least their distinguishing characteristics, and the

barriers of distinction are horribly erased. The result of mediation, in this case but to some degree in any poetic predication—
since poetic predications are virtual and *outside their frame* possess no other illocutionary force than that of "being poetic"—is to
dissolve entirely the distinctness of the items mediated, into some
larger whole.

The couplet, by tagging fourteen lines with its click, brings
mediation back home; it reinforces the sense of proverbial truth
inhering in the aphorism as it summarizes the doctrine.

Even without rhyme, the proverb, in its formulated syntax,
implies a *prima facie* truth-value, as well as a predication. The
proverb is not only propositional: laying down a truth for future
discourse, it is also meant to be summary: summing up past discourse in a *sententia*, a single sentence of opinion so normative as
to be taken for hoary social truth. *Frailty thy name is woman* or
ripeness is all do more than to voice the opinion of a single character at a single moment, or even to muster a commonplace for
specific application to the drama; they ring the drama in on a
world of codified wisdom which, among other things, the whole
play may be said to exemplify. The whole plot of *King Lear,* especially on the model of the medieval *De Casibus Virorum Illustrium,* may be taken as an expanded proverb, as the schematism
of the Morality, or such early plays as *The Spanish Tragedy, Edward II* and *Doctor Faustus* may be said to imply.

Furthermore, as F. P. Wilson says, "What the proverb meant
to Shakespeare is best shown not by the number and variety
which he uses, although those so far identified are indeed many,
but by his use of them in the gravest and greatest passages in his
plays. Proverbs are mingled with folk-tale and ballad in the
snatches, half sense and half nothing, spoken by the mad Ophelia:
'They say the owl was a baker's daughter, Lord, we know what
we are, but know not what we may be.' In *King Lear* Shakespeare puts into the mouth of the Fool the silliest catch-phrase—
'Cry you mercy, I took you for a joint-stool'—with poignant effect
and the Fool's last speech is a reference to the homely, ironical
proverb: 'You would make me go to bed at noon.' " [32]

Proverbial utterance may be expanded by fresh image and

varied by rhetorical device: this is what happened to the speech of Macbeth above, whose rhetorical conditionals imply their own contradiction ("If the assassination/Could trammel up the consequence and catch/with his surcease success"—but it can't). And yet every proposition uttered by Macbeth refers not only to law ("plead," etc.) and not only to theology as well ("judgment") but, at every point, to that folk wisdom which proverbs succinctly formulate, the immemorial social usage preceding law and underlying the sacredness of the social contract. "If but this blow/Might be the be-all and the end-all here" formulates, in trenchant coinages where the deep structure of whole clauses has been compressed into a single substantive "be-all" and "end-all," something not too far different from the proverb "Dead men tell no tales," and by ways of shying up to confront what amounts to a countervailing proverb, "The murderer of a good man is doubly despised." "Strike while the iron is hot" or "A stitch in time saves nine" ("then 'twere well/It were done quickly") is also set against "Haste makes waste."[33]

Behind the proverb may lie Proverbs, a book of the Bible, or a general register that Scripture may strike. So Macbeth's "done quickly"[34] echoes Christ's words on Judas, John 13.27. "Return to plague the inventor" recalls Proverbs 26.27 and the general scriptural context of retribution. "Vaulting ambition" suggests Proverbs 29, "Pride goeth before destruction, and an high mind before the fall."

The enrichment of proverb by metaphor is a standard linguistic resource in this panoramic theatre. It is much favored by Chapman, and the purple passages in *Bussy d'Ambois* will be found to rest their force on a proverbial substratum. The newness of the phrasing often reinforces the venerableness of the idea. So:

> 'Tis immortality to die aspiring,
> As if a man were taken quick to heaven
> (*Byron's Conspiracy*, I,ii,31-32)

The forceful second line, suggesting an analogy possible for all souls to the Assumption of the Virgin, directs the strangeness of

the first line toward a Christiañ commonplace so fully accepted as
not to need explicit proverbial expression, that the one goal of
every life is to die saved.

> Truth is a golden ball, cast in our way
> To make us stript by falsehood.
>
> *(Ibid.,* II,ii,155-156)

This applies the Atalanta myth to a homely version of the sub-
Machiavellian notion, proverbial even if no explicit proverb be
found to embody it, that in the give-and-take of power-jockeying,
the attention to truth is an encumbrance to competition as something over and above the considerations at hand. This is a kind of
inference from "the race is not to the swift nor the battle to the
strong, neither yet bread to the wise, nor yet riches to men of
understanding, nor yet favor to men of skill" *(Ecclesiastes,* 9:11),
and it may also echo "the children of this world are in their generation wiser than the children of light" *(Luke* 16:8). Much of
Shakespeare's own Biblical allusion has such proverbial force.

Uttering such pithy statements, a character like Bussy or
Byron or Macbeth will seem, through the forcefulness of his utterance, to be embodying prodigious energies of a personal sort
and at the same time to be drawing on the funds of wisdom provided by the social order. They seem to be asserting, constantly
and triumphantly even as they succumb to outer hostility or inner
evil, the same basis for extending language that Beckett, for
example, is questioning, in Olga Bernal's reading:

> Il apparaît que le rapport du mot à la chose est le même
> que le rapport du mot au Je.[35]

Or, in this case, putting the statement into the mouth of a character on stage is parallel, as an act, to making a statement at all.
This is an observation which may be said to be implied already
in the *Poetices* of Julius Caesar Scaliger,[36] who asserts that
poetry is primarily language in two relationships, to things and
to audience. In order to distinguish poetry from any language

whatever, one would have to define audience in some sense more explicit than "auditor," a sense that would already be approaching the audience of a play. In this realm of sixteenth century discourse, a model for the high verbal art of the Renaissance in France and England as well as in Italy, poetry aspires to become drama; drama fulfills as a kind of telos the goals of poetry. This valuation, in turn, is implied in the reliance of such critics, and their English imitators like Sidney, on the *Poetics* of Aristotle.

The refined style holds language to a reasoned normalization, a moderated control analogous to, and paralleled in, the control of meter. Interrelated limits are added to the principles of selection —a poetic diction, and of combination—a rhetorical balance. These limits overdetermine and constrict the utterance, and at the same time fill it out, much as meter both overdetermines the sound-patterns of an utterance and provides a further pattern wherein all elements are accounted for through being referred to a principle outside the rules of the language.

In the large classification of styles available to the Renaissance playwright, the types defined by C. S. Lewis for nondramatic poetry may be found to be equally applicable, the *Drab*, sometimes called the *plain* style, and the *Golden*, sometimes called the *sweet*. The *drab* is less than the *refined* syle: Cordelia's *And so I am, I am*, is too simply colloquial to be refined; and the *golden* is more, full of the very *magnificence*, to use the Renaissance term for the splendor of the courtier, which the refined style eschews as an excess. Shakespeare, in tending towards the magnificence of the golden style, subjects his dramatic afflatus to the high Siren-call of a hyperbolic ring.[37]

The pace of conversation in ordinary language goes at what is apprehended as a normal rate. It does not call special attention to itself, it flows into what it names; it effaces itself in the implicit assertion that the order of the world is stable and maintained by the act of speaking.

Any stylization calls attention to itself, making explicit some special assertion about order. So rhetoric emphasizes the leader's claim to leadership as he addresses a largely silent audience. Courtly turns of phrase emphasize the courtier's membership in an upper class and assert his adherence to the values of that class. Courtly rhetoric asserts class values not only as these cohere among themselves but as they maintain themselves against the rougher order of the lower classes or even against the last things of a church where the category of class is not final, and possibly not relevant. When courtly turns of phrase are systematized by the rhetoric of poetry into a refined style, an additional value of literacy, the value of permanence, is asserted. Writing allows the preservation of what oral tradition blurs into archetypes or oblivion. The refined style developed contemporaneously with literacy in Greece, and questions of permanence are a common topos of refined poems, "Not marble nor the gilded monuments/Of princes shall outlive this pow'rful rhyme" (Sonnet 55,1-2). The normal rate of conversation is itself specially systematized into the measures and recurrences of poetry, implying the assertion that the writer of the sonnet is dedicating values of literacy, permanence, and courtliness to the lady who in the act of celebration both evokes and transcends those values. In so far as she evokes them, she is the highest form of courtier; in so far as she transcends them, she is analogous to the divine order. And she is often praised particularly for courtesy, for a union of beauty in body and loveliness in soul which is analogous to another Hypostatic union.

Refinement is a kind of norm for style. For a dramatic character to depart from it in the direction of conversation is not just to return to the normal rate of ordinary language, but rather to suggest that the moment is so intense no words will do but those of common use and rhythm. Coming at pitched moments in the flow of refined or golden utterances, the plain utterance constitutes a kind of preterition—it advertises its self-effacement by straining to be able to do no more than use the normal flow. And it also constitutes a kind of reduction, to a rock-bottom of humanity as of speech wherein last things are the first and only things.

A "golden" utterance, rising above a refined base, performs another turn: it asserts the gorgeous and mysterious complexity of the orders it is glorying in. When mostly the utterance is golden, as in *Antony and Cleopatra*, a return to the refined base constitutes a pause or breathing space. Then the play rests for the time being on the values of one principle of order, as in the dialogue between Octavius and Antony (II,ii,27-174), where the strain that is present is apprehended, in these refined terms, only as a strain upon this particular order, negatively, with no positive or countervailing assertion of the other, finally triumphant order. Empire dominates all the way, and Love can only be sensed in the vacillation of the "triple pillar of the world."

The spectrum from plain to golden is defined two-dimensionally, so to speak, in order to characterize the style of lyric poems. In dramatic verses, another dimension has been added, the future-oriented purposiveness of the speaker in his complex of relation to other purposive speakers on stage; and this panoramizing dimension is enlivened by the fact that the silent auditor is not a reader but seated in the flesh listening to the quick of what is being said. In this posture of attention, the cues fade in and out, the registers blur into one another.

In a lyric poem we need attend only to the order of the words. But in a play there is a corresponding, resulting, and inspiriting order of actions. Shakespeare's freedom of range along the spectrum of styles derives not only from his dexterity with words but also from his resourcefulness at putting the action into intimate reciprocity with the words, all within the seemingly fixed externalizations of a recitative convention. So Hamlet's shifts of style are not just movements along the scale of possible utterance; they betray changes from moment to moment in the attitude of the speaker; and the changes themselves constitute an underlying pattern of action-with-words (action by means of words, and words responding to actions).

One may, consequently, characterize the styles according to the notions of the time: the *mel* and *fel*, the sweet and the acrid styles of Scaliger's classification for small lyrics,[38] for epigrams, producing the ideal of *point*, a rhetorical ideal obtainable in both plain and golden styles. Or one may extrapolate the qualities of either style according to Richard Carew's census of desiderata, to define the way in which each may exemplify *significancy, easynes, copiousness,* and *sweetnes.*[39] Or one may make the distinction congruent with Puttenham's two kinds of stylistic operation, *enargia,* which "giveth a glorious lustre and light" (a phrase which anticipates Shakespeare's effect!) "to satisfy and delight," and *energia,* which has "wrought a strong and vertuous operation . . . to work a stirre in the mind."[40] "*Figure,*" Puttenham says, "breedeth them both," but he goes beyond conventional rhetoric in offering the set of organizing terms for style: *Analogia* (proportion), *Tasis* (tuneableness) *Syntonia* (brevity), *Synthesis* (orderliness), *Ciriologia* (sounding proper and natural), *Tropus* (lively and stirring). The suggestion that one attempt to characterize Shakespeare's stylistic effects by this nearly contemporary set does almost all the work of so characterizing them. Performing this exercise, or invoking the exercise of Sister Miriam Joseph's catalogue of rhetorical devices in the plays,[41] would help to focus on the intricacy of Shakespeare's stylistic effects—but always two-dimensionally, without reference to the action.

4

Action can be both rich and controlled and still in a sort of stiff relation to the words of its characters. Marlowe's *Edward II* offers a set of alternations where the Barons fail to control the king (A), then succeed in controlling the king (B), then succeed in controlling the new king (B[1]), then fail in controlling the new king (A-B-B[1]-A[1]). In the last scene, when the boy Edward III condemns the protector Mortimer for murdering his father, he does so while the body of the old king, Edward II, is brought in. He also sends his mother to the Tower—a boy king more resolute than Hamlet is, who also faces a mother in league with the lover-murderer of his father. Since his quarrel with her repeats, and varies, and leads from the initial grievance of the barons, Edward II's favoritism towards the homosexual Gaveston, this boy-king's final actions may be said to make all four stretches of the action visibly present before us—A, as the final result of the quarrel over Gaveston, in which the spurned queen sided with the barons led by her new lover; B, as Mortimer has been the agent of undoing Gaveston at the queen's skillful and surreptitious suggestion that he not be sent into exile; B^1, as the Queen and Mortimer open the scene by attempting to dominate the boy; and A^1 as he asserts the continuity of divine right, in father as in son. The boy weeping on the throne with the casket of his father standing nearby, the head of his recent protector displayed, and his mother just excluded, offers a rich and powerful summary of all the action, for which his tears are an adult and audience-like response as well as a yielding to the impulse of his tender years. At the same time Marlowe has steered just one verse-line clear of having Isabella register the shock of facing her lover's severed head. There is the further long-range double-take that at first, scandalized by the shock of Edward's adherence to Gaveston, and the replacement of Gaveston by the Spencer who had also been his lover, we side with the Barons and with the spurned, legitimate Queen. So that the act of usurpation has to be dramatized—the act of the legitimate grievance appears in the long-run light as a recourse to an illegitimate and self-seeking rebellion—before the silent principle of divine right turns Mortimer and the Queen, through the action of the play, from noble sufferers into arrogant usurpers.

The Shakespeare who speaks convincingly of "Desiring this man's art, and that man's scope" (Sonnet 29.7) never equalled the presentational concision and paradox of this scene, which sets all these progressions forth in visible form, though he does reproduce its slow double-take by translating the noble sufferer Bolingbroke into the usurping Henry IV. Here the politics, the human emotion, are more concentrated, more schematically resumptive, than any conclusion Shakespeare can bring off. Nor does anything in the degradation of Richard II equal for sharp impact the gratuitous scene where Edward II's captors shave him in puddle water so that he will not be recognized.

Still, Edward's addresses to his crown present a stiffness of attitude. They have no recourse to the "inwardness," which really derives from the interplay of action and words, in the speeches of Richard II, in his hollow crown speech, or in the later, parallel one of Prince Hal with the crown from his father's pillow. And, concurrently, the final words of Edward III find no interaction, and even no equivalence, for the richness of the scene in which he finds himself; nor has he been silenced, since there are no pregnant speeches in the play by which we may measure his presumed taciturnity:

QUEEN ISABELLA:
Then come, sweet death, and rid me of this grief.
                                    (*Exit with Second Lord*)

        (*Enter First Lord, with the head of Mortimer Junior*)
FIRST LORD:
My lord, here is the head of Mortimer.
KING EDWARD III:
Go fetch my father's hearse where it shall lie,
And bring my funeral robes.
  (*Exeunt Attendants*)—Accursed head,
Could I have ruled thee then, as I do now,
Thou hadst not hatched this monstrous treachery!—
Here comes the hearse; help me to mourn, my lords.
  (*Re-enter Attendants with the hearse and funeral robes*)
Sweet father, here unto thy murdered ghost
I offer up this wicked traitor's head;
And let these tears, distilling from mine eyes,
Be witness of my grief and innocency.
                            (*Edward II*,V,vi,92-102)

"Grief," in this concluding line, looks all the way back at all the play; "innocency" summarizes the present state of a king who starts with a clean slate. But no impetus in this language gives us any vision of a future beyond itself; Faustus' marvelous final soliloquy, also, only tries to stave off a certain, and timed, damnation. Shakespeare, on the other hand, invests his plays with impetus at every point, so that they can, as they usually do, refer to an altered futurity in their conclusion; the energy whereby futurity has been embodied has been pitted throughout into the relation between ordered action and re- cited words. When a genuinely grieving Prince Hal tries on with genuine delight the crown lying beside his sleeping fa- ther, he recapitulates and unifies all his attitudes, from sport- iveness to dutiful dedication; he looks toward the future his father admonishes him for craving and blesses him for deserv- ing.

So even in the beginning of an early play, we are made to feel a propulsion forward in the assumption of the golden style to actions that are as yet to unfold:

BEDFORD:

> Hung be the heavens with black, yield day to night!
> Comets, importing change of times and states,
> Brandish your crystal tresses in the sky
> And with them scourge the bad revolting stars
> That have consented unto Henry's death!
> Henry the Fifth, too famous to live long!
> England ne'er lost a king of so much worth.
>
> *(Henry VI, Part One, I,i,1-6)*

The speaker here is on the surface merely uttering a standard public compliment, a ceremonial variation on "The King is dead, long live the King." But by way of doing so he invokes such a diapason, and touches base on so many different ideas, that he already is active; he already embodies the energetic principle of quick change, and of the mystery of death which will centrally define and undermine all the action in this tri- logy of plays. He looks powerfully ahead while looking back at a beginning. No such change takes place in the similarly end- stopped, similarly "mighty" lines Tamburlaine speaks at the death of Zenocrate:

TAMBURLAINE:

Black is the beauty of the brightest day;
The golden ball of heaven's eternal fire,
That danced with glory on the silver waves,
Now wants the fuel that inflamed his beams,
And all with faintness and for foul disgrace,
He binds his temples with a frowning cloud,
Ready to darken earth with endless night.
Zenocrate, that gave him light and life,
Whose eyes shot fire from their ivory bowers,
And tempered every soul with lively heat,
Now by the malice of the angry skies,
Whose jealousy admits no second mate,
Draws in the comfort of her latest breath,
All dazzled with the hellish mists of death.

(*Tamburlaine, Part Two*, II,iv,1-14)

This is the same *topos*, but it has yet to plow its recitation back into psychological reaction. It is a response, but it does not evidence the materials out of the quick of which responses come into being, except in so far as it is splendidly cumulative. Both these passages are Senecan; but still less, in English rendering, can one feel an informing attitude, any more than a public recitation, behind the presumed words of what the Renaissance thought was Seneca turned into English:

OCTAVIA:

Now that Aurore with glitterying streames,
The glading starres from skey doth chase,
Syr Phoebus pert, with spouting beames,
From dewy neast doth mount apace:
And with his cheerefull lookes doth yeeld
Unto the world a gladsome day.
Go to, O wretch, with ample Fielde
Of heavy cares oppressed aye,
Thy grievous wonted playntes recount

(*Octavia*, I,i,1-10)

This is a comparable *topos*, the linking of celestial phenomena with grief (here contrastingly, and as it were through *meiosis*, since this dawn shines on "heavy cares"); and yet there is nothing in the speech to take it beyond the lyric set-pieces with which Thomas Newton's rhymes associate it.

Kent rises to antithesis, suggesting the refined style, across the enjambed break whose colloquialism is also in the plain style, refinement not taking over completely in the pith of a strong response that has begun with a more refined and more mannered prior speech:

KENT:

> Royal Lear
> Whom I have ever honour'd as my king,
> Lov'd as my father, as my master follow'd,
> As my great patron thought on in my prayers—

LEAR:

> The bow is bent and drawn; make from the shaft.

KENT:

> Let it fall rather, though the fork invade
> The region of my heart. *Be Kent unmannerly*
> *When Lear is mad.* What wouldst thou do old man?
>
> (I,i,138-145)

And Kent swells, after this, back into trenchant and refined antithesis based on proverbs. The sentence I have italicized retains the balance of the courtier, echoing the control of Kent's interrupted speech, and so continuing that control. The maxim sets forth the felicity conditions (to retain Austin's term) under which all the code of the court may absolve a courtier for acting contrary to it and still remaining courtly, the conditions under which "Kent" may be "unmannerly"—"When Lear is mad."

Further, it exemplifies of itself the leverage built into the antithesis by giving a mannerly expression to the unmannerly act, suggesting a notion of high mannerliness, the large human

code that the purgative actions of the play will invest in the
survivors.

By contrast, as well as echo, the plainness retained in Kent's
refinement looks back to, and implicitly as well as explicitly cri-
ticizes, the easy afflatus of the king's description of the map:

> Of all these bounds, even from this line to this,
> With shadowy forests and with champains rich'd,
> With plenteous rivers and wide-skirted meads,
> We make thee lady
>
>   (I,i,62-65)

This sentence is already contrasted, as an over-facile gorgeous-
ness, with Cordelia's immediately preceding aside:

> What shall Cordelia speak? Love, and be silent (61)

a line which offers its own refinement on a plain, proverbial
base (*Still waters run deep, all is not gold that glitters*, etc.).
Counterpointed at every turn, the king's golden magniloquence
spends itself in the ineffectuality of *flatus vocis*:

> For, by the sacred radiance of the sun,
> The mysteries of Hecat and the night;
> By all the operation of the orbs
>
>   (108-110)

The curses are bound to fall unfulfilled not only because these
"powerful" gods have only a virtual existence for a Christian
audience, and not only because the will of the old man will
undergo one modification after another, but because such speeches
as Kent's are set in a register that defines their hollowness by a
contrast of solidity—just on the verbal level, since of course at
this point what the king says is law, and what others say can
so far only be words, words whose trajectory is implicit in the
extensiveness of their effects. Lear is merely enacting a fond, if
powerful, charade, giving away lands to get mere pledges of love.
Kent, observing this, gives, in the sentence I continue to expound,

an instant and alert (alertness being another trait of the courtier), and therefore faithful, diagnosis of what the king's actions imply. They imply Lear is acting so irresponsibly, so "mad," that he lays on his courtier the fiat of unmannerly truth-telling, "*Be Kent unmannerly*/When *Lear is mad*." This diagnosis, both correct and prophetic, looks ahead prospectively to all the fool says in his different register of parable and song:

> Then they for sudden joy did weep,
> And I for sorrow sung,
> That such a king should play bo-peep
> And go the fools among.

> (I,iv,173-176)

—this being the theme of much that the fool voices. And of course Kent's blunt, refined statement looks ahead to all the tragic accumulation of real madness, through all the chaos that has to clear before the note of plain refinement can again be dominant:

> I have a journey, sir, shortly to go.
> My master calls me; I must not say no.

> (V,iii,321-322)

The rich onward flow of the action, underlying and buoying up all these turns and levels of style, makes every stylistic gesture, even the simple laconic utterance, a kind of "heightening" or "prominence".[42] In such a complex of significative structures, as between both actions and words, it would be partial to single out some special trait of the words as a "deviance" from normal speech. In normal speaking, of course, where the background is given, some possibility of deviance or heightening or prominence can be sensed and even described. There the background is given. And in lyric poetry the background is neutral. But in a drama the background, which includes the action immediately foregoing, is all invented; it possesses of itself the interacting significative function which keeps the language afloat. Certainly we do not feel Shakespeare is forever altering his styles, or his stylistic emphases, from plain to refined to golden: we are absorbed in the action to which the words are pointing; that action is conceived to be set before our eyes. The poetry thereby is released for a gratuitous magic; the centrality of the action keeps us from being wholly absorbed in picking up the single cue that an orotund, ostensive name is repeated in end-stopped position: Tamburlaine not only revels in the word "Zenocrate"; he also dotes on the presence of the lovely creature who is artificially, in the strutting of a boy actor, set before us. So Juliet with the name "Romeo" or Henry V with the name of Agincourt and St. Crispin's Day. But Milton's "Looks toward Namancos or Bayona's hold" absorbs us wholly in the country whose power and mystery of unfamiliarity the name of the Spain where they are located would not conjure up. He puts our eyes and the eyes of the angel "homeward" toward a home that is actual for the angel and an aspiration for us. We are, for the moment, wholly absorbed in that moment of magic naming, whereas in a play we are also attentive to past and future actions that the magic naming arrests, but never wholly.

Against the moderately bare boards, or conventionalized scene, of this stage, the physical universe is as spiritual as the words make it. In Macbeth's address to the witches above, when they can affect weather, as perhaps also the future, by their witchcraft, creating for themselves the "filthy air," his description of the apocalyptic side-effects of their naming what they call a "a deed without a name" may be taken for an accurate measurement of possibility, as also an imaginative assimilation to it (the tormented evil man corresponds to whirlwind destruction as he had begun by imagining cherubim or a naked babe riding the blast):

[WITCHES]:
    A deed without a name.
MACBETH:
    I conjure you . . .
    Though you untie the winds and let them fight

Against the churches; though the yesty waves
Confound and swallow navigation up;
Though bladed corn be lodg'd and trees blown down;
Though castles topple on their warders' heads;
Though palaces and pyramids do slope
Their heads to their foundations; though the treasure
Of nature's germens tumble all together,
Even till destruction sicken—answer me.

(IV,i,49-60)

Here is imagined a universal cataclysm more miraculous than
Birnam Wood coming to Dunsinane, but in the same spirit,
and we cannot say it is not in response to the cue from him
that the witches prophesy the form that his own downfall will
take, an upheaval in vegetative nature. Winds strong enough
to drive a seed into something solid, a cataclysm in which huge
stone structures are not shaken down but reduced by a kind of
melting (slope), in which creation's seeds are so confused that
destruction sickens—this is an apocalypse indeed. And it serves
to tell us of the state of soul of a man who would bring such a
condition about merely to get an answer: a desperation of
supernatural evil in which the utterance partakes, for which
it stands, out of which it defines the fusing trans-metaphoric
connections. The heavily-structured signs of such a speech render possible, so to speak, the conception of such energetic connections.

Timon moralizes a universal landscape when beset by thieves;
his attribution of moral qualities to physical processes, again,
performs an act of combination wherein the pregnant aptness
of poetic characterization spiritualizes into communality the
physical attributes whose items are meant "only" as emblems
in a list:

Do villainy, do, since you protest to do't,
Like workmen. I'll example you with thievery:
The sun's a thief, and with his great attraction

Robs the vast sea; the moon's an arrant thief,
And her pale fire she snatches from the sun;
The sea's a thief, whose liquid surge resolves
The moon into salt tears; the earth's a thief,
That feeds and breeds by composture stol'n
From general excrement—each thing's a thief.
                        (*Timon of Athens*, IV,iii,432-440)

By all these quantitative connections, within the intense range
of a word and from word to word, poetry prepares a qualita-
tive leap. Such pressure does not have to be constantly maintained to be constant; and when it is made to seem to characterize the speech of people in the "normal" interchange of life,
it invests that life, its time and its space, its motives and the
gardens and chaos of its surroundings, with some of the same
all-imbruing energy. Valences do not have to be stretched in
every clause for that larger possibility to be suggested, nor
metaphor to be generated in every period or metonymy linked
in every pairing to sense the presence of a heightened language
where metaphor and metonymy are themselves, unless defined
"metaphorically" to include almost any linguistic act whatever,
only an especially salient and schematic, if prevalent, kind of
connection[43] for a language which can, when it must, do without
them.

There is, as C.L. Barber asserts, even so early as *The
Spanish Tragedy*, a point of nearly idolatrous, or flagrantly
profane, investment in mere language on this stage,[44] a reliance on hyperbole as a hypercathected verbal magic in response to the sort of intolerable pressures in the imagined
drama that would otherwise drive a Hieronymo, or a Hamlet,
truly mad. The ritual recourse of Oedipus, the ritual demise of
Pentheus, are not open to them. Their reliance on language
attests to that closure in the action, as well as to spiritual open-
ings that only the language, again, can give glimpses of because the action, at that point of complication, is in the process
of producing its own mortal closures. The possibility that Hamlet
holds out to Horatio, "Absent thee from felicity awhile" (V,ii,

339), is one the play had not demonstrated to it, a world whose paradisal harmonies (felicity echoes the Latin *felicitas*, condition of the blest) can be imagined to supersede the harrowing action only, so to speak, because Hamlet has resolutely worked his language round to the point of envisioning it so, a restoration at a new level of "the glass of fashion and the mould of form" (III,i, 153). In this sense, while the action may silence the words, as Barber says, at the same time the words go beyond the action.

5

In ordinary language people either mean what they say or have some sort of reason for not meaning what they say. The frame is stable, the addressee is conceived of as standing in place, and the message does a definable task whose coordinates its own cues will completely define. In this stability of "meantness," statements very different in character—"Bring me the nails," "I love you," "You know I only like Vivaldi sometimes"—are alike in not raising doubts.

Poetry that exhibits (and poetry of its very nature does exhibit) such a stability of meantness will ring as plain-spoken: Greville, Landor, Pushkin. But stable meantness is only a pendulum dead center for the possibilities open to poetry, which can use its fictiveness to play with many aspects of the frame; and in dramatic poetry to play with many aspects of the addressee, both the addressee(s) on the stage and the collective addressee in the audience.

At one end of the pendulum, poetry can be so labile in its meantness that the very richness of language seems to empty it of content, or nearly. This tends to happen when the ostensible subject and the real subject of the poem diverge, as in *Lycidas*. The ostensible subject is mourning for the death of a friend. The real subject is the bearing of mortality on the literary vision. Hovering in that uncertain frame, directed at an iridescent and vanishing addressee, are injunctions whose very fullness of suggestiveness seems to undermine their force. What meantness can reside in *Weep no more, woful shepherds, weep no more?* or in *Look homeward, angel, now, and melt with ruth/And, O ye dolphins, waft the hapless youth?* Keats offers a rich vision; but statements like *Thou wast not born for death, immortal bird,* and *No, no, go not to Lethe, Neither twist/Wolf's bane, tight-rooted, for its amorous wine* are labile in their meantness. They do not bear the credibility (the frame is not as stable) of *And all that mighty heart is lying still,* a statement of stable meantness made by a poet who seems to have tried to hold his verse at this center of the pendulum, defining it as the "language of man speaking to men."

This lability cannot be ascribed to the artificiality of the verse, to any analyzable syntactic or stylistic devices; nor is stability just an effect of the plain style: Greville, Landor, and Pushkin, among others, are notable masters of artifice. It might be found to correlate with complexity of verse pattern; certainly, so far as we can judge, Pindar swings in his intentional pendulum over to the labile side, meaning what he says less stably than in ordinary language.

At the other end of the pendulum the statement in verse possesses an urgency of meantness, as though it were trying to forge an entirely new frame, a new addressee. Such verse resounds with a prophetic intention, in the work of Blake, Whitman, and Rimbaud. It tends to consume the life of the poet; the words are coals of fire on his tongue. The prophets in Scripture are the great exemplars of urgent meantness. In such urgent verse the categories of vision and of command break down, and other categories tend to break down too. The words carry not only the permanence of artifacts, which all verses pretend to do; they are also eschatological and apocalyptic. They announce a judgment they are calling for, they cleanse and ask to cleanse, they render null the whole question of stability or instability since their invocation is directed at a sort of fully established Eden where such questions could not be asked.

Now dramatic verse in Shakespeare's hands possesses a meantness that draws on the whole range of the pendulum: it advertises its fictiveness, it is notably labile; and at the same time it holds almost always to the directness of ordinary speech. It means what it says; its meantness has the neutral stability of the morality play. And at the same time it thrusts forward in a mighty rush that at nearly every moment carries with it the air of urgent meantness, of the prophetic onus. His language, his style, set forth not an Eden but a world whose rich possibilities are Edenic in seeming fulfilled, at being both charged at every point with past and future, invented just for the moment, and rationally continuous with anything one might possibly know. This is true of Homer and Dante too, but Shakespeare possesses in the dramatic form, and uses fully, a set of divisions between speaker and speaker, actors and audience, which keeps alive both the provisionality of the utterance and its largeness of inclusive aspiration.

SIX
Endings

The endings of Shakespeare's plays remain open to a future
that is presented in the often elliptical bent of rounding the play
out. The freedom of the Renaissance stage in this exceeds the neat
five-act adaptation of the Terentian version of beginning, middle,
and end, the protasis, epitasis, and catastrophe of Renaissance critical formulation which would have been inculcated at school in the
boy Shakespeare.[1]

Beginning, middle, and end, the Aristotelian structuring of
plot-orders, only adapt, truistically, for particular application to

the stage, the necessary subjection of human life to time. All plays, to be put on, would have to have a beginning, a middle, and an end; and any proportionate attention to coherence would bring the middle to an increase of complication (*epitasis* in Renaissance terms, *desis* in Aristotle's), the end to a somewhat striking resolution thereof (*catastrophe, lusis*).

But Shakespeare notably renders this pattern, which would seem to be universal, into an enunciation of mysteriousness by bending it at the end of a play away from itself. Every one of his history plays looks behind at its action by looking ahead to an interaction of forces which will either be markedly more complicated than what it has shown, or markedly less so, as the conclusions of *King Lear* and *Cymbeline* emphasize.

This openness is felt not just at the end, of course. The third acts of Shakespeare's plays, their midpoint, are often especially strong in a merely tonal way, when we would expect them to be concentrated on just furthering the action. At that point Lear is raging against the thunder, Claudio contemplating death with a false friar, Hamlet frighting the king with the "false fire" of the play-within-a-play, Macbeth staging his banquet, Othello not hearing the lute music Cassio stages for him, Coriolanus turning away, Timon staging his trick banquet.

And a tonal effect can intrude on the play out of nowhere at any time: the beginning of the thunder in *King Lear*, the music under the earth in *Antony and Cleopatra*, the knocking at the gate in *Macbeth*, the unheard music in *Pericles*.

The title of·*Twelfth Night*, and the festive circumstances of its court performance,[2] relate the meaning of the play not just to the seasonal ordering of time in the Christian year, and not just to the conjunction of kingly order and divine in the visit of the Magi to the Christ Child, but to the no-man's-land in time of the age-old intercalary interval, the spell in the dead of winter when time-reckoning is out of time, the "twelve days of Christmas." This mid-winter intercalary period, in pagan counterparts all the way back to Egypt and Babylon, up to our own day, for the week between Christmas and New Year's, is an occasion for a sort of counterfertility celebration of timelessness in a short period of "endless" time.

Immobility and timelessness haunt *Twelfth Night*, from the opening words about music, "Give me excess of it, that, surfeiting,/ The appetite may sicken and so die." (I,i,2-3), all the way to the actual singing of the closing song, an elliptical enunciation by an elliptical character, whose refrain is a fertile-infertile timelessness, "the rain it raineth every day." This immobility of rhythmic undertone, set in a play whose title announces it as coming at the end of the intercalary run, suggests an endless-time/no-time/miniature year whose spatial counterpart is the enchanted space/associationless space/miniature dukedom of Illyria.

The melancholy Duke Orsino begins in an immobile posture, and his erotic insight is not sufficient to induce him into an effective mobility.

He senses already at the beginning that a feminine approach may, as it does, open Olivia's heart:

DUKE:
> O, then unfold the passion of my love,
> Surprise her with discourse of my dear faith!
> It shall become thee well to act my woes:
> She will attend it better in thy youth
> Than in a nuncio's of more grave aspect.

VIOLA:
> I think not so, my lord.

DUKE:
> Dear lad, believe it,
> For they shall yet belie thy happy years
> . . .
> And all is semblative a woman's part.
> I know thy constellation is right apt
> For this affair.

> (I,iv,23-35)

The Duke here seems keener than Viola, whose doubt still presents a mild disinclination masking the already formed powerful inclination of love for him. And yet he will not, until events force him to do so, put two and two together; he will remain stalled from the proper "constellation" of what shines between the feminine-seeming of his "dear lad" and the fact that, as he has already told us, "I have unclasp'd/To thee the book even of my secret soul" (I,iv,12-13).

The wooing proceeds with this strange indirection throughout, stalled into a graceful and wholly subliminal prescience of non-becoming. Yet at the same time the wooing is realized in an aftermath that thus defines itself as one for already having happened: Olivia is the first to rush to the altar, who had been the most reluctant to approach it when everything seemed decorously propitious; she marries Sebastian before she knows he is not Cesario, and Sebastian strings along because he literally thinks it a dream.

The difficulties are so extreme they can only be resolved in an undercurrent, subliminally, out of the normal, waking nexus of time; thus do Viola and Orsino discover each other in the by-blows of a jealous anger quickly resolved by the discovery. The elation of actualizing what time alone can bring to light in the pureness of no-time, is matched by the depression of true impossibilities—the matching of Sir Andrew Aguecheek and Malvolio, who are fully stalled, and in fact checked, through the aspirations of their wooing Olivia, a central figure mysteriously passive until she becomes mysteriously active. Towards her all characters are defined in their erotic contours: Orsino, Viola, Sebastian, Sir Andrew, Malvolio, and even her Uncle himself, since his horseplay in the wings of punishing unwarranted courtship of his niece becomes, in retrospect, a courtship between himself and his collaborator Maria. The lady in waiting gets the overwhelming reward of marriage for her cleverness at counterfeiting Malvolio's hand (as it is archly, and no doubt ironically, put), "Maria writ/The letter, at Sir Toby's great importance,/In recompense whereof he hath married her" (V,i,349-351).

And this marriage, too, is distanced for being recounted rather than presented, as an aftermath of something that has already happened rather than in the immediate perspective of the multiple marriage round-up that normally concludes a comedy. The festive exuberance of comedy is present only in its echoes. This play is a school of liberality, in Barber's terms, perhaps for us, but not for the characters, who are as susceptible to feeling as they are impervious to other than erotic change. Fertility comes about without exuberance, without at any time undermining the chaste responsiveness of Viola, who in the last scene, responding to some subliminal echo of murder-as-sacrifice, offers the sacrifice of her death. So in the time-scheme of the play, its subtle progression and its enigmatic events, the pagan side of Misrule festivity, are brought into harmony with the charitable inklings of the hopeful Christmas season in the sequenced perceptions of the audience, a harmony audible in the music and words of the final song, which says nothing whatever about the events of this play and cannot be applied to it, the Clown never being a Lover in any play, and the "I" of the song belonging to a different social class from our characters. He is also at a point in age, too young for many of them, and too old, in his experience at least, for Viola:

> When that I was and a little tiny boy,
> With hey, ho, the wind and the rain,
> A foolish thing was but a toy,
> For the rain it raineth every day.

> But when I came to man's estate,
> With hey, ho, the wind and the rain,
> 'Gainst knaves and thieves men shut their gate,
> For the rain it raineth every day.

> But when I came, alas! to wive,
> With hey, ho, the wind and the rain,
> By swaggering could I never thrive,
> For the rain it raineth every day.

> But when I came unto my beds,
> With hey, ho, the wind and the rain,
> With toss-pots still had drunken heads,
> For the rain it raineth every day.

> A great while ago the world begun,
> With hey, ho, the wind and the rain,
> But that's all one, our play is done,
> And we'll strive to please you every day.
>
> (V,i,375-394)

This reasserts the melancholy hanging over the play, as it re-phrases the sense of stalling, of getting nowhere, that the play both presents in its progression and denies. This conclusion, at the same time, completes an order nowhere referred to in this song. If music be the food of love, this song manages to speak of wedding and bedding while avoiding any mention of the love which songs are supposed to be about—and *are* about, elsewhere in this play. Moreover, elsewhere the love songs are sung by the Clown, who in the tradition of the Fool[3] will be present at the festivities of love but is nowhere assigned the role of a lover. He is given the love songs in the course of the play because the lovers are checked for celebration: they cannot so much as serenade one another.

When they whisk through to fruition, they have taken love, so to speak, out of the song of the clown; and in this sense the action of the play is present here, but only in its absence.

Even "beds" could be indifferently the bed of marriage or the bed of impotence and old age, depending on whether one takes it as an equivalence for "wive" in the previous stanza—since "wive" could be coordinate in time with "man's estate" in the stanza that precedes it—or in the life-cycle series from "little tiny boy" to "done," the course of a life that, in the telling, brings life back around again to the stage: it's "our play" that is done, and the fact is offered as being "all one"—in space and time, so to speak, as well as in the logic of colloquial disclaimer ("that's all one" means "none of it matters").

The song does stall. It offers two refrains, not one; and refrain takes up fully half the line, the extreme of "redundancy," in Bateson's sense,[4] being the flow of nonsense which one refrain often enlists the way Renaissance songs do but no other song in this play does, "hey, ho" being only exclamatory or pausing.

And a stalling redundancy is offered in the alternate, open slots of the song. The sentences that are inserted in the slots themselves present the surprise of their increased-valences often by way of redundancy: *what that... and; little... tiny;⁵ foolish thing... toy; knaves... thieves* (all thieves are knaves and all knaves in some metaphoric sense thieves; the poem is strong on metaphor): *toss-pots... drunken heads; a great while ago... world begun.*

In this redundancy there is a marked lowering of the threshold of meaning, disestablishing the very linearity that is the theme of the song, since the song is forced to be circular, though it tells about the course of a life from childhood to death, and then about the entire course of time, and then about the end of the play whose own linearity of events it displaces not only in form and in theme (the play is about love, not about the seven ages of man) but also in reference.

Instead of rounding out this play, by an elliptical variation of its own stallings and redundancies, the song proceeds to unfold a new, totally different order: of eventless progress through life instead of the deep, breathless event of falling in love; of bad outer weather instead of the benignant inner weather that brings lovers together in their magic, distant kingdom; of a hostility that might accord with the world of *Troilus and Cressida, Macbeth,* or *King Lear*, " 'Gainst knaves and thieves men shut their gate," but not with a small Arcadia in which all gates are open even to smalltime knaves who would never be guilty of thievery; of an illness banished from this play except, perhaps, in the remembered precedent death of Olivia's brother and father.

In its very last reference to persons, the song does touch on the embodiment of the pleasure principle in the play, Sir Toby; but Sir Toby is more than a quintessential "toss-pot," and his head is clear enough to do that which would be inconceivable for Falstaff; he too marries, and so in that sense he does not remain in the condition illustrated by the maxim "toss-pots still have drunken heads." The origin of the world, the concluding reference, is an anticlimax, a crescendo which is at the same time a decrescendo, since it merely announces the conclusion of an afternoon's entertainment through the wrong end of a telescope that makes the play a little tiny event indeed seen in the perspective of the whole course of time.

The whole play offers a crescendo that is at the same time a decrescendo, and the rich surprise of the song increases the enigma of that progression by offering the succinct account of an almost totally different order, in a world where also the weather is always the same, since "the wind and the rain" are as constant in the song as Illyria lacks any of the associations that England or France or Italy would have. So this Illyria can be both a real place and something like the Elysium off-rhymed with it in Viola's first couplet. Standing rescued on the seacoast, she picks up the last couplet that the Duke utters in his palace:

DUKE:
> Away before me to sweet beds of flow'rs:
> Love-thoughts lie rich when canopied with bow'rs.
>
> (I,i,40-41)

VIOLA:
> And what should I do in Illyria?
> My brother he is in Elysium.
>
> (I,ii,3-4)

This pair, who have not yet met, will enter their own Elysium when the Duke finds himself mated not to that other woman absorbed in thoughts of her brother's death but to this very one; her own brother will find his Elysium by marrying that other woman. This circle, of mating already closed by implication here, is re-opened by the final song.

2

A play shows us, in the span of a single sitting, a whole sequence of events that crucially affect the whole lives of the imagined persons before us. The events on the stage scene, as though miraculously, foreshorten the events of actual life. And in the process of doing so they lift the veil of taboo by rigorously maintaining the tabooed veil of the stage barrier (in real life all lines may be crossed under certain conditions, but not the proscenium line). No longer are we forbidden to see the intimate, formative sequences of others' secret lives, their love lives (comedy); no longer are the circumstances leading to death hidden from view (tragedy). The celebratory conclusion of a comedy, the marriage, brings round to the public of the wedding festivities the public of the dramatic audience: the circle is all but closed, and assimilating one private union into a public context is re-transposed on the fictive public context of the theatre. The mirth of our relief unbinds the risk of our looking on.

Shakespeare reopens that circle in *Twelfth Night* by the song; in *Midsummer Night's Dream* by introducing the bungled tragedy of Pyramus and Thisbe at the wedding festivities; in *Love's Labour's Lost* by delaying the marriage for death, "Jack hath not Jill" (V,ii,863)—and also by a dramatic presentation on the part of the rustics, who offer it in the form of two songs, both of them discordant from the charm of the play, since the "Spring" one centers on the charivari of cuckoldry and the "Winter" one on an unpastoral village of unattractive women: "Marian's nose looks red and raw," "Greasy Joan doth keel the pot."

The pressure of what has been foreshortened, of all that must be cleared up before an ending can come about, is induced by ordering the events into intricate combination—and sometimes, on the panoramic Renaissance stage, by orchestrating the action and reactions in several spheres, the partial ignorance of people in each,[6] so as to bring about disruptions in the measured progress through time of the play's rhythms. In *Much Ado About Nothing* the camp of Don John and Borrachio works to bring about a striking disruption at Hero's wedding ceremony; uncovering the dirty work proceeds not by any gradual, reasoned investigation, but rather by fits and starts. The effect of the fits and starts is first to mate, and then to enlist, the odd couple of Beatrice and Benedick, who balance the even couple of Claudio and Hero. It is not till the first major disruption, till the fourth act, that the odd couple are tricked into love: the stalling allows them to draw together, and the evenness of the ending is a restoration of harmony in the world of love, which the concluded military campaign of the beginning had allowed the exogamous warriors to enter.

Shakespeare's theatre does not offer a three-quarter Grecian circle, but a space oriented towards the future, so to speak, since we look to the end of that space for the action to take place, up front, as at the altar of a church at the far end of a nave. As Duvignaud says, relating the space of the theatre to the time of its events, "In the lateral extension of the fresco scene, destiny has less sense than the story and its unfolding: life develops in a two-dimensional universe in which the will imposes itself immediately, where the acts operate one upon another, in which the connection of the actions brings a visible consequence, where a temporality-against-the grain confronts a modern temporality turned in the direction of freedom."[7]

And still, in the breadth of his conception, Shakespeare adopts as well as transforms a sense of destiny: some vestige of the Stoic attitude towards Fate, absorbed as it were into the impartiality of the panoramic presentation, is still discernible in his plays.

The death of a king implies not only closure to one ending but, in what the doctrine of the divine right implies as a normal course of events, the continuation of the prior order, a cyclic repetition of the process. The king's "two bodies," the mortal body and the body politic,[8] come together in the succession at the moment they come apart. This is the process preordained in the orderly transmission viewed at the end of *The Winter's Tale*, which uses a pastoral or seasonal order of the generations not just to affirm a closure of that circle, but also to envision a deeper and more singular process of charitable repentance redeeming the mortal ravages of morbid suspicion.

In none of Shakespeare's other plays is the transmission, orderly or not, a transfer to the beginning of a comparable cycle. In *Richard II*, a dying king enunciates the notion of the two bodies; but it is a king who stands under condemnation by a usurper. *Henry IV* envisions a different order, and *Henry V* still a different one. The opening of *Henry VI*, back at the beginning of Shakespeare's career, announced that the change of kings would involve such a change of order; Henry V was "too famous to live long" (*Henry VI, Part One,* I,i,6). And the very lesson of the tetralogy that *Henry V* concludes must mean that this single play is only a phase. Or, as the Chorus puts it in their final speech, "Small time, but, in that small, most greatly lived/This star of England. Fortune made his sword;/By which the world's best garden he achieved." (*Henry V*, Epilogue, 5-7). And they go on to say that the successful total control by this monarch which the play exhibited before us, will be succeeded not even by maintaining it (which would still offer a different temper if not a different order) but by losing it in the dissolution of that control, under not one steady hand but many unsteady hands, "Henry the Sixth ... /Whose state so many had the managing/That they lost France and made his England bleed" (Epilogue, 9-12). The order Fortinbras establishes is neither the order imagined by Hamlet the son nor that maintained by Hamlet the father. Brutus discovers that to change the ruler of a commonwealth is to change not just what one has defined as needing change, but everything, and so radically that one may go under. So Lear learns; and the reign that succeeds the dual rule of Albany and Cornwall will differ from that, and also from his own: those two forms of unenlightenment, ignorance and malice, will have enlightened the successors—or the successor, since of the two, Kent resigns, leaving Edgar in power to "Rule in this realm and the gor'd state sustain" (V,iii,320). And Edgar replies that he is compelled to observe the lessons of ignorance and malice, "The weight of this sad time we must obey," (323) the royal "we" mingling the cooperative-collective and the regal-personal in a way that instantly exemplifies what it is asserting. The deaths have not brought the order to a full circle; they have changed the order.

The representation of change on stage, without referring that change to the closed circle of an enunciated order, awakens in the audience either delight that their surrogates to whom they have surrendered their speaking capacity are leading a charmed, joyful life (comedy) or the awesome sense that the closest one can come to understanding is to have a cycle of events open to the future, rather than closed, in a visualization of a *Sein-zum-Tod* that has been compressed into the time of an afternoon while still retaining some mark of the openness that life itself presents. Thus the signifier, the play, presents, in its very gaps and ruptures of causality, a homology to the signified, the pattern of events in life. Moreover, if the play hangs together mostly in a classical pattern of causality—if the open end does not dominate the entire play— then the play will still predominantly more than echo the over-determination of events. It will demonstrate overdetermination by the *a fortiori* presentation of an enchainment of events closer than that in life, as well as on a shorter span; the open end will only qualify such an enchainment, as the effect of the song at the end of *Twelfth Night* is not so much to break the spell of Illyria's charm as to distance it by offering another cycle of life on a millennial scale (*a great while ago the world begun*).

The Shakespearian play thus offers an enactment of overdetermination. Its sequences offer neither the constancy of a closed order nor the alternation of two competing systems, but rather a powerful and impressive dissymmetry in which either desirable forces unpredictably triumph over undesirable ones, as in *Measure for Measure*: or *vice versa*, as in *Troilus and Cressida*, where the value of love does not exactly counterbalance the value of chaotic war but rather, unpredictably but overdeterminedly, goes under to the undesirable value. This play "misses," in Charles Williams' words, "a dramatic, a theatrical, conclusion; it ends indeed with the vague statement by both armies and individuals, 'Well, we'll all fight again tomorrow'...the abandonment (of the themes of the play) is not only on the side of action, but of intellect also."[9]

These "problem" plays are only problems if we insist that the sense of order, or of chaos, be more than tangential; or if we try to impose some sort of pluralism on them, when what they offer is a single sense not of constancy nor of alternation but of a dissymmetry at the heart of their action, and of our lives.

All this holds in retrospect, if one looks back at the play; and to look back is to look ahead. "What's past is prologue" (*The Tempest*, II,i,244). Without looking ahead there can be no *Sein-zum-Tod*.

Any play is essentially a construct-in-prospect. We formulate its meaning after we see it, as we summarize a life after a person has died. But the process of a life is in the living, and the process of a play is as it moves ahead, unseen and unpredictable, into the hypostasized futurity of an unknown plot that, for being unknown, is in that way, too, analogous both to our sense of our own death and to our sense that a future may, by a backward look, reveal a meaning to the lives we live, still open for their mortality as Shakespeare's play presents an order that remains open when much of its action has taken on causal closure.

This theatre generally tends to have its moments refer both back and ahead, on more tangents than in classical tragedy. In Jonson's play, *The Poetaster*, Caesar suddenly intrudes on a masque-like scene where his daughter Julia mocks and revels in her love for Ovid (IV,iv):

> What would you have me let the strumpet live
> That, for this pageant, earns so many deaths?
> (IV,iv,15-16)

Such thunderbolts clear the scene; they unleash an order of absolute rule that breaks up the family in the course of asserting the value of the family. They also look back at the conventionally illict amour, and ahead to the banishment of the poet, about which the classically trained audience will be supposed to know something in advance. Such a process is intensified in the later acts of *King Lear* and *Cymbeline*, which are dazing to assimilate not only because there are so many strings to the plot but because those strings are being pulled every which way.

The realistic play, which maintains a firm distinction between the inforcements and elisions of closure in the effect of cumulative latency of words and the manifestness of actions, affords itself re-

repetition—the mother's eerie offstage piano playing in *A Long Day's Journey into Night*, Regina's final entrance in *Ghosts*.

Film intensifies realism by presenting sequences of shots of what is "really" there. The evidence of the eyes seeing a film is a firm anchor. Where the stage theatricalizes the real, the smile of Cabiria at the end of *Notte di Cabiria* takes in and resolves her sequence of self-deceptions.

Nothing can disturb the linearity of sequences in montage but a reflexive comment on the sequence. Nothing can change their temporality but a posed suspension of temporality. The film's triumph of visual singleness, of significant surfaces, makes absolute the achievement of Ibsen, loading his surfaces with latencies. In the showy language of Shakespeare, and in the rhythms that are free to change at every moment, the surfaces comment on each other, and the conclusion, as often as not, is angled so as to produce a still further comment.

There is, to borrow Angus Fletcher's adaptation (in a lecture) of Van Gennep, a kind of virtual liminality in the end of these plays, a powerful threshold which plants at the door of the theatre, for the audience to cross as it reemerges into life, something at once fuller and more tentative than the terms "comedy" and "tragedy" can be made to comprise, since they can only be understood as bestowing some kind of order on events, and these plays can only be understood as transcending such kinds of order. Those terms, applied to the plays of Shakespeare, are no more than tone signatures. In other respects they are part of the rhetoric, a general heading for a title page under which the title poses its own enigmas (*Measure for Measure, The Winter's Tale;* "a sad tale's best for winter" but there are ways in which this play is not sad, and it is classified under the heading "comedy"), or else refuses to do more than name its occasion or protagonist (*Twelfth Night; A Midsummer Night's Dream*), describe its circumstance (*The Taming of the Shrew; Much Ado About Nothing; The Tempest*), or advertise the refusal to summarize that is implied in the powerful nuances of its ending (*As You Like It* and the alternate name for *Twelfth Night, What You Will*).

SEVEN
Justice

His actions illustrate his words—as they should, since words are symbolic actions. But who else has spoken without an element of self-condemnation? All the rest of us are Oedipus. Jesus has some claim to be an authority on words. More exactly, he is word. The man himself, in both action and suffering (which add up to refusing to be the Messiah), is what he advocates. The Mediator is the message.

John Pairman Brown
The Liberated Zone

1

Keeping the endings open in these plays has the effect of allowing the rightness of a conclusion not deducible from the causal pattern its higher say in the action. Justice, at a moment of time, or in a closed order of times, locks the definitions. Opening the order allows room for Providence,[1] or whatever one may call the higher principle of ultimate justice that weighs the effect of a final outcome. The open event emphasizes the mystery of the outcome, the powerlessness of men to do other than, say, dramatize stories about it; and the effortlessness "not strain'd" of whatever remote agency brings it about.

Justice, freed from logic, becomes mercy. "The quality of mercy is not strain'd;/It droppeth as the gentle rain from heaven/ . . . It blesseth him that gives and him that takes" (*The Merchant of Venice*, IV,i,179-182). The actor becomes one with the acted upon; in this, mercy resembles, and exemplifies, love; it is also like love in having a lightness of touch and a nobility (two senses of *gentle*); it is a natural effect, "as rain." And it is possible for a man to take it upon himself; it is a person that Portia is enjoining to show mercy, before the necessity of defining justice is sharply invoked. It is of the defining essence, the "quality," of mercy to be effortless, to proceed freely. It is not forced, by logic or any other agency, to its conclusion. Using it is a way man may imitate God ("from heaven").

This doctrine, at its point of connection in a double causal sequence (marriage and bond-redemption) transcends the temporality of that causal sequence; the appeal in fact is not met; and it does not matter.

In *Henry IV, Part One* there is, within that time sphere, an unreconciled division as between a world of duty managed by the king and a world of pleasure managed by Falstaff. But the play is part of a tetralogy, and in the further sequence of time-phases, Falstaff gets the complex justice not just of contrasting definition but of receiving his deserts from the authority of the old playfellow he has been expecting to welcome him. He must assimilate the blow of being ignored, and then of being arrested. When he dies, he is eulogized by the woman he stayed shy of marrying. Doll Tearsheet, too, has been arrested; the cruelty of narcissism the two embody receives its check from the events. It is Pistol who marries Mistress Quickly; together they run an Inn whose "gentlewomen that live honestly by the prick of their needles" (*Henry V*, II,i,33-34) are perhaps persisting, in the perennial looseness of the social order, at the old trick, which we have already been shown will be given its due. Sir John of Lancaster does not allow Falstaff to ransom Colville (*Henry IV, Part Two*, IV,iii,23-69). And the last echo of the Gadshill episode, the final definition of the injustice of its self-indulgence, is found in the fate of Bardolph, who is executed after having his nose slit for plundering French churches (*Henry V*, III,vi,96-103). Falstaff does see an ultimate pastoral-celestial glimpse of pleasure as he dies, " 'a babbled of green fields."

Still, the counterbalance between self-indulgence (prose) and duty (verse) is now weighted, by *Henry V*, heavily in favor of the latter. The prose world gasps in insufficiency, as braggadoccio, hypocrisy, squabbling, marital self-satisfaction and idleness held sway for Pym, Bardolph, Quickly, and Pistol on the eve of Agincourt. A minor defalcation over a gambling debt, and the illness of Falstaff equally hold their attention. Their piety in recounting his offstage visionary death (II,iii,1-26) quickly evaporates into the mustering of predatory expostulation:

> Let us to France, like horse-leeches, my boys,
> To suck, to suck, the very blood to suck.
>
> (55-56)

Bardolph is executed for stealing a pyx, but Pym and Pistol also emerge as thieves (III,ii,40-54). So much for the camaraderie of Gadshill, except for the apotheosis of self-sacrificing comradeship in the verse part, Henry V's exhortations on the eve of the battle itself.

One criterion of just order in a state, based at least partly on the scriptural tradition of subordination to constituted rulers that the current of Lutheran discussion only reinforced, asserts the divine right of kings. Another criterion, that for which Machiavelli stands, holds that only someone who is adept at manipulating the actual forces of human self-interest, by force or by deceit, will be able to maintain himself in power. If a king has got to the throne by force or by deceit, then his very adeptness will work against him and inspire rebellion (e.g., Richard III). If he has some just cause, then the momentum built into his defending himself may carry him to the throne (Bolingbroke-Henry IV), though there will still be something left over both in the unresolved forces of the outside world (the rebellions against Henry IV) and in his conscience. The theory of divine right, and the theory of the sway of the most powerful, both are shown as holding in Shakespeare's plays, and yet both, taken at a point in time, or even for the reign of a single king, are inescapably in conflict, the moment either assumption is tested at all, when either a legitimate king is in some way weak or a strong man is in some way not the legitimate king. The divine right could only be demonstrated if it could be shown to hold in spite of a king's weakness, and the Machiavellian principle of power could only be demonstrated if applied to someone whose right was in some question.

Shakespeare's histories present the view that usually one or the other of these testing conditions tends to be the case in fact, though in theory neither principle would be tested if you had a legitimate king who happened also to be strong, as with *Henry V*; in such a case, one would get only the air of felicitous triumph which that play radiates.

The tetralogies, eight history plays taken in groups of four, refer the deadlock between divine right and countervailing force to a longer span of time, to a series of reigns in the second tetralogy and to a sequence of many disparate events in the first. Justice is resolved, and the deadlock broken, only by a time so long, and a causal sequence so mysterious, that only such a duration and such broken patterns could equal it.[2] Even *Henry V* presents its victorious king not as a resolving case of divine right combined with effectually wielded power, but rather as the end of a line: if a king is sensitive but captious and weak (Richard II), he will be replaced by a strong man he has wronged by his captiousness: one so insensitive, however, that he will not embody the glories of a regal ideal but only wrestle as a power-broker (Henry IV). It takes the third generation (Henry V), a youth forced to defend his princely sensitivity against the insensitivity of a father whose protectiveness would effectually limit him; and who therefore goes through a psychic dynamism that gives him, as he undertakes the succession, both the strength of his father and the sensitivity of the dispossessed king: an unquestioned embodiment of the divine right whose particular angle towards it had brought him through the complicated course of earning the sensitive adjudication of power without manhandling others in the process.

The king must die. Such is the expectation of immemorial social traditions still dimly alive in a society ruled by kings who still wield some vestige of a magical power while embodying a large measure of divine right. To set a king involved in strenuous events before the people on a stage that is a locus for exhibiting the full swing of fortune, is in itself to overshadow the future of the short-spanned events with some higher likelihood that the central figure will die. In the sense that to invoke this possibility is to bring about that sequence, the protagonist, even in a history, is a sort of involuntary and unwitting sacrifice. And in Shakespeare's ten history plays we hear of the deaths of at least nine kings (*Richard II*, *Henry IV*, Henry V, Edward III, Edward IV, *Richard III*, *Henry VI*, Henry VII, *King John*), five of whom (the ones in italics) meet their end in plays that bear their name.

Tragedy centered on mere intensity of circumstance, like Ford's *The Broken Heart*, tends to seem merely perverse, rather than profound, when it does not enlist such deep and dim expectations. The process of history itself does offer them; if for no other reason than that kings are mortal, and that the whole body politic must readjust when one dies, participating to that extent in the sacrifice, at a point where the ritual is indistinguishable from the practical. A random continuity is offered by the chronicles which Shakespeare adapted for his histories—a genre he can be said to have given the fullest treatment of any of his contemporaries, and in that sense to have invented. Random continuity likewise dominates *A Mirror for Magistrates*, from which he borrowed too, and Daniel's *Civil Wars*, which cover the same ground as the two tetralogies. These offer set pieces of moralization, effectually, on either Fortune or Virtue, where the time-frame of Shakespeare's histories complicates each of these terms and tries to connect them with each other in striking ways, a virtue complexly embodied in character in some kind of interaction with the not quite predictable fortune of event. The medieval *De Casibus Virorum Illustrium* is a ground on which he works many figures,[3] just as the word "chance" (*casus*) meaning both a random and a fitting occurrence[4] is as changed in his contexts from his medieval sources as the deaths in his plays are from the bull and bear baitings that were performed in one of the same arenas[5] and derive from a comparable ritual source, like the bullfight itself.[6]

The old king dies, the new king heals. At the beginning of the first tetralogy, however, the new king has not quite assimilated the full magic powers of the old. Kings are persons as well as figures, and the person Henry VI, the play tells us at once, is no match for the person Henry V, as the conclusion to the play that bears his name will also tell us.

At the end of the play about an ideal king such a statement is a ceremonial assertion of total loss. At the beginning of a group of plays it has a portentous effect: it suggests that the king will be even more subject to mortality than kings, as human beings and also as ritual surrogates, usually are. And the first tetralogy does finally, after many byways, bring round the death of Henry VI, by assassination.

The byways themselves, in fact, involve other deaths in the *Henry VI* group—sequences of deaths. Each single death comes in a way that is at once unpredictable and, at its point, a redefinition of an order in the event, an order which otherwise is closed by the adjudicated counterbalance between the divine right and the realities of power. A weak king will simply be surrounded by many power brokers: Henry VI has a Protector and also a Chancellor. This adaptability, however, is perilous, because it simply increases the chances of redefinition by death, when older men are necessarily involved, because, if not born to power, one must spend part of one's life attaining it; and also simply because many persons are involved and not just one.

By the time the second or third unexpected death has broken the order of events in *Henry VI, Part One*, we begin to expect deaths, without being made any the wiser as to when they will occur or what particular pattern of justice they will exhibit. In retrospect, we can provide an answer: people who meddle in power may get snuffed out; so Winchester is poisoned and Gloucester dies strangled. But in prospect no one, except the king who exhibits a dangerous weakness, lets himself in for a sequence that seems to draw death as a predictable end.

The pattern, taken in retrospect by the audience of the whole tetralogy, is a simple one: the king can count on not being able to count on the order of events. An unscrupulous king could take advantage of such a situation if he were also strong, but Henry VI is both scrupulous and weak. Doing so does not save Richard III anyway. *Henry VI* begins a motif in Shakespeare's work that does not find fulfillment till *The Tempest*: that of the ruler too pure to meddle in the sordidness of worldly affairs. Taken in prospect, then, as centering on such a king, the pattern is wide-meshed. The simplicity emphasizes the singleness of the stage, while the breadth of the action stresses the panoramic nature of its enactments. In such a panorama a principle of justice is so abstract that it tends to be indissociable from the whole sequence of events. But neither is the tetralogy a chronicle.

Its most salient recurrence, the death of a principal, serves as both a limit, taken singly: that is the end of a life; and also as a cycle, taken cumulatively: we are back around at the point where a death breaks the pattern. *Tamburlaine* already begins such a pattern, and its series of triumphant deaths takes place in a mortal time that must eventually bring the death of the woman who enhances it all, and then of the conqueror himself. This is, as we say, poetic justice. But the justice of *Henry VI* is poetic in another sense. The deaths are sometimes deserved, as Suffolk's and Cade's and even Joan of Arc's are shown to be. And they also sometimes follow the principle of decorum in their mode: it is fitting that the proud unscrupulous Suffolk be done in by unscrupulous commoners who hold a grudge against him, while he is carrying out a flight from the center of the power he has mismanaged. It is fitting that the interloper Cade be killed by a householder who is accidentally a fellow countryman. And it is fitting that a witch die a witch's death, that the false virgin be unmasked as a pregnant strumpet. But other deaths are more poignant than fitting, and they are striking because of the absence of decorum. This is the case for the first deaths, those of Salisbury and Gargrave, snuffed out by a boy who has pulled a successful trick at a siege. Justified and decorous or not, all the deaths have in common the feature of thrusting into the action, and none is produced by a causal sequence, except that of the king himself, who may be said finally to have brought his death down upon himself by his long series of vacillations.

Scene by scene the tetralogy tends to square its opposing forces off into the immobility of simple, locked opposition, Winchester against Gloucester, the White Roses against the Red, Talbot against the Countess, Gloucester against Suffolk, Edward IV against Henry VI; and then, later on, Richard III tends to square off schematically against whoever confronts him, man or woman, restive conspirator or hostile widow or prospective mother-in-law. At a point of the play it would seem either impossible to adjudicate between the forces (*Henry VI*, all parts) or else impossible to bring justice to bear (Richard III seems consistently to outsmart his interlocutors, as he himself boasts in his opening speech). And yet, in the long run, justice is brought to bear; a contender dies, or a death alters the conditions of contention, "Just Death, kind umpire of men's miseries" (*Henry VI, Part One*, II,v,29).

The political deaths typically take a long time to effectuate; their preparation is protracted through many scenes. So the impeachment of Gloucester and the exile of his wife takes more than an act to bring about; and still his death by strangling comes as a sudden blow (*Henry VI, Part Two*, III,iii). Soon thereafter, in demonstrated justice, Winchester, the opponent responsible for the strangling, dies in the same bed, also by foul means. The nexus of forces slows retribution, but the unpredictability of factors speeds it: Suffolk is attacked at length, starting from the point when his·connection with the queen brings him into suspicion; but his death comes suddenly and speedily (*Henry VI, Part Two*, IV,ii). Cade sustains his rebellion through several scenes, and through the execution of Cromer and Say; he dies in the same scene where he fatally strays into Iden's garden (*Part Two*, IV,x).

The deaths on the battlefield, simpler and more expected, are still given many turns. The first death in the tetralogy is a false one, the mistaken report of Talbot's death (*Part One*, I,i,141,*ff*). A commander who braves combat is a natural target for the enemy, fair game to die at any time. But Talbot is many times sought in vain. He wriggles out of the trap the Countess believes she has caught him in (*Part One*, II,iii). At a low ebb of battle he expects to die and enjoins his son to carry on in his stead. And then, suddenly, the son is struck down, Talbot bears the boy across the field in his arms, and he is finally himself struck down (*Part One*, IV,vii)—a motif that is varied much later when a large battlefield exhibits the schematic succession of a son who has killed a father, and then of a father who has killed a son (*Part Three*, II,v). Bedford is brought to the battlefield sick on a litter, groans on stage, and expires (*Part One*, III,ii). Salisbury, the first nobleman killed on the field of battle, is despatched by a boy who sneaks in upon him with a linstock (*Part One*, I,iv). Clifford is shot through the neck (*Part Three*, II,vi).

These deaths are beyond justice; they result from the interplay of forces, like the culminating death of all, the death of Henry VI himself, who is stabbed by Richard. His son, Prince Edward, is stabbed by many in concert (*Part Three*, V,v), as York has earlier been mocked and stabbed (*Part Three*, I,iv). Young Rutland is struck down and his bloody napkin used cruelly by the queen (*Part Three*, I, iii).

Just as the action is balanced between a short span of deadlocked forces and a long span of realignments defined by death, so the deaths are divided between those brought about through poetic justice and those brought about through blind force. As though to emphasize the disparities of complex action, the deaths are classifiable in this way into two groups (justice, blind force), in another way into two groups (political, military), and in still another way into as many groups as there are deaths, the play seeming to avoid the commoner causes of mortality, direct death by combat or death because of old age—except in the death which precedes the tetralogy, that of Henry V. No one death of the more than twenty in the first three plays occurs in a way exactly like any other, except for the three stabbings of leaders.

Richard III, a pendant on the first three plays, steps up the schematization: an evil man whose ambition causes him to snuff out many people is finally dethroned through the collaboration of his surviving victims. The schematism finds its final expression in his climactic battlefield line "A horse! a horse! my kingdom for a horse!" (*Richard III*, V,iv,7)—an exact assessment of exchange values, like that of a dying man on a desert island who realizes a glass of water would literally be worth his entire fortune. But the quick mind able boldly and instantly to produce this equation, whereby he might at least escape, is caught hopelessly in the poetic justice of his situation; the pattern of events will not allow him to escape. Richmond will not only succeed him but also bring about his death.

Shakespeare varies many of these themes throughout the rest of his work but he never again produces so large and so schematic a canvas, with a pattern of increasing complexity and multiplying correspondences as we stand close to it. As we stand away from it, it offers a *memento mori* as simple as its own doubling confrontations, and as Warwick's dying words:

> Why, what is pomp, rule, reign, but earth and dust?
> And live we how we can, yet die we must.
> (*Part Three*, V,ii,27-8)

Death, as the final common demoninator for differentiating the lives of persons in time, informs two of the most thoroughly realized literary works of the middle ages. In the *Divina Commedia* the spirit of a living man compasses level by level the dead in the other world. In the *Testaments* of Villon the poem takes on the rhetorical form of the will, of commands to effectuate a transfer of property appropriate both to the testator and the legatee, in the commonality of the future's equality—"*Frères humaines qui après nous vivez*"—as the rotting bodies of the hanged are imagined to say, those who have nothing to will.

On Shakespeare's stage this first tetralogy offers a partial, rather than a total, accounting. The general medieval current—there is no evidence that these splendid forerunners impinged in any informing way upon his consciousness—is assimilated centrally, and then subjected to a Renaissance questioning. Villon, as it were, becomes Montaigne without ceasing to be Villon. Or Dante becomes Ariosto without ceasing to be Dante. The wide lens of the panorama, the break in both space and time of the proscenium, overlays the events it includes with a single determinant, with a complex pattern, and in deliberate failure to carry through all-inclusively. For there is still another sequence, that of the reigns, not here explained with full characterological causality. Henry VI is weak enough to form the bad bargain of a misalliance; Edward IV amorous enough to do the same; and Richard III evil enough to gloat in his power to make alliances at will. These situations are in a sense too simple to admit of working out into any satisfactory equation the implicit contradiction between the divine right of kings and the elementary facts of power. Unpredictability does duty for resolution.

Concurrently with its run through the sequence weak-sensitive king, strong-insensitive king, strong-sensitive king, the second tetralogy aligns forces of a complexity that increases arithmetically from *Richard II* to *Henry IV, Part One*, continues in *Henry IV, Part Two*, and is expanded to the international plane in *Henry V*. In *Richard II* the attraction-repulsion of the king's narcissism succumbs to a series in which first the king outdoes his barons, then stands counterpoised to a baron who silently contains a future king within his purpose, and then goes under to the new king. In *Henry IV, Part One*, Bolingbroke copes with problems in Wales, in Scotland, and in the North—from all directions except that of the Ireland where Richard II fatally withdrew—and he lingers in the kingdom's center, not withdrawing, as it becomes clear that what seem to be separate problems are really one problem; and he manages the problem by putting down the rebellion that is staffed from all three quarters. In doing so he has failed not only to carry out his expiatory pilgrimage but also to adjudicate, in a way satisfactory to himself, a balance within his won succession: Prince Hal is given over to narcissism, and the play is divided between the two worlds of Duty and Pleasure. In the second part the rebellion is weak enough, and the king far gone enough in life, to assimilate and adjudicate Pleasure in the perspective of Duty: Falstaff is arrested in the last action of the play. The sphere of Duty encompasses Pleasure, and now another sphere dominates the stage, the sphere of Mortality, which compasses Duty also (as well as Pleasure; Falstaff grows even older), both for the old king who dies and the new king who is caught in the psychodrama of having to expose his desire, secretly enunciated in an earlier soliloquy, for the crown. His meditation on the crown (*Henry IV, Part Two*, IV,v,21-47) parallels that of the doomed Richard II.

But Prince Hal is fated rather than doomed, and he carries on to fund his narcissism in the political, military, and amorous prowess of an ideal king. Though it is against an entire kingdom that he wages war, rather than against allied rebels, most of *Henry V* is given up to his glorying in the tests of winning. His *sprezzatura* carries along all the sorrow and all the life of battle. On the field of Agincourt there is no room for the cowardice of Falstaff, and Bardolph's sacrilegious greed has already been exposed and punished. Here prose and verse mirror a single world, as do chorus and actors. Playing with the battle-pastoral of going in disguise among his soldiers, Henry receives just one check for his narcissism, the refusal of Williams to accept the money-stuffed gloves casually rewarding him and forgiving him for having been trapped into half-treasonous mutterings against the king. The disguised "common soldier" presents the gauntlet, calling Williams on the challenge he has uttered. This resolution of a duel into no contest parallels Richard II's imperceptive justice in calling off the duel between Mowbray and Bolingbroke, except that there are no feelings to be pent up here. The king's narcissism oversteps itself in offering the money-stuffed gloves, and Williams need only assert his dignity of refusal to leave the whole episode in a transitoriness of the past, from which both he and the king can proceed, defined but untrammelled.

The unmanageable complexity of the first tetralogy is driven inward in the second: it is the psychology of the king that determines whether the complexity of events is manageable or not. As Sigurd Burckhardt puts it, "In the first tetralogy the crown is striven for as though it were a final goal—as though time would stop once the goal were reached. In the second tetralogy it is the symbol of an office, simultaneously desired and feared, a goal and at the same time a beginning."[7]

Death, too, here loses the randomness of the first tetralogy. Richard II dies at the end of the first play, as the end product of a weakness dramatized before us. Hotspur is killed in combat at the end of the second because a complete warrior must compass more than warring to be fully adequate, even on the battlefield. In the third play Bolingbroke succumbs to a mortality which cannot be regarded as premature, in the light of how long it would take in a life to manage the sequence of events we have been shown: working out a long rivalry and then going into exile and then returning to fight his way to the throne and then planning a victory against several sets of rebels and then putting further rebels down, cleaning rebellion up just in time to enter the Jerusalem Chamber for the justice of finally facing the penitential meditations he has been both approaching and delaying. The last words of *Henry V*, and of the tetralogy, declare the personal and national fealty of marriage, "And may our oaths well kept and prosp'rous be!" (*Henry V*, V,ii,365). The chorus takes over for a wider conspectus, declaring that the union between the "wooden O" and what it has enacted will have been brought about in the time-span of the play's presentation:

> Our bending author hath pursu'd the story,
> In little room confining mighty men,
> Mangling by starts the full course of their glory.
> Small time, but, in that small, most greatly lived
> This star of England.
>
> (Epilogue, 2-6)

"Small time," looking back, is the time of the play; looking ahead (in the sentence) it is the time of the king's life as well.

King John combines the random incursion into a set order of the first tetralogy with the psychological demonstrations of the second. This condensed play serves as an epitome, or as an *a fortiori* proof, of all the others.

In *King John*, at any point, the forces are foreshortened into what would seem to be order. The dispute between Faulconbridge and his brother Robert begins in the sort of deadlock which, when it happens between Mowbray and Bolingbroke, ends only with the transfer of the kingdom. But here it is resolved in a double-take, first by Lady Faulconbridge's unexpected confession of the Lion-Heart's paternity, and then in Faulconbridge's renunciation of his claimed lands in favor of campaigning. This is a sort of double double-take; and we are shortly given another. Arthur's challenge to the throne would appear to be no contest; until the French back him; they suddenly give up doing so when John matches Blanche to Lewis; but they suddenly revert again when the papal legate forbids them to assist someone recalcitrant to the Holy See. This pattern has another double double-take in store; John *does* submit; but it is too late.

The new force is always a distraction, and it is always at the same time a culmination for the old forces. Proposals are not carried through—the sacking of Angiers for example. But then, when they happen they are a blow: instead of a battle scene, we are given an exciting call to arms, "To arms let's hie" (III,i,347), and then, at once, the Bastard's re-entrance carrying the head of his antagonist, Austria (III,ii,1).

At this point, suddenly, the incursion into the order of events, the double-take of surprise, involves death, as in the first tetralogy, but with a shock more direct and a relevance more far-reaching to questions of justice. And death remains the intrusive element in a stepping-up of pace to the end. The death now to follow comes about through the longest series of double-takes in the play, those built into the harrowing emotions and adjudications between justice and power surrounding the death of Arthur. The death is first ordered, then predicted by the heartbroken mother; then prepared for with the extra injustice and cruelty of an iron heated on stage to sear out the boy's eyes; then abandoned by the drafted citizen of Angiers, Hubert, who does not have the heart to carry through; then countermanded by the king after he has learned that the repercussions of the execution might rebound to his disfavor and unseat him (this involves a little double-take in which the king deplores that the deed has been done, curses Hubert, and is told the deed was not done); then all this power is foiled by Arthur's terrified attempt at escape; then that is finally foiled when Arthur falls and breaks his neck, to be discovered in the ditch by the king's antagonists, who believe that Hubert has in fact executed him and cannot be convinced otherwise. Purposes are shown here, as always, falling too short to compass the complexity of motives and actions. When reversals come so thick and fast, partial ignorance, dramatic irony, results not from some particular combination, it would seem, but rather from the general condition of political existence; and the audience escapes into a charmed omniscience not from some privilege of vision but for the very reason that it is uninvolved.

In the middle of all this complication the king stages not his coronation but his re-coronation, an act whose gratuitousness seems designed to outface the political murder of Arthur, or so the nobles think, who break up the solemnity of the event and pull away, leaving the King to change his mind. He does not confront that issue at once, because their exit to seek out Arthur's grave (when he is not yet dead) is immediately succeeded by the entrance of a messenger who announces two deaths that have in fact taken place, that of the Queen Mother, and that of Constance, Arthur's mother, who has fulfilled the prediction of how she will react to her own prediction of Arthur's death before he has even died. Events come so fast that they terrify even the king, as he says:

> Withhold thy speed, dreadful occasion!
>
> (IV,ii,125)

And the crown he here puts on again, he will very soon hand over as he expires on stage (V,i,).

The conclusion, a scene of succession, restores the tempo of pageantry, but not before the suddenness of a death which is at the same time protracted in its final hour. We are put through the infernal sufferings of the cruel king's just fate as the fires of the poison consume him before our very eyes. Here is no sequence of reigns, but a short span, in which a higher power swiftly brings poetic justice on the capable and the incapable alike. The Bastard exhibits a capacity which he seems to regard as compassing the events in a combination of cynicism and loyalty: but neither the Commodity speech with which he concludes the first half, nor the oath of loyalty with which he concludes the play, can do any more than offer a momentary principle of coherence in a mortal existence whose only principle of coherence is a fitness that is both unpredictable and unmanageable from any partial vantage of formulation.

2

After worrying the question of justice and equilibrium in the social order through nine history plays, Shakespeare distanced, simplified, and idealized his questions by locating them in the exemplary home of statecraft where social degrees obtained, but no kings, and where a legendary sense of duty dominated those in authority without benefit of a Christian dispensation, around a story whose central event was well known to his audience. Trading Holinshed for Plutarch, he dealt with the consequencess of removing a ruler whose power was proverbial for its absoluteness, while still without benefit of the divine right—so that he would have to be done away with at the center of the government itself, at the Capitol, at the height of parliamentary business, too busy even to read the hurried message that he was in mortal danger.

Brutus is not an *anima naturaliter Christiana*, but a declared Stoic (*Julius Caesar*, V,ii,100-107); and Cassius not exactly an atheist but specifically an Epicurean (V,i,76-77). In sternly forcing the state to remain short of kingship, they lay claim to virtues which are short of the Christian ones, and which cannot be translated into Christian ones without an effort which would add to the play that which Shakespeare has strongly subtracted from it.

There is no divine right of succession, but just successive dominance of the powerful, Pompey before and Octavius hereafter, but

Caesar now. This being the case, the question of power is balanced not against the question of divine right but against the naked question of justice. And that question itself poses the ambivalence of a Brutus who will not face what it means to permit Antony to remain alive, and also to speak; who at the same time retains a sense of justice for which the successor, in the generosity of the victor, can praise him, as "the noblest Roman of them all" (V,v,68). The ambivalence remains in terms of his justification for killing Caesar, since Caesar had thrice refused the crown; he has to assert that he is a *potential* emperor, rather than the actual one the audience would have known that Octavius later became. "I am constant as the northern star" (III,i,60), Caesar himself does say, as he should let others say for him (though Shakespeare may be adding, as he does in the first scenes of the play, local Roman color and illustrating the traditional lack of modesty in Romans). Yet Brutus' conclusive reasons for snuffing out Caesar rest not on how he now acts but on mere possibility:

> and to speak truth of Caesar,
> I have not known when his affections sway'd
> More than his reason. But 'tis a common proof
> That lowliness is young ambition's ladder,
> Whereto the climber-upward turns his face;
> But when he once attains the upmost round,
> He then unto the ladder turns his back,
> Looks in the clouds, scorning the base degrees
> By which he did ascend. So Caesar may.
> Then, lest he may, prevent. And since the quarrel
> Will bear no colour for the thing he is,
> Fashion it thus—that what he is, augmented,
> Would run to these and these extremities;
> And therefore think him as a serpent's egg,
> Which, hatch'd, would as his kind grow mischievous,
> And kill him in the shell.

(II,i,19-34)

His concession that "the quarrel/Will bear no colour" is not permitted to take over the argument, nor does the psychology of the successful ruler's attitude towards his ascent really bear on whether or not he will domineer once he succeeds. To refuse to look backwards, and even to condemn actions which he took himself, does not necessarily lead a ruler to perilous aggrandizement. Henry V, indeed, as recently presented by Shakespeare, has himself done both and remained an ideal ruler.

This argument is no better than Cassius' two arguments, that Caesar's fallible body involves a fallible policy, and that his preeminence throws everyone else into the shadow. Moreover, Brutus shortly denies his very own doctrine of potentiality when Cassius adduces it to urge the corollary necessity of killing Antony (II,i,155-180), responding with a fable that the limbs are powerless when the body is dead. And then he does not see—susceptible to music himself (IV,iii,256-268) as Cassius is not (I,ii, 204)—that Antony's penchant for revelry does not make Antony nugatory:

> If he love Caesar, all that he can do
> Is to himself take thought and die for Caesar;
> And that were much he should, for he is given
> To sports, to wildness, and much company.

> (186-189)

No sooner does Antony appear than he belies this estimate by coolly offering a mask of frankness, pretending to lay his mind open in all political conjecture:

> Gentlemen all—Alas, what shall I say?
> My credit now stands on such slippery ground
> That one of two bad ways you must conceit me,
> Either a coward or a flatterer.

> (III,i,190-193)

Here he confects a subtle policy which escapes these alternatives by pretending to be nonplussed between them, and this in the face of both a threat from Brutus:

O Antony! beg not your death of us.

(III,i,165)

and a justification first promised (179-182) and then referred to by counter case, "Or else were this a savage spectacle" (III,i,224); but the justification is not given more than rhetorical allegation in Brutus' funeral speech, a piece of policy which Antony undoes by a craftier piece of forensic policy.

Brutus' reasons alone, his sense of his own justice, without reference to his actions or his psychological network of relationships, will not fully pass the play's muster; but neither will Caesar's actions, which are seen in the double light of infallibility and arrogation.

It is not, finally, the balance of justice that causes the conspirators' downfall, or even Brutus' one mistake in military strategy of leaving the high ground, eagerly seized at Phillippi by the experienced soldier Antony. Rather it is something outside the equilibrium of the public arena, a destiny coming in a Roman play as the fate foretold by a series of portents, and an inner psychology taking the form of dreams, visions, and fantasies.

Destiny and psychology are brought to converge. Cassius, who scoffs at astrology and other forms of portent, is subject, both ironically and with psychological consistency, to rash conclusions: and so in seeing his tents burnt, he falsely imagines he has lost the battle which in fact he has won (V,iii,13), his suicide leaving alone a Brutus who has borne up under the double shock of Portia's suicide and the lingering threats of Caesar's ghost. It is unresolvably obscure whether Brutus loses because his co-general is dead or because he is himself distracted.

The toll showed in Portia at the beginning: she wounded her thigh to prove her steeliness (II,i,300-301). Left alone back in Rome because Brutus must now engage in distant combat, she has swallowed fire. The action of the assassination is measured in such contingent effects. There are many portents—thunder and lightning; a slave's flaming hand; the lion in the streets; men "all in fire"; the owl shrieking at noon (I,iii); the brilliant exhalations (II,i); Calpurnia's dream; yawning graves; warriors in the clouds; rains of blood; a beast of augury without a heart (II, iii); the soothsayer's warning (I,ii;III,i); Caesar's ghost (IV,iii); gorging eagles; flocking ravens (V,i,79-88). Between all these portents and the military adjudications, there is, then, a congruence. But there is no definite causal connection between them, except that the portents turn out to be resoundingly right. At the same time, Brutus comes as close as anyone to heeding them. Both Cassius, except at the end (V,ii), and Caesar himself, except on momentary impulse, ignore them.

The play, then, offers no ground on which the question of justice, its central question, can be fully adjudicated, for Caesar or for his chief antagonist. Nor is a bearing on the question focused by balancing out the opposing views. Brutus is both over-scrupulous and incorruptible, Caesar both peremptory and infallible. The line Shakespeare may have changed in the light of Jonson's criticism, if restored to the text of the play from Jonson's remark to Drummond, perfectly comprises this situation:

> Caesar never did wrong, but with just cause
> (III,i,47 emended)

This line does not even offer a paradox, since the act is judged by the cause, and also by the effect, and a deflecting temporal sequence is offered which perpetually refers the judgment of "wrong" ahead to the circumstance "just cause," then back again to the act "did wrong," which is then referred back. A paradox is a logical balance, whereas this quasi-paradox involves a temporal situation which is built to evade the very criterion it raises, very much as the temporal sequence of the play operates.

The play refers the audience back to portents, or to supernatural appearances of ghosts, or to vacillations of character. And it also refers the questions of justice to the impact of the events on the characters, as do *King John* and *King Lear*. In those plays, however, the impact helps us measure the justification of Hubert's final response to Arthur, of King John's final sufferings, of Lear's final military victory. Here, again, the death of Portia is invested only with pathos.

Her death comes as a dramatic surprise at the end of a scene in which Brutus and Cassius have been working out their cooperation in the face of Brutus' just, and at the same time disproportionate, complaint against Cassius for passing over, and possibly sharing in, his underlings' depredations. The death works to bring Cassius to an apology, but only for a lack of timing. It works also to increase our admiration for Brutus' practice of the Stoicism he had earlier professed and will later act on when he impales himself.

Caesar's dying words to Brutus, famous before they were adopted by Shakespeare, are also relegated to mere pathos: *Et tu Brute*, and we are made to share the pang of Caesar, and possibly of Brutus himself. In the quick of this response we do not alter our sights on justice, brought merely to a sharper sense of Caesar's humanity (and so the conspirators' misapprehension) and also his unswervable decisiveness and self-reference (and so their justification).

Antony's funeral oration turns that reaction outward: we see it operating on the crowd and are taken at once with its capriciousness and its inevitability. Antony operates on the same assumptions, in fact, which Caesar himself used to "silence" the tribunes who had tried to keep him from mounting too high by "disrobing the images" "deck'd" with "Caesar's trophies" (I,i-ii)—an act on Caesar's part which evidences at once his infallible vigilance and his overconcern for his reputation, suggesting that Brutus may be right in his assumption that Caesar may eventually accept a crown. Antony is proving Brutus wrong and Cassius right as he delivers the funeral oration—but also proving Brutus generous and Cassius niggardly. The emotional effects are felt here as in other cases to bear on, but not to affect, the ultimate definition of justice about the acts they accompany. And this audience subscribes at least officially to the doctrine of the divine right, as the playwright would also seem to do, and it subscribes at the same time to the notion that the classical virtues of the noble Roman are held up for admiration.[8] How then are they to react to Cassius' words about Brutus, given the point of anachronistic Christian phrasing:

> There was a Brutus once that would have brook'd
> Th'eternal devil to keep his state in Rome
> As easily as a king.

(I,ii,159-161)

This Brutus proves he still exists by acting on Cassius' suggestion, which is at once enlisting and corrupting to a cause which the play takes as both honorable and short-sighted. The faint possible echoes from contemporary theological discussion of Rome as the Whore of Babylon and the Holy Roman Empire as a diabolical contrivance only serve to give our impasse another branch leading in. None leads out.

Coriolanus' passion for justice is likewise trammelled in an absoluteness that may be taken either for the incorruptibility of an heroic soldier or the simple-minded stubbornness of a proud man. It involves effects on the state that are either deserved for his vacillation or undeserved for the base of his loyalty, and on a family whose sufferings may be taken either as inflicted by its head or as involved in a larger political pattern.

The emotional impact, on him and on us, that calls forth his next-to-last soliloquy, in the face of his supplicating wife, mother, and son, occasions not a definition of justice so much as exclamations of incongruity in his situation:

> What is that curtsy worth? or those doves' eyes,
> Which can make gods forsworn? I melt, and am not
> Of stronger earth than others. My mother bows,
> As if Olympus to a molehill should
> In supplication nod; and my young boy
> Hath an aspect of intercession which
> Great nature cries, 'Deny not'.

(Coriolanus V,iii,27-33)

Coriolanus never did wrong but with just cause. He was either wrong to seek a world elsewhere or wrong to yield to claims so strong that they make even "gods forsworn." He proves either his common humanity in being "not of stronger earth than others"; or else he fails the very sternness his mother bred in him, ceasing to be subordinate to her ideal as he subordinates himself to her person, in the very act of doing her the tribute of contrasting her godlike bearing (Olympus) to his proto-impotence (molehill). The sway of feeling over justice, and the possibility that feeling is a higher justice, get enacted as Coriolanus and his mother kneel to each other—the gesture that tips his balance towards Rome.

Timon in his first acts begins as someone of unquestioning generosity. In the strongly schematic Morality-like presentation, others are first measured against this positive quality as more prudent/ less generous than he. He regards the lilies of the field, how they sow not neither do they reap; but he is also a rich man who cannot get through the eye of the needle, who is giving his lands away not as a matter of principle but only out of careless prodigality. When he is stripped of possessions, he becomes not an ordinary man but a hermit-with-a-Midas-touch. And then others are measured against this negative situation for being more involved in the business of life/less pure than he. The senators of Athens are justified/timorous in expelling Alcibiades, who is justified/rebbellious in conquering them. Military campaigns, government, prostitution, thievery, painting, poetry, are all measured against the quizzical central figure, whose extreme purity, or extreme perversity, does not come any clearer for the obvious injustice involved in some of these activities.

He is in turn measured by one who is a scorner of mankind from abreaction and habit rather than from principle: by Apemantus; and by a man loyal on personal attachment and ordinary probity rather than on ostentatious principle and heroic incorruptibility: by Flavius. Timon himself throws Apemantus into the same selfish light which Flavius throws him into. But that is no resolution.

Timon's death is causeless, announced by a soldier who cannot read the epitaph he brings in (*Timon of Athens* V,iv,65-73). The epitaph is anticlimactic; the passer-by is not likely to curse, and in any case he needs not Timon's injunction to pass by; or else the injunction is almost phatic, a convention of epitaph-writing. Alcibiades' praise of him as "noble Timon" (80) finds no evidence in the epitaph. There is indeed more than a hint of policy in this soldier-conqueror's adoption of an incorruptible dead man as a patron. What he says to the subdued senators could serve to define not only his own actions but Timon's as well:

> Till now you have gone on and fill'd the time
> With all licentious measure, making your wills
> The scope of justice;
>
> (V,iv,3-5)

Timon himself, too, is devoted in equal measure both to justice and to the scope his wealth afforded him, inextricably. He would never have predicted, and nothing in the action leads us either to hope or to fear, the claim of Alcibiades' concluding words, which declare a soldier's goal of statecraft that other soldiers in Shakespeare, notably Henry V, have carried off, but that his past does not promise (as, to be sure, Prince Hal's did not either):

> Bring me into your city,
> And I will use the olive, with my sword;
> Make war breed peace, make peace stint war, make each
> Prescribe to other, as each other's leech.
> Let our drums strike.
>
> (V,iv,81-85)

Will he really beat his swords into ploughshares, or at least turn them into swords of Justice? The language is rife with the kind of contradiction that everything in the play up to this point has mocked. So much for the assertion, looking backward. Looking ahead, he seems to understand that what he must do is what Henry V must do. "Not Amurath an Amurath succeeds/But

Harry Harry" (*Henry IV, Part Two*, V,ii,48-9). Which is Alcibiades?

3

Success is easier to understand in the person (Imogen) than
failure (Ophelia), but harder (*Cymbeline*) in the action (*Hamlet*).

When it is enacted, understanding is justification.

The tragic hero may be someone who either falls away from his
success, like Macbeth: *corruptio optimi pessima.* Or he is worked
upon, like Hamlet or Timon, Coriolanus or even Othello, by action of so full an effectiveness that the proscenium is a strong
spell that cannot be broken.

For justification, we cannot get beyond Othello's own self-
definition: he is an "honourable murderer" (V,ii,297). He is measured by the impulsiveness-in-deliberation by which he stands in
awe of his beloved victim: "It is the cause, it is the cause, my soul
/Let me not name it to you, you chaste stars" (V,ii,1-2). If honourable, he cannot escape being a murderer. "But why should
honour outlive honesty?" (V,ii,248). This despairing definition
of justice judges the tempter who has corrupted his own honesty.
Something humble, transcending class, is at the substratum of the
honour in the honourable murderer. "Why should honour outlive honesty" means also, as a corollary, why should Honourable
Othello, who has nothing but his honour, outlive Honest Iago,
who never possessed the honour (Othello, so to speak, withheld
honor from him for just cause) which Othello retains as an honourable murderer—or does not retain, because honour should not
outlive honesty? The rhetorical question announces that injustice.

Is Othello himself justified? Our angle of vision, the comprehensiveness of the dramatic irony, makes an answer impossible. The disproportion in Iago's effectiveness is not the same
thing as its inadequacy: it does his horrid work. The partial exon-

eration of Othello must in some way break the proscenium; it must shuttle among disproportion, effectiveness, and inadequacy; then it must go to the success of a person, Iago, who is easy to understand in that collected purposiveness, but harder to understand in his deep failure of malignity, so hard if we try to fix it he will seem either "motiveless" or moved by too much. And then the exoneration will proceed to the "honourable murderer" himself, beyond which it cannot go.

It is, perhaps, the unbearable sense of not being able ever to resolve this question, in addition to his unbearable sense of loss, that leads Othello to do away with himself. He dies because the question of justification is too much for for him, and his death seals us in that same perplexity, about his life—and also about the death, which itself has in it both a Christian scandal and a Stoic justification. But it is also his feeling of loss that is unbearable, questions of justification aside. Like Coriolanus and Brutus, Othello bodies forth a state where complexities of justice and imperatives of feeling have a distinct bearing, and, while separable, are inextricable.

King Lear opens in the schematic situation with which *Othello* ends: the victim of "practisers" becomes himself an evildoer; credulity entails malefaction. As in *Othello*, the terms of justice are uncertain only as they apply to the protagonist; everyone else acts in the blinding light of good or of evil. Even Emilia does, once she is called upon to do so. Here, of course, her counterpart, Kent, goes unheard when he makes his outcry; he is not heeded but banished, though he stays on disguised. The counterpart of Desdemona lives and returns to support her misguided father.

A king so distant in time as Lear would seem as much father as king, and the kingdom small enough to have some of the air of a family estate.[9]

If we discount Lear's disaffection as personal and captious rather than as a judgment on his daughters' managing the kingdom, Kent is left virtually alone (the Fool's remarks do not have political weight because a fool excoriates any political present; that is his job). The first scene of the second act involves an exchange of compliments over alertness to the "treason" of Edgar, which takes in everyone but the man who devised it, Edmund himself. Gloucester refers to Cornwall as "The noble Duke my master" (58). Cornwall is strutting rather than grinning when he delivers his own compliment to Edmund "Whose virtue and obedience doth this instant/So much commend itself" (113-114). Even Edmund perhaps believes the promise he utters, since he can hope for advancement, "I shall serve you, sir,/Truly." And there is no reason to think Regan does not have a sense mainly of her own graciousness—her lust will await the death of her husband—when she herself addresses him as "noble friend." The adjective, in fact, contains the promise of what Edmund hopes for; and what by their law he has every reason to hope for, if Edgar is the traitor he seems to all the others to be—to his father, who pronounces a death sentence on him, no less than to the noble Duke and his wife.

The irony that weighs on them is made ponderous by the certainty of our judgment. In the kingdom itself, by the lights of rulers oblivious to their own injustice (as rulers often are; the trait makes the sisters, in fact, true children of the oblivious King himself), there seem to be only ineffectual checks on this process.

"Men must endure/Their going hence, even as their coming hither:/Ripeness is all" (V,ii,9-11) is a general statement. This is aimed at how to handle unjust actions, not how to redress them. In context it is a charitable injunction from a wronged son to a harried father not to give in to suicidal despair. The redress has come in the charitable action, which provides its own unqualified demonstration of what true justice entails.

In the light of such actions, for the play's sense of justice as for the final bearing of its enactment, such prevailingly harsh formulations as Lear's are special in their application to persons and provisional in their effectiveness to time: words disappear and actions remain; the moods that words voice disappear, and such despairing formulations as the anti-theological ones are evidence of a mood that may pass as much as of an attitude that actions may belie. "Thou, Nature, art my goddess; to thy law/My services are bound" (I,ii,1-2). Edmund's dying act belies this declara-

tion, even though he casts his "good" in the context of the statement, "Some good I mean to do/Despite of mine own nature" (V,
iii,243-244).

> As flies to wanton boys are we to th' gods—
> They kill us for their sport.
>
> (IV,i,37-38)

> The gods are just, and of our pleasant vices
> Make instruments to plague us
>
> (V,iii,170-171)

Indeed it is true that "these remarks refute each other," as Lionel
Abel says.[10] And the second can be read by the rule of the first,
"the 'justness' of the gods is as wanton as their sport," as Laurence Michel argues.[11] But only by exaggerating the context can
one take these statements as definitions of the play's action. The
first would be true—by what principle of justice should Lear and
Cordelia die?—if we stood far enough off from them to see them
as flies and were imperceptive enough of their reactions to look
on them the way "wanton boys" would, heedless of all but the
sadism that Lear elsewhere excoriates. The second is true only of
someone who feels the justice of the remark: all vices may not be
pleasant, and to the unpleasant vices of Goneril and Regan, Cornwall and Oswald, there is no instrumental handle for the gods to
catch. None of these is "plagued" in the sense of prolonged operation upon them: all die sudden deaths. A "plague" has in fact a
purgatorial value, and is instrumental in the restitution to dignity, to "joy" as well as "grief," for the Gloucester of whom his
son is speaking. .

There is also the converse of the second proposition: the gods,
of our virtues, make instruments to rescue us. The action of the
play exemplifies the second proposition, and it is by the converse
of the second proposition that the first is belied, not by the proposition itself.

The first statement is made by Gloucester as he reels away
from his blindness in despair over the son who appropriately

comes to his mind while the servant leading him is describing the
Mad Beggar crossing their path:

> He has some reason, else he could not beg.
> I'th' last night's storm I such a fellow saw;
> Which made me think a man a worm. My son
> Came then into my mind; and yet my mind
> Was then scarce friends with him. I have heard more since.
> As flies to wanton boys are we to th' gods—
> They kill us for their sport.
>
> (IV,i,32-38)

The dramatic irony here is heavy to the point of sentimentality.
Gloucester is suddenly acute in his sympathetic discrimination as
his first line lays out the condition under which a man will find
himself capable of begging at all. The lines about the gods are
simply wrong, and we know they are wrong as he states them,
since the son he assumes to have died is alive before his unseeing
eyes; and the person whom the servant sees is only disguised for
life-saving prudence as a mad beggar; and he is not another instance of what Gloucester remembers (so two cases plus the third
of his son make a general law) but the same person (and also his
son: there is only one case). And his son lives not to be killed but
in fact to rule the very kingdom in which for the moment both
father and son are outcasts. And Gloucester himself will not be
snuffed out like a fly but die only after he has gone through a
whole series of purgatorial reconciliations.

The second statement does, as Michel asserts, contain a hint of
sanctimoniousness, but only a hint. It does not entirely undo the
charitable forgiveness—of a nearly mortal injury—to which it is
appended:

> Let's exchange charity.
> I am no less in blood than thou art, Edmund;
> If more, the more th' hast wrong'd me.
> My name is Edgar, and thy father's son.
> The gods are just, and of our pleasant vices
> Make instruments to plague us:

> The dark and vicious place where thee he got
> Cost him his eyes
>
> (V,iii,166-173)

The second line is a courteous obfuscation, a gentle *meiosis* or litotes. Edgar knows very well that by the law of primogeniture he would inherit the title even if Edmund were legitimate, because Edmund is, in his own words, "twelve or fourteen moonshines/ Lag of a brother" (I,ii,5-6). Hence Edmund's special pleading, "Why bastard, wherefore base?" is a distortion, and Edgar does not impose more than gently—in the fulfilled condition of his third line—a correction on his dying brother. Edmund often accuses the father, and now Edgar accuses the father—thereby joining the other son charitably rather than standing under the old man's protection against his brother, as Edmund himself had done through the play. Edgar avoids accusing his brother, Edmund himself, of the lust that has brought Edmund to this pass: the adulterous letter has incited Edgar to the challenge. The blanket effect of his statement about the gods is to imply "like father, like son," a stern confrontation, but one that is good for Edmund's repentence, if Edmund is equal to it. He has implied he is, by making the statement which Edgar is here answering, "I do forgive thee" (166). And he justifies Edgar's expectation in his own answer to the implied accusation of a wrong equivalent to the father's lust. Moreover, to blame the gods for Gloucester's blinding is also to exonerate Edmund, who is certainly as guilty as anyone, since it is he who gave Gloucester's letter to the French forces into the hands of Cornwall. Edgar says, then, "it is justice, not only you, who are responsible for our father's blinding" and "he as well as you has paid for his lust; we brothers may contemplate that," as well as "do not forget, on this deathbed of yours, that your death exemplifies poetic justice if his death—rather than his blinding—would not". And Edmund rises to this:

> Th'hast spoken right, tis true;
> The wheel is come full circle; I am here
>
> (V,iii,173-174)

This response kindles the wronged husband's act of forgiveness; Albany speaks up. Edgar's speech has been the first in a quick series of perceptions Edmund must assimilate—the account of his father's suffering death, the depiction of Kent's extremity, the sight of Goneril's and Regan's dead bodies—which culminates in Edmund's order countermanding the execution of Lear and Cordelia. Edgar's statement about the gods has been, in fact, the beginning of Edmund's exemplifying the counter-instance of the maxim: a residuum of honesty in him becomes the instrument of redemption in him after his vice of ambition and craving for admiration have plagued him in stroke after stroke—one of the strokes being Edgar's very maxim.

In *The Winter's Tale* there is a pastoral cycle of nature-and-art, fruition-and-decorum, celebrated in such annual rounds as the sheep-shearing of the fourth act, in such activities as the gardening of Perdita's compliment-exchanges. This cycle proceeds at an easy pace; its justice is effortless as it orders the classes of society and the times of life through birth, marriage, and death—so effortless that a retrospective, courteous look at a youth spent in its shadow assimilates easily to a banter conflating the pastoral activities of "lambs" and an Edenic freedom from original sin (I,ii,27-37).

This cycle does triumph in the play; *The Winter's Tale* is virtually alone among Shakespeare's plays for showing a kingdom which will stay on an even keel of rule in the (otherwise never attained) ideal of one generation succeeding another after an exemplary royal love match: the reign of Florizel and Perdita will reproduce all the excellences, further on, that the early and late reign of Leontes will have embodied.

But the heir is dead, Mamillius, before he reaches the point of matchmaking, though his own banter with his mother's maids naturally takes that as its subject, as his boy-courtly conversations with his father are preoccupied with military *virtù*. The cycle of transgression-and-forgiveness overarches the pastoral cycle, a massive intrusion on it, and a deep challenge for long redress before the pastoral cycle can be reconstituted.

The middle reign of Leontes is sidetracked by a jealousy that takes only an instant to spring into being and sixteen years of intent purgation to exorcise.

What unites the two cycles, and what also separates them by a "gap," is the Time who interposes between the earlier series of dissolution and the series a generation later of restitution.

The pastoral cycle proceeds at a serene, even pace, measured by years and by lifetimes, producing echoes in the imagery as well as a frame for the plot. But the gestures of evil or charity in the transgression-cycle are instantaneous. Leontes gives a death order, and Camillo at once disobeys, employing his authority over the gates as the means of instant escape. Antigonus flounders in executing Perdita's death-warrant and is almost instantly torn to pieces by a bear, the possible humor of whose entrance must be transfixed in the surprise and horror of the violence that is shortly recounted.[12] The "Clown" saves Perdita, and immediately starts the series of events which will lead to her restitution and his own ennoblement. He is caught, sixteen years later, all at once in Autolycus' Good-Samaritan confidence game, and then in his false agency; but the evil immediately misfires, and the good of its main product operates as though it were a by-product, dramaturgically placed and timed for self-transcendence. Autolycus' thefts are covered in oblivion, but also without the profit to himself that he has been jockeying for. Part of the play's distancing magic is the movement towards centering incidental evil in a merry but disreputable character, who is the locus also of song in the play.

Earlier in The Winter's Tale, on royal and not rustic ground, the psychology is deeper, the effects of evil are more mortal. Leontes unjustly accuses Hermione, and she is thought to have died from the shock; their only son Mamillius, who in the scene of initial suspicion is Leontes' only personal consolation as well as his only heir, dies "with mere conceit and fear/Of the queen's speed" (III,ii,141-142)—a sudden blow, in the dramatic sequence, coming at the very moment when Leontes rejects the oracle proclaiming Hermione's innocence! He says "There is no truth at all i' th' Oracle" (III,ii,137) and pat comes the messenger to announce Mamillius' death.

Leontes assumes, without saying so, that his only remaining descendant, the baby girl, is too far away for his order that she be exposed to be successfully countermanded:

> We enjoin thee
> As thou art liegeman to us, that thou carry
> This female bastard hence, and that thou bear it
> To some remote and desert place, quite out
> Of our dominions; and that there thou leave it
> (II,iii,172-176)

Leontes himself, obsessed after his instantaneous superstition, does not flounder. Under illusion his gesture is absolute—"There is no truth at all i' th' Oracle," but he retracts instantaneously at the news of his son's death, "Apollo's angry; and the heavens themselves/Do strike at my injustice" (142-143). Paulina, however, instantly interprets (as we much later learn) the queen's swoon as her death, and the long, complicated cycle of repentance has been initiated at this stroke. In contrast to the vacillating Antigonus, Leontes remains regal enough to compass that deep cycle. He is one of those figures frequent in Shakespeare—the list includes Bertram, Oliver, Parolles, Angelo, Antonio, Edmund, and others—presented as almost scandalously unforgiveable, and then forgiven.

4

The purposive angling of these definitions energizes them towards, and away from, the action they would define. "What's past is prologue" (*The Tempest*, II,i,244), a statement aimed at convincing a king's brother to kill a king. The statement holds further ironies for the action: the speaker is a duke's brother who deposed a duke. In that sense the past merely repeats: deposition is prologue to deposition. But after twelve years Antonio's own deposed brother has gained power in exile, a magic power under whose spell they are all operating without knowing it, at the very moment of deposition. So "what's past is prologue" will repeat repetition in the form of unwilling purgation: part of the purgation involves being led to such plots, to saying "what's past is prologue." They are led by their own evil natures. Without a disposition toward scheming, Antonio would not be inducing Sebastian to imitate him by killing a brother. And there is an important missing piece of information which, in not being firmly past, serves all the more as prologue: Ferdinand, the next in line to the Neopolitan throne, has not died after all; he has been led forward and astray by the very same magic power.

The impotence of the speaker here breeds mild laughter, which breeds indulgence, which breeds a climate corresponding to the forgiveness that rounds out the play, and so heavily influences most of its verbal interchanges. Justice on the face of it is simple. The angling in which the magic entraps the shipwrecked passengers qualifies them, distorts them, ripens them quickly into fantasy, and allows them to fall back into place, their spiritual garments made fresher as their physical ones have been.

Such multiplicity of dramatic bearing intensifies these recitative speakers away from the set stances of the agonists in classical tragedy. We are not invited to pause and weigh criteria of justice, however deep. Rather, the criteria undergo metamorphosis in the very quick of being firmly bodied forth: the strategy remains recitative, but it subjects its enacting progressions to heavy qualification, to rapid fusions and transfers. The witty leads to the oracular, Frye can assert of the soft-spoken clown in *All's Well That Ends Well*.[13] "In watching tragedy," he later says, "we are impressed by the reality of the illusion . . . in watching romantic comedy we are impressed by the illusion of the reality." And in both, the reality is made to qualify the illusion, and vice versa, even in comedies other than romantic: we cannot believe there is a law in Vienna that punishes the fornication of engaged couples by the death of the man alone. Singling Claudio out, and leaving Juliet unprosecuted, refers the measure of that measure away from any common law, before which both sexes would equally stand, to some dim tribal memory of the fitness of retaliatory sacrifice for a male who participates in adult sexuality before initiation. Claudio is matched by someone who has delayed adult sexuality, Angelo: the two are set in relation by a fraudulent and improper bride-exchange without marriage. Are such tribal patterns illusion or reality? For the civilized they become that which unites the two, dream. The play is an equivalent for the dream, and it is in the dream atmosphere, a faint equivalent thereof, that measure is dispensed for measure, justice reestablished.

The Duke is a consciousness manipulative to the point of casuistry, setting the unconscious to rights; Angelo must be trapped, Claudio must face death, Isabella must believe he has been executed, for each to emerge into a proper relation to justice, for Angelo to become a husband, Isabella a wife, and Claudio more devoted to the wife he has chosen than to the dowry for which he delayed their wedding (in this, repeating a version of the fault of Angelo), "She, Claudio, that you wrong'd, look you restore" (V,i, 523).

The audience is also perturbed, or at least transported. Hamlet bases his staging of the play-within-a-play on such evidence of perturbation:

> I have heard
> That guilty creatures, sitting at a play,
> Have by the very cunning of the scene
> Been struck so to the soul that presently
> They have proclaim'd their malefactions
>
> (II,ii,584-588)

This irresistible contagion is a "primitive" reaction—except that it would be unimaginable in a ritualized presentation, in a spectator at a Greek play. It is the skill of the playwright that effectuates such evocations, "by the very cunning of the scene."[14]

The guilty creatures produce in real life a set of gestures more indirect than any we are usually shown on stage; their proclamation consists not of a recitative confession but of revelatory gestures, "For murder, though it have no tongue, will speak/With most miraculous organ" (II,ii,589-590). Claudius' starting up, with almost "no tongue," is an extravagant and perhaps novel effect for this theatre.

Prospero concludes his epilogue by pretending that our transposition of response into judgment, judgment into mercy, and mercy into an act of prayer, will produce across the proscenium a sort of mutuality, wherein everyone in the audience is a guilty creature who is "set free," and sets him free, not by leaping up like Claudius but by repeating in his management of a response to the play the purgative actions he has just seen the guilty go through on stage:

> But release me from my bands
> With the help of your good hands.
> Gentle breath of yours my sails
> Must fill, or else my project fails,
> Which was to please. Now I want
> Spirits to enforce, art to enchant;
> And my ending is despair
> Unless I be reliev'd by prayer,
> Which pierces so that it assaults
> Mercy itself, and frees all faults.
> As you from crimes would pardon'd be,
> Let your indulgence set me free.
>
> (*Tempest*, Epilogue, 9-20)

The adaptiveness of the action to the principles it is unfolding, the provisionality that keeps alive a sense that a conclusion is not yet, is managed by Shakespeare through an unevenness of pacing from scene to scene that is characteristic of his work.[15] Final scenes tend to deliver quick blows that settle the fate or the business of the principles. To concatenate these blows at a slower pace, the action must swell in conclusion, because it has so many characters to accommodate. The very retardation of a conclusion suggests a further broadening of application to the life outside the stage of the adjudications on it; if to settle is to slow down, then what is most like the pace of life is most amenable to being settled.

The drama mightily seizes the ground of enactment and translates the features of play, as Huizinga formulates them,[16] back into a vision of reality: the voluntary participation of the spectators, their freedom, is transposed into a sense of the priority in destiny; the sanctum of a make-believe removed from real life is made a vehicle for submitting real life to judgment; and the time-span of the play is handled in such a way as to suggest its total application to the time-span of a mortal life.

5

In the space of *Pericles*, the only unity is the water of the Mediterranean,[17] a sea whose name tells us it is at the center of land, though in fact that sea is named only once in his works (*The Tempest*, I,ii,234). Pericles crosses that sea to kingdom after kingdom, driven on each time by the closure of the events in the last. Each set has its own poetic justice, but his life escapes laterally from that episode, linking the episodes in a chain of justice-analogies that only luck or virtue or time can resolve.

As it unfolds, the allegiance between justice and fate is arbitrary, and the more reassuring for that. It is certain that evil will receive poetic justice in the long run, but less certain in the short run what will happen to the good. The first, exemplary action of Pericles himself teaches us what his daughter's resourcefulness later reinforces, that the good, in the clarity of their virtue, possess a very openness that gives them accessibility to a future that the evil have closed upon themselves.

The gold thread linking episode to episode is discernible only to the eyes of charity, which is not empowered to recognize it for what it is, only to follow it for its own sake. Suffering here is *not* purgative, though we are misled to believe, when we see Pericles facing death with alert tact, that the subsequent tact of the rulers of Tharsus in the face of famine implies a corresponding virtue in them. Even the wise Pericles is taken in at this point, enough so to entrust his daughter to their care. So much does momentary gratitude have the air of permanent charity.

In *Cymbeline* suffering is purgative, even for those who would not seem to need purgation. Shakespeare notably refrains from illustrating, for any but the evil characters again, the Biblical maxim that is quoted at the beginning of Janekyn, one of his sources for this play, a maxim he had earlier adapted for a title, "With the same measure ye mete shall it be meted out to you ferred to in a source but not, again, by Shakespeare), heads a state again" (Matthew,7.2; Mark,4.24; Luke,6.38). Cymbeline, ruling at the normative and also miraculous time of the birth of Christ (re-whose features look back to the primitive kingdom of Lear, and out to the model of the ideal empire of the Roman plays. Yet this ideal comprises "garboils"; in the persons of the Queen and Cloten it recalls the world of *Titus Andronicus*, as its entanglement of love in its military struggles recalls that of *Antony and Cleopatra*. By hinging sovereignty ultimately on capability, it also looks ahead to the time examined in the history plays. And its question of justice may thus be said to assimilate much of the questions that occur in the histories and the tragedies generally. All this reality is glossed over by the distance and simplicity of the kingdom.

A lack of charity may intrude and be quickly passed over: Posthumus strikes the disguised Imogen; Imogen seems to show ingratitude to the Lucius who has saved her life, by refusing to ask for his life to be saved. But charity pervades not only the statements, but also the small actions, sometimes to dire but temporary embroilment. Posthumus enters the house of Philario in the first place, where the consolation of masculine camaraderie entices him into the ill-advised wager over Imogen, because Philario was a fellow soldier of his father's "to whom I have been often bound for no less than my life" (I,v,27), charity manifesting itself on the very battlefield, as pronouncedly later on in the play. The Queen proposes animal experiments (I,v,18-23), which the courteously independent Cornelius describes as hardening the heart, in addition to being "noisome and infectious" (26). Cymbeline pays the tribute to Rome even though he wins the war, and this act has to be ascribed to the same mysterious resignation of temperament, now become positive, which had permitted the queen to dominate him. The act is beyond policy, since there is no immediate reason for it, and beyond the justice he refers to in urging that the queen dissuaded him (V,v,458-463).

In *The Tempest*, the air of magic is replaced by the reality, and the masque is performed by spirits whom this father has conjured up, by way of restoring himself to his kingdom and renewing his family, producing justice for both the state and the family. Ferdinand and Miranda provide their own magic, "They have chang'd eyes." The others, in their more appropriate ways, undergo the purgations which magic brings about, and the spirits, like those that perform the masque of Ceres, set them a banquet table that vanishes before they can trust it enough to touch it. Ariel is not purged—he does not have to be—but is simply freed. Caliban cannot be; he is simply punished. The sphere of justice is slightly narrower than the sphere of existent beings. It is not narrower than magic, which is used by being justified.

And even Sycorax was the beneficiary of justice, having escaped the death penalty on a technical count of pregnancy at the same coast of North Africa from which the wrecked ship has been returning, after the celebration of a marriage that does something for the state, presumably, but nothing for the family that believes it will never again see the bride.

The long time is envisaged; Prospero has been there twelve years. But the time is made congruent with that of the actual play: it takes only so long to happen as it takes to put on. At the end of the life there is much left over, but it takes on the character of a story to be told to someone who has been changed from political opponent to companion and fellow in-law. "I long/To hear the story of your life, which must/Take the ear strangely" (V,i,311-313), says Alonso in his last speech to Prospero. Old men are self-possessed enough to have reached Gonzalo's point of Utopian benevolence, a possibility for all. Prospero has recognized his own survival of the magic that restores him, and he has buried his book. "Now my charms are all o'erthrown,/And what strength I have's mine own,/Which is most faint" (Epilogue, 1-3). Mortality approaches as justice comprises it.

Notes

CHAPTER 1: THE MASTERY OF DIVERGENCES

1. Leslie Hotson in *The First Night of Twelfth Night* (London, 1954) argues that *Twelfth Night* was acted at Whitehall before the Queen during Epiphany, 1601. *Measure for Measure* was put on before James I on December 26, 1604, and the play arguably incorporates various references to that occasion in its plot and language, as discussed by Josephine Bennet, *Measure for Measure as Royal Entertainment* (New York, 1966).
2. M. C. Bradbrook, *Themes and Conventions of Elizabethan Tragedy* (Cambridge, 1960), 39. She is borne out by J. V. Cunningham's reading of Donatus (*Woe or Wonder; The Emotional Effect of Shakespearian Tragedy*, Chicago, 1951) and by T. W. Baldwin, *Shakespeare's Five-Act Structure* (Urbana, 1947).
3. Albert Cook, *The Dark Voyage and the Golden Mean* (Cambridge, 1949).
4. Marion Bodwell Smith, *Dualities in Shakespeare* (Toronto, 1966).
5. Reuben Brower, *Hero and Saint: Shakespeare and the Graeco-Roman Heroic Tradition* (Oxford, 1971), 121.
6. All quotations from Shakespeare are from Peter Alexander, ed., *William Shakespeare, The Complete Works* (New York, 1952).
7. René Girard, *La Violence et le sacré* (Paris, 1972).
8. Harold Brooks, "Themes and Structure in *The Comedy of Errors*," in Kenneth Muir, ed., *Shakespeare: The Comedies* (New York, 1965), 14-15.
9. Thomas McFarland, *Shakespeare's Pastoral Comedy* (Chapel Hill, 1972), 60.
10. *Ibid.*, 30.
11. *Ibid.*, 31.
12. More technically, J. L. Austin (*How To Do Things With Words*, Oxford, 1955) distinguishes these uses in ordinary language: saying something propositional in a statement (locutionary), doing something such as promising or warning (illocutionary), and bringing about an effect such as persuading or pleasing (perlocutionary). An act of ordinary language may carry out two or three of these functions at once. Following Richard Ohmann in his application of this theory to drama ("Speech, Action, and Style," in Seymour Chatman, ed., *Literary Style: A Symposium*, London, 1971, 241-259), I am

asserting that the condition of the dramatic communication across the stage barrier seals all three of these functions inseparably together. Questions concerning these distinctions in ordinary language are discussed in J. R. Searle, ed., *The Philosophy of Language* (Oxford, 1971), especially 6-7, 39-53, and 23-38.

13. Corneille and especially Racine make the tightness of their plots do duty for suggesting the power of human possibility by enacting the opposite of an open situation. The future comes to seem like a past (and so vice versa).

14. The clown's imagery later gets transposed to verbal violence, the instruments "speak i' the nose," and it is Cassio's nose that Othello will throw to the dogs, in a delayed rejection of this music's appeal, "Oh I see that nose of yours, but not that dog I shall throw't to" (IV,i,140-141).

15. C. L. Barber (*Shakespeare's Festive Comedy,* Princeton, 1959) analyzes the ritual component with a generally unexceptionable perspicacity. However, even of the comedies only *The Merry Wives of Windsor* draws on popular festival to the near-exclusion of other elements, where all the strains combined in Greek comedy or tragedy can be derived from elements contributing to the festivals of Dionysus. *A Midsummer Night's Dream* does dramatize a Night of Illusion and a Feast of Fools like the Maying festivals from which it derives much of its form and some of its tone. But at the same time it presents in Theseus an ideal of the ruler that is ultimately derived from the secular aristocracy, an ideal expounded in such literary works as *Il Cortegiano* and the *Mirror for Magistrates*. This ideal is to be found nowhere in folk festival and its conventions. Popular festival and aristocratic ideal are enough at odds to refer almost wholly to distinct classes of the society. The folk festival, on its own ground, can only accommodate the aristocratic ideal by turning it topsy-turvy; while Titania undergoes something like this upset—and at the same time touches magical and courtly strains quite other— Theseus and Hippolyta pointedly do not.

16. George R. Kernodle, *From Art to Theatre: Form and Convention in the Renaissance* (Chicago, 1944).

17. Emrys Jones, *Scenic Form in Shakespeare* (Oxford, 1971), 11.

18. Angus Fletcher made this point in a Colloquium at the State University of New York at Buffalo, February, 1973.

19. Sigurd Burckhardt, *Shakespearian Meanings* (Princeton, 1968), 266.

20. Albert Cook, *Enactment: Greek Tragedy* (Chicago, 1971), 43-44.

21. The list Bacon recommends in his essay "Of Travel" will serve as a convenient summary. I underline the items of public gather-

ing which offer some analogy to or influence on the theatre: The things to be seen and observed are: *the courts of princes, specially when they give audience to ambassadors; the courts of justice, while they sit and hear causes,* and so of *consistories ecclesiastic;* the *churches* and *monasteries,* with the monuments which are therein extant; the walls and fortifications of cities and towns, and so the havens and harbours; antiquities and ruins; libraries; *colleges, disputations and lectures,* where any are; shipping and navies; houses and gardens of state and pleasure near great cities; armories, arsenals; magazines, *exchanges; burses;* warehouses; *exercises of horsemanship, fencing, training of soldiers,* and the like; *comedies* such whereunto the better sort of persons do resort; treasuries of jewels and robes; cabinets and rarities; and, to conclude, whatsoever is memorable in the places where they go. After all which the tutors or servants ought to make diligent inquiry. As for *triumphs, masks, feasts, weddings, funerals, capital executions,* and such shows, men need not be put in mind of them, yet are they not to be neglected.

22. Dowland is explicitly parallelled with Spenser in *The Passionate Pilgrim*, the ability of music to "ravish" set in a frame with the "deep conceit" of poetry:

> Dowland to thee is dear, whose heavenly touch
> Upon the lute doth ravish human sense;
> Spenser to me, whose deep conceit is such
> As, passing all conceit, needs no defense.

(8.5-8)

23. J. V. Cunningham, *op. cit.*
24. Francis Fergusson, "*Macbeth* as the Imitation of an Action," in Norman Rabkin, ed., *Approaches to Shakespeare (New York, 1964),* 126-127.
25. William R. Elton, *King Lear and the Gods* (San Marino, California, 1966).
26. The law in 3 Jac I, 21 Jan.-24 Mar. 1606, as noted by Edgar I. Fripp, *Shakespeare, Man and Artist* (Oxford, 1938), II, 653.
27. L. C. Knights puts it effectively in "King Lear," Anne Ridler, ed., *Shakespeare Criticism 1935-1960* (Oxford, 1963), 288-289: "What Lear touches in Cordelia ... is, we are made to feel, the reality, and the values revealed so surely there are established in the face of the worst that can be known of man or Nature. To keep nothing in reserve, to slur over no possible cruelty or misfortune, was the only way of ensuring that the positive values discovered and established in the play should keep their triumphant hold on our imagination, should assert that unconditional

rightness which, in any full and responsive reading of *King Lear*, we are bound to attribute to them."

28. J. V. Cunningham, "Plots and Errors: *Hamlet* and *King Lear*," in *Tradition and Poetic Structure* (Chicago, 1960), 102-3.

29. *Op. cit.*, 270-271.

30. The impact of Albany's normativeness on the audience may be inferred from a fact that Robert H. Darby brings to our attention: "When Shakespeare wrote *King Lear*, there was a Duke of Albany, and that Duke was James I." (Helmut Bonheim, ed., *The King Lear Perplex*, San Francisco, 1960, 75.)

31. "Passion" is a word that occurs frequently in Shakespeare—115 times. In this passage it comprises the sense of suffering generally (sense 3 in the NED), of being subject to extreme force (sense 5), of exhibiting a powerful affective condition (sense 6), along with some hints of a painful disorder (sense 4), like Lear's "*Hysterica passio*, down, thou climbing sorrow" (II,iv, 57) when this "extreme of passion" is "grief." It may even touch on the sense of outburst (sense 7), since Gloucester's heart burst smilingly under the two extremes; and on the martyrdom (sense 2) which is based on analogy to the Passion (sense 1), since he does die because of it.

32. An approach to what happens in the affective patterning of audience response would be to subject the sequences in the plays to a series of Freudian analyses in order to define, within that terminology, the kind of resolution a normative spectator might expect to derive from each particular sequence. But one does not have to go all the way in each instance with the technique refined by Norman Holland (*The Dynamics of Literary Response*, New York, 1968) in order to retain a concentration on what is perceived and apprehended during the course of a play. And it might be distracting. The lechery of Lear's utterances is off-target in his life; not even Freudian analysis can bring it on-target, since to see it so is to see him as destroying the normal barriers between subliminal-sexual motivation (the Freudian pleasure principle of the unconscious) and the actual discourse in the real world, where the reality principle asks that we not talk too much in public about sexual matters, and especially if we are eighty years old.

In one of his phases, Lear does destroy those barriers, but he recovers; and when he does, his concerns are beyond their mere negative definition as freedom from psychic obsession.

Lear's main problem, the king's blindness to the implications of selfishness in others, gains depth but not redirection by being seen in the context of childish pleasure-passivity or sublimated incestuous desire. And yet lechery is on-target in his kingdom. In its extensions it deeply motivates women as well as men; his daughters have been proving as much before our eyes. The lucky hit of his off-target shot might be ascribed to deep social roles as well as to psychological structures: to the anthropological fact that madmen are supposed to have special insight as well as something like the license of fools (who are licensed to act like madmen)—as Timon and Hamlet also demonstrate.

The plays may also give rise to a rich, but thematically distracting, series of evidential inferences about the life of the playwright. Joyce sees as biographical the plays' preoccupation with banishment. We know that men with powerful imaginations often have powerful mothers, as Robert Greer Cohn has pointed out for such as Sartre, Baudelaire, and Rimbaud. Goethe, Rilke, Nietzsche, Schopenhauer, and perhaps Rembrandt might be added to the list. Such speculation can neither fully ground itself nor fully cease over a Shakespeare who married a much older woman, idealizes virgins and brides, and rules queen-mothers for the most part out of his plays after Gertrude, except as step-mothers. Even Hermione is driven off-stage for sixteen years. Lear, Prospero, Pericles, Cymbeline, Leontes widowers are all at some point.

Or again, one might speculate on the association for Shakespeare in the name "Arden," when he places a serene and quasi-Utopian society in the Forest of Arden near his home, with the fact that Arden was his mother's maiden name.

33. Alexander Pope in the preface to his edition of Shakespeare, 1725.

34. "Reduction and Renewal in *King Lear*," in Thomas McFarland, *Tragic Meanings in Shakespeare* (New York, 1966), 127-71.

35. Puppet plays or "motions" were shown at Elizabethan fairs, perhaps not unlike the Pulcinella (Punch) recorded in Genoa as early as 1600 (E. K. Chambers, *The Medieval Stage*, II, 159-160), since they came from Italy. A puppet theatre, indeed, is shown in a miniature from the "Romance of Alexander," ca. 1340, Bodleian Library, Oxford, as reproduced in George R. Kernodle, *From Art to Theatre* (Chicago, 1944), 194.

36. Robert H. Darby in Helmut Bonheim, ed., *The King Lear Perplex* (San Francisco, 1960), 63, citing Sigmund Freud, *Works* (London, 1958), XII, 289-301.

37. Enid Welsford, *The Fool: His Social and Intellectual History* (New York, 1935).

38. Kenneth Muir, ed., *King Lear* (London, 1963), 200, *ad loc.* quoting Thomas Carter, *Shakespeare and Holy Scriptures*.

39. William Sylvester, "The Existence of a Disjunctive Principle in Poetry," *College English,* January, 1967, 266-272. See also his *Poetry and Disjunction,* The Swallow Press, Chicago (forthcoming).

CHAPTER 2: THE SOUNDING OF THE THEME

1. The co-presence of constituent elements in the figures on a stage make it misleading to interpret these staple forms as only sequentially presented. Othello, for example, is drawn as (1) a black man (larger, wilder, more potent, more evil, stranger, than a white, with charged interactions among these traits—as, wilder equals more potent, etc.); (2) a Moor (anti-Christian background with overtones of magic); (3) a mercenary, in the Machiavellian context of service for an Italian city-state; (4) a statesmanly general; (5) a middle-aged bridegroom. All these stand together under one skin, and when he opens his mouth for utterance, all may be felt to have some bearing. In Lear, on the other hand, madman and king are co-present, but in proportions that differ as the sequence of the action unfolds.

Stylistic analysis, too, would distract from, and possibly blunt, the pointed thrust of dramatic interchange in a play. In narrative, Roland Barthes (*S/Z,* Paris, 1970, 27) finds... "sont ... toutes les inflexions d'un *fading* immense, qui assure à la fois le chevauchement et la perte des messages." But in drama the declarative presence is always dominant; it has always picked up and totally redeployed any "fading" in its enacted, confronting presence. The silence of the reader at this moment is like the silence of what he remembers having read; the spectator hears loud voices and sees live persons acting, as distinct from his silent memory of what transpired on stage a few moments ago. So, to take Barthes' five codes, when Desdemona banters with Iago, Emilia, and Cassio to while away the time till Othello lands (II,i,103-180), the *hermeneutic* enigma is posed in more than just those terms and involves all her emotions towards the three persons present, and also towards her husband. These active emotions direct the *seme* of any statement she makes, locate the *symbol* she utters or hears (as "angel"), define and coordinate the *act* of her small interchanges, while subordinating the *reference* of any gnomic utterance Iago or she herself may invoke or exemplify. Or again, any one of the five social types combined for the character "Othello" may be seen at any point as hermeneutic, as seme, as symbol, as act, and as reference. So "black" is an *hermeneutic* enigma till the very end, one determinant of the *semes* Othello will utter, a self-evident *symbol* of (ironic) Manichean force ("a black ram/Is tupping your white ewe"), a condition of *act*, and the *reference* of phraseable and phrased gnomic utterances. And so for "Moor," "mercenary," "general," and "aging bridegroom." When Othello is on stage, all this stands before us as what we are seeing; when he is off, what we hear includes each of these, and all this, among its references. That is, whatever he may be saying, Iago is always in a sense talking about "Othello," who always means all of the above.

Or again, to put it more simply, as Robert B. Heilman says in *Magic in the Web: Action and Language in Othello* (Lexington, 1956), 12: "Othello's farewell to arms (III,iii,348,*ff*) is relevant to the specific situation of the moment, to Othello's personality generally, to Shakespeare's conception of the modes of response to disaster possible to human beings. Emilia's picking up of the handkerchief helps advance the action by contributing to Iago's deception of Othello but it is also relevant to her character and to Shakespeare's conception of the modes of wifely devotion and marital relationship (not to mention its relations by contrast with actions of Desdemona and Bianca and of Emilia herself later). The theories of sex which Iago advances to Roderigo are relevant to his purpose of controlling Roderigo, to his modes of thought generally, and to Shakespeare's awareness of the whole realm of philosophies of love."

The rich emphasis of the dramatic moment gives it the power to pack all this in, and one may unpack it by various methods—by Barthes', by Kenneth Burke's pentad of actional constituents (*A Grammar of Motives and A Rhetoric of Motives* , Cleveland 1962, 3-20), or by such an empirical keenness as Heilman's here.

Or if the roles are sequentiàlly presented before us, they do not fade one from the other: they gather cumulatively. Our initial image of Cordelia standing taciturn, demure, and wronged, is gathered up in the further images of her—the absent bride in France who writes a letter to Kent; the resolute planner of rescue for her father; the Queen distracting herself from military duties to tend him; the captive blissfully listening to him. At last the dead body borne by Lear gets its range of pity from all these prior, distinct images of Cordelia—as from all our prior, distinct images of Lear: the king, the madman, the pilgrim, the old man. These roles also persist for him; he is "every inch a king" (IV,vi,107) while a wandering madman. The *rex* and the *senex* comment on each other, and also qualify each other: he is enough of a king still to retain the vigor and resistance that one associates not with a "very foolish fond old man" (IV,vii,60), but with someone in the prime of life. Moreover, the comprehensiveness of the king-role allows him to manifest the qualities of his subjects; at times he resembles Kent and Edgar, and even Edmund and Cornwall; his tendency to appeal to supernatural power recalls the superstition of Gloucester; his recalcitrant slipping away into oracle and satire echoes the posture of the Fool and of "Mad Tom." Hamlet shows splendidly a comparable countertension of roles, son against prince, courtier against philosopher against madman.

Barthes' codes generally offer a "spatial" metaphor for what is irreducibly a temporal art. Their successiveness, and the very lexical unconnectedness of their application, make them distracting when applied to the drama, which deals with some successions, but not with these codes successively. And it does not deal with its own successions mainly in terms of the code, as *Sarrasine* does not do either, since its whole signification is a "word" in a large paragraph called "*La Comédie Humaine,*" where *connections* are made between youth and old age, sexuality and artistic aspiration, money and family, native and foreign (or metropolitan-sophisticated and provincial-initiate), the public display of luxury and the deep secret of organized vice. *Sarrasine's* "meaning" of connection among all these does not exist just by itself but mainly, and intentionally, as its own particular *connections* are transposed into other handlings of equivalent connections elsewhere in the *Comédie.*

2. Thomas McFarland, *Tragic Meanings in Shakespeare* (New York, 1966), 73-4, adapting the idea of Bernard Spivack, *Shakespeare and the Allegory of Evil* (New York, 1958).
3. Reuben Brower, *op. cit.,* 1-28.
4. McFarland, *op. cit.,* 60-5.
5. T. S. Eliot, *Selected Essays 1917-1932* (New York, 1932), 51-88, 107-20.
6. Guillaume Du Vair (T. I.), *The Moral Philosophie of the Stoicks,* (London, 1598), A4, "Let it not seeme strange unto us that Philosophie should be a meanes to help Divinitie, or that Christians may profit by the Stoicks."

The treatise goes on to stress a voluntaristic line quite in accord with the active thrust of a dramatic protagonist, and a management of "passions" in the midst of crossfires such as those which the dramatic plot tends to produce.
7. McFarland, *op. cit.,* 80-3.
8. And as it happens, the *Octavia* is spuriously attributed to Sen-

eca (*Der Kleine Pauly, sub Octavia,* München, 1972, IV, 230), though of course it was assumed to be genuinely his in the Renaissance.

9. Bacon in "Of Love" hits close to the assumption: "The stage is more beholding to Love than the life of man. For as to the Stage, love is ever matter of comedies, and now and then of tragedies, but in life it doth much mischief, sometimes like a syren, sometimes like a fury."

10. The parallels are tabulated schematically in F. L. Lucas, ed., *The Complete Works of John Webster* (London, 1927), III, 3-9.

11. The evidence, statistical and other, for the special prevalence of sexual license at court under Elizabeth, James, and Charles, is summarized in Lawrence Stone, *The Crisis of the Aristocracy, 1558-1641* (Oxford, 1965), 662-668. As he characterizes the general situation, (664): "One of the most striking features of Early Stuart society was the growing cleavage in outlook and behaviour between Court and Country. An aspect of this development which attracted much contemporary attention and criticism was the sexual license at the Jacobean Court, which may well have rivalled or excelled the more notorious conditions at the Court of Charles II."

12. To use the terms of Harold Bloom (*The Anxiety of Influence: A Theory of Poetry,* New York, 1973), one could regard Shakespeare's handling of his convention either as a *clinamen,* a swerving, in so far as he distorts it; as a *tessera,* in so far as he completes it by its opposite; *kenosis,* or an emptying of it by active discontinuity; *askesis,* or an energic redefinition by reworking its premises.

Of course here Shakespeare relates not to a prior poem, Bloom's discussed condition, but rather to a contemporary matrix of rhetorical forms. The elements Bloom separates out do in fact recombine in the active practice of any poet, with reference to the codified literary *langue* out of which he writes or to some particular exponent of it.

Shakespeare would seem, in fact, to have set himself early the task of exploring the byways of desire, of contemplating the main line by triangulating its peripheries. *Venus and Adonis* dwells, lovingly as it were, on what happens when the woman is the wooer. His manhood fatally escapes to the self-assertion of hunting:

> Since thou art dead, lo, here I prophesy
> Sorrow on love hereafter shall attend ...
> That all love's pleasure shall not match his woe.
>
> (*Venus and Adonis,* 1135-40)

Tarquin is all too willing to bring mortal shame on someone accessible to him only by rape. The poem presents a series of set-pieces meditating on the extremity of this situation.

> What win I if I gain the thing I seek?
> A dream, a breath, a froth of fleeting joy.
> Who buys a minute's mirth to wail a week?
> Or sells eternity to get a toy?
>
> (*The Rape of Lucrece*, 211-214)

The Sonnets combine the theme of infidelity with the theme of bisexuality in ways nearly impossible to extricate, while *The Phoenix and the Turtle* describes love as a kind of universal miracle. *Love's Labour's Lost, The Taming of the Shrew, A Midsummer Night's Dream, Twelfth Night,* and *All's Well That Ends Well* all study the problem of love when some form of disinclination is present.

13. Shakespeare even reverses the bed trick. In folklore, as in *The Changeling* and *Bussy d'Ambois*, someone other than a wedded partner is bedded under cover of darkness. But in *All's Well That Ends Well* and *Measure for Measure* it is a wife who substitutes for an illicit partner.

14. Othello, having chosen his "great arithmetician" in Cassio, "evades" the "three great ones of the city" whom Iago, it would seem, incited to intercede for his appointment. Othello's bureaucratic skill at handling influence by forestalling it, "Certes . . . . I have already chose my officer," is matched by his resoluteness at passing over someone like Iago who had proven himself in the field (I,i,8-20). Iago, who shows he understands all this by recounting it with the etched accuracy of resentment, then falls away from his own account and falsely redefines the choice as one between *influence* and service:

> Preferment goes by letter and affection,
> Not by the old graduation, where each second
> Stood heir to the first.
>
> (I,i,36-7)

Shakespeare moves on abruptly to weightier matters before making it clear that Iago understands, as Othello seems to, the bureaucratic principle of never making the second-in-charge successor to his superior—"A new broom sweeps clean"—and Cassio is a Florentine, though friend enough to have accompanied Othello on his courtship visits.

15. Thomas Rymer, "A Short View of Tragedy" (1693), Chapter VII, as reprinted in Joel E. Spingarn, ed., *Critical Essays of the Seventeenth Century*, II (Bloomington, 1963), 224.

16. William Empson, *The Structure of Complex Words* (London, 1951), 185-249. The large repertoire of senses Empson sees in

"honest" only partially focuses the contradiction Iago has dared to embody. As someone universally reputed to be (1) honest in all its senses, he is a good (2) servant who is also (3) clever and (4) evil. All the senses of (1) honest extend only to (2) servant; they stand in antithesis to (4) evil, and they shade into difference from (3) clever, since Renaissance "honest" implies plain and therefore a little stupid. Iago glories in exploiting these contradictions of role, and it is by ringing the changes on applying "honest" insinuatingly to Cassio that he first arouses Othello to suspicion (III,iii,103-140). "Honest" remains the pivot of the contradiction, providing a cover under which the (4) evil (3) clever (2) servant can perform the actions of the Vice. Servants are not supposed to be too clever anyway, and it was for qualities related to intellectual ability that Cassio was appointed over Iago, who can be getting his own back by revelling in the cleverness others have overlooked.

17. Even Coleridge, who gets the sense of disproportionate restlessness in Iago's "motive-hunting of a motiveless malignity," falls wholly under the stage spell of attributing a fixedness to the malignity. S. T. Coleridge, *Lectures on Shakespeare* (London, 1907).

18. On the map Desdemona has travelled more than half the distance to Palestine herself.

19. Truman Capote's *In Cold Blood*, a report of an actual crime, established a comparable pattern—a pair close enough for their connection to be a sublimated homosexuality, an Iago (Dick) who plots the crime and an Othello (the half-breed Perry) who executes the victims.

    In this connection we may take at some face value (as often) a disclaimer of Iago's which also has a purposive point:

> Yet do I hold it very stuff o' th' conscience
> To do no contriv'd murder. I lack iniquity
> Sometimes to do me service.

(I,ii,2-4)

20. David P. Willbern, "The Elizabethan Revenge Play: A Psychoanalytic Inquiry," unpublished doctoral dissertation, University of California, Berkeley, 1973, partially published in "Thomas Kyd's *The Spanish Tragedy*: Inverted Vengeance," *American Imago*, XXVIII, 1971, 247-267.

21. Fredson Bowers, *Elizabethan Revenge Tragedy—1587-1642* (Princeton, 1966), 3-4.

22. Stuart Schneiderman, "Shakespeare and Psychoanalysis," unpublished doctoral dissertation, University of Indiana, 1975, partially published in "The Saying of *Hamlet*," *Substance*, No. 8, Autumn, 1974.

23. Travis Bogard, "Shakespeare's Second Richard," *PMLA*, LXX, 1955, 192-209.

24. Sense 1 in the NED, *sub voc.* The lovers often, too, feel as gods: Antony is a "demi-god" and Cleopatra dresses up as Isis.

25. The imagery of the entombing earth comes at the time of Romeo's separation from Juliet, not when the lovers are together. The condemned suitor-expectant father Claudio in *Measure for Measure* can evoke the powerful connection as a way of substituting a welcoming courage before death for the marraige forbidden him with his own Juliet:

> I will encounter darkness as a bride
> And hug it in mine arms.
>
> (III,i,85-86)

The connection between love and death is lightly asserted in Orsino's prescience about a woman unattainable to him:

> How will she love when the rich, golden shaft
> Hath killed the flock of all affections else?
>
> (*Twelfth Night*, I,i,35-36)

26. Horace Howard Furness, ed., *Romeo and Juliet, Variorum Edition* (New York 1963), 367-395—all a discussion of the one phrase, "runaways' eyes."

27. In connection with the timelessness of love's development, it is worth remarking, though it may be a pure accident, that *Romeo and Juliet, Troilus and Cressida,* and *Antony and Cleopatra* are among the six plays given no act or scene divisions in the Folio.

28. "...the distinction between the Greek words *agape* and *eros*... is blotted out in English, where both meanings are included under the single word 'love'." Roland M. Frye, *Shakespeare and Christian Doctrine* (Princeton, 1963), 48.

29. Ernst Bloch, *Das Prinzip Hoffnung* (Frankfurt, 1959), I, 381.

CHAPTER 3: DRAMATIC IRONY

1. Albert Cook, *Enactment: Greek Tragedy* (Chicago, 1971), 30-34.

2. Francis Bacon, *Novum Organum*, XLI-XLIV.

3. Jackson Barry, *Dramatic Structure: The Shaping of Experience* (Berkeley, 1970), 156.

4. Murray Schwartz, "Between Fantasy and Imagination: A Psychological Exploration of *Cymbeline*," in Frederick C. Crews, ed., *Psychoanalysis and Literary Process,* (Cambridge, Mass., 1970), 219-283.

CHAPTER 4: PLAY

1. Angelo Poliziano in *Panepistemon* (as summarized by Bernard

Weinberg, *The History of Literary Criticism in the Italian Renaissance*, Chicago, 1956, 3) classifies *Teatrica* as among items under *Actualis Philosophia*, as opposed to *Spectative* and *Rationalis* (under which are included *Poetica*, along with *Grammatica*, *Dialectica*, and others), saying that *Teatrica* leads to useful activity (his sense of *actualis*).

2, 3, and 4. Jonas Barish, George Hibbard, and Clifford Leech in William Blissett, Julian Patrick, and R. W. VanFossen, eds., *A Celebration of Ben Jonson* (Toronto, 1973).

5. Duvignaud, *Spectacle et Société* (Paris, 1970), 97.

6. The writers themselves, if they were actors, were thus classed as servants. And chiefly, but not entirely, because of censorship, they were often in trouble with the law. In *The Cambridge History of English Literature*, V (Cambridge, 1932), 371, A. W. Ward points out: "A list of the writers who suffered from the interference of authorities comprises the names of Cartwright, Chapman, Daniel, Dekker, Drayton, Fletcher, Heywood, Holinshed, Jonson, Kyd, Lodge, Marlowe, Marston, Middleton, Munday, Nashe, Rowlands, Selden, Shakespeare, Smith, Stowe, Stubbes, and Wither." For the complex social situation, Chambers' "The Control of the Stage" (*The Elizabethan Stage*, I, 236-388) provides elaborate detail. Stubbes' remarks (*Ibid*, IV, 221) of 1583 show how sweeping the condemnation could be.

7. Michel Foucault, *Histoire de la folie à l'âge classique* (Paris, 1961).

8. T. S. Eliot, *op. cit.*, 51-88, 107-20. F. R. Leavis expands this point with a comparable over-emphasis (*The Common Pursuit*, Harmondsworth Middlesex, 1963, 136-159).

9. Anne Righter, *Shakespeare and the Idea of the Play* (Harmondsworth, Middlesex, 1967), 21.

10. Lionel Abel, *Metatheatre, A New View of Dramatic Form* (New York, 1963).

11. Anne Righter, *op. cit.*, 82, quotes W. J. Lawrence (*Speeding Up Shakespeare*, London, 1937, 4-14) on this question: "It is to be noted that Shakespeare most frequently uses the word 'act' in the sense of deed or action, and yet rarely, if ever, without giving it some associated theatrical coloring."

12. Fripp, *op. cit.*, II, 533-534, further shows that Shakespeare has Jaques burlesque the seven-ages topos.

13. Bertold Brecht, *Versuche*, Vol. 11 (Berlin, 1951), 93.

14. Albert Cook, *Prisms* (Bloomington, 1967), Chapter Five.

15. C. L. Barber, *op. cit.*, 123, 144, where he points out, citing Minor White Latham's discussion (*The Elizabethan Fairies, the Fairies of Folk Lore, and the Fairies of Shàkespeare*, New York, 1930), that the fairies of folklore tended to be malevolent. "Shakespeare

... entirely alters the emphasis so as to make the fairies either harmless or benign."

16. J. Dover Wilson, *What Happens in Hamlet* (Cambridge, 1935), summarizes the various doctrines of the time concerning ghosts.

17. Williams, *Superstitions of Witchcraft* (1865), 220, as quoted by T. F. Thistleton Dyer, *Folklore of Shakespeare* (New York, 1966).

King James' *Demonology* discusses all the supernatural classes in Shakespeare—fairies and ghosts as well as witches and devils. When King James particularizes "all these kinds of spirits and spectres that appears and trobles persones; those that troble houses and solitary places, those that follow people along, those that possess them, and Faeries," every one of these finds some instance in Shakespeare's work.

18. On Shakespeare's achievement of having the make-believe of pastoral and the vision of comedy reinforce each other, McFarland (*Shakespeare's Pastoral Comedy*, 32, 37) is particularly apposite: "From these two perspectives supplied by the Platonic tradition—the view of Plotinus in which even the tragic confrontation of death and catastrophe is annulled by play, and the view of Plato in which play assumes a sacramental character— the final meanings of comedy may be sighted ... The alliance of comedy and pastoral realizes what neither mode could adequately achieve by itself: the representation of paradise. An alliance is necessary, for such a representation must be conceived simultaneously as happy society and blessed place."

19. Gregory Bateson, "Redundancy and Coding," in Thomas A. Sebeok, ed., *Animal Communication* (Bloomington, 1968), 622-3.

20. C. L. Barber, "The Form of Faustus' Fortunes Good or Bad," in Paul A. Bates, ed., *Faust: Sources, Works, Criticism* (New York, 1969), 157-71 (reprinted from *The Tulane Drama Review*, Vol. VIII).

21. *Op. cit.*, 614-615.

22. Jacques Derrida, "La Double Séance," in *La Dissémination* (Paris, 1972), 199-318, citation from 225. "Ce que Mallarmé a donc *lu* dans ce livret, c'est la prescription *s'effacant d'elle-même*, l'ordre donné au Mime de n'imiter rien qui de quelque façon preexistât à son opération: ni acte (*"la scène n'illustre que l'idée, pas une action effective"*) ni parole (*"ode tue ... soliloque muet que, tout du long à son âme tient et du visage et des gestes le fantôme blanc comme une page pas encore écrite."*)

23. William Frost, "Shakespeare's Rituals and the Opening of *King Lear*," *Hudson Review*, 1958, 577-585.

24. The Donatan view of tragedy, summarized by J. V. Cunning-

ham, *op. cit.*, sustains this emphasis on "poetic justice." So does the retribution frame of the "medieval inheritance" of Elizabethan tragedy, the *De Casibus Virorum Illustrium*. In this connection, Greville's attitude may have been typical, as cited by L. G. Salinger: "In Fulke Greville's *Life of Sidney* (c. 1610-1612) there is a striking comment on Renaissance tragedy. Ancient tragedy, according to Greville, had been ultimately rebellious; it had sought to exemplify the disastrous miseries of man's life ... and so out of that melancholic vision, stir horror, or murmur against Divine Providence. Modern tragedy, on the contrary, was dominated by moral law; it sought 'to point out God's revenging aspect upon every particular sin, to the despair, or confusion of mortality.'" (Cited in Boris Ford, ed., *The Age of Shakespeare*, Harmondsworth, Middlesex, 1955, 334).

25. Abel, *op. cit.*, 113.

CHAPTER 5: STYLE

1. Jackson Barry, *loc. cit.*
2. John Aubrey, *Life of Bacon.* This is just the function Shakespeare has the dying Henry assign to music in a neighboring room:

    KING:
    > Let there be no noise made, my gentle friends;
    > Unless some dull and favourable hand
    > Will whisper music to my weary spirit.

    WARWICK:
    > Call for the music in the other room.
    >   (*Henry IV, Part Two*, IV,v,1-4)
3. Bertrand Bronson, *Traditional Tunes of the Child Ballads* (Princeton, 1959).
4. Puttenham (*The Art of Poesie*, II,XI) classifies rhyme according to "distaunces." A couplet is the first distaunce, alternate rhyme the second, and outer rhymes, such as those of *The Phoenix and The Turtle*, the third.
5. Albert Cook, *Enactment: Greek Tragedy* (Chicago, 1971), 90-91.
6. The liveness of this question at the time appears in Thomas Campion's *On English Verse* (1602), when he speaks of the "unaptness of rhyme" and in Samuel Daniel's answer, *A Defense of Rhyme.*
7. These terms are classified in John Hoskins, *Directions for Speech and Style*, 1599, as edited by Hoyt H. Hudson (Princeton, 1935), 45-48.

8. In "The Naked Babe and the Cloak of Manliness" (*The Well-Wrought Urn,* London, 1949, 21-46), Cleanth Brooks analyzes the consistency in the imagery of Macbeth's sense of inadequacy for rule, "now does he feel his title/Hang loose about him, like a giant's robe/Upon a dwarfish thief (V,ii,20-22)." In his correlative reading of the "babe" as a recurrent image in the play ". . . the babe signifies the future which Macbeth would control and cannot control" (p. 42).

9. Albert Cook, *The Classic Line: A Study in Epic Poetry,* (Bloomington, 1966), 141-176.

10. John Thompson, Jr., *The Founding of English Meter* (New York, 1961).

11. Puttenham, *op. cit.,* in the section "Of Proportion," discusses the poetic use of monosyllables and bisyllables.

12. Philip Wheelwright, "On the Semantics of Poetry," in Seymour Chatman and Samuel R. Levin, eds., *Essays on the Language of Literature,* (Boston, 1967), 258-259. "The principal poetic meaning in the passage is expressed in the thematic use of the word 'done,' repeated three times like the tolling of a dirge . . . a tragic reminder of the irrevocability of a deed once performed. The reminder is expressed obliquely, but in some mysterious way it gains in power by its very obliquity." Picking up later iterations of "done" by Lady Macbeth, Wheelwright asserts the word "done" to be a plurisign. It is not, however, a plurisign taken in itself, but only as its repetitions charge with significance the sequentiality, random in the ordinary language and here structured across an enjambment. The near repetitions and the far echoes, Macbeth's three "dones" and the ones later in the play, turn the monosign "done" into an intensification of itself, to signify not only "completed" but also "completed beyond any possibility of undoing"—a meaning that shadows and undercuts the later forward monosign of "tomorrow and tomorrow and tomorrow," where the futurity of the lexical sense is lost in the "dusty death" to which future and past alike are relegated as Macbeth expresses his impassivity on receiving the news of his wife's death.

13. Puttenham, *loc. cit.,* also discusses "stirre" or "motion" in words.

14. Roman Jakobson, "Linguistics and Poetics," in Chatman and Levin, *op. cit.,* 296-322.

15. Charles Hockett, *A Course in Modern Linguistics* (New York, 1958).

16. Arnold Stein, "Yeats: A Study in Recklessness," *Sewanee Review,* LVII, 1949, 603-626.

17. Owen Barfield, *Poetic Diction: A Study in Meaning* (New York, 1964), 118-120.
18. Milton Klonsky, "A Guide Through the Garden," *Sewanee Review*, LVIII, 1950, 16-35.
19. William Empson, *Some Versions of Pastoral* (London, 1950), 119-145.
20. Paul Valéry, *Oeuvres*, I (Paris, 1957), 314-39.
21. Elizabeth Sewell, *The Structure of Poetry* (New York, 1952).
22. Gustav René Hocke, *Manierismus in der Literatur* (Berlin, 1965), 91-92. Hocke relates this ambivalence to the anxiety Bacon exemplifies before the question of nominalism: "Eine Generation von Skeptikern versuchte, der konventionellen Sprache das zu verleihen, was wir 'Illusionsperspektive' genannt haben. Worte werden, in diesem Skeptizismus, anamorphotisch. Im Umformen sieht man ihren Grund. Wieder wird der Einfluss des Nominalismus spürbar, und wir werden daran erinnert, dass Francis Bacon mit der realistischen Tradition gebrochen hatte, um neue Beziehungen von Wort, Ding und Subjekt aufzudecken. 'Ein Wort lieben, schreibt Bacon, Wittgenstein und a. vorwegnehmend, 'heisst ein Bild lieben.' 'Worte sind nicht Zeichen der Dinge selbsts'. . . . Doch Shakespeare, und das ist seiner tiefsten Wesenszüge, stand mit geradezu begnadeter Überlegenheit mitten in diesem Taumel einer sich selbst ent-wortenden und gleichzeitig verwortenden Welt. Er stand in der Spannung, aber er verfiel weder dem nihilistischen Hyper-Manierismus mancher seiner Zeitgenossen noch der Kompromissbereitschaft der stets als Ausweg vorhandenen Klassizistischen *'Augusteans.'* [sic]"
23. M. M. Mahood, *Shakespeare's Wordplay* (London, 1957), 23-24.
24. Roman Jakobson, *op. cit.*, 315.
25. Jacques Lacan, "L'Instance de la lettre dans l'inconscient," *Écrits* (Paris, 1966), 493-528.
26. Prosopopeia is discussed at length in Abraham Fraunce, *The Arcadian Rhetoric*, I, 31; by Sir John Harrington in *A Brief Apology for Poetry* and George Chapman in *A Defense of Homer* (both in G. Gregory Smith, ed., *Elizabethan Critical Essays*, Oxford 1904); and in Julius Caesar Scaliger's *Poetices Libri Septem*, III, XLVIII, as prosopopeia or "attributio."
27. Self-reference in language poses an irreducible indeterminacy, and dramatic speeches must be composed in self-reference. Seeing them as *prosopopeia* gives prominence to the referential determinacy of a rhetorical figure. In a more modern kind of analysis, Edward Kissam (unpublished doctoral dissertation, SUNY-Buffalo, 1975) forcefully suggests the substructure of "asymmetry" that first-person utterances, and notably dra-

matic speeches, involve: "The syntactic well-formedness of the sentence-token:

I hate Ed Kissam

is undecidable. Only the utterance can be said to be well-formed or deviant. This interplay between knowledge and language is not, as a theory of language as a self-contained entity would have it, random; it is systematic and central to language-use.

"It is notable that a huge amount of the form of dramatic narrative is derived from this feature of language. The function of language in *Macbeth* is deeply reliant on referential opacity which is not a random phenomenon. Macbeth does not simply happen not to know who the witches are referring to; it is a fundamental part of the speaker/listener relationship. And the prophecy is mirrored by the theme of treachery. Whereas Macbeth feels himself secure due to a speaker/listener asymmetry, the king feels himself secure due to the same asymmetry. Similarly, the social implications of the 'royal' *we* are not exhausted in an analysis of the cultural identification of king and his people or, perhaps king and deity, but has the linguistically entrenched ambiguity of reference which is at the heart of *King Lear*. The question 'Who are we?' is not only a psychological and a social one, but a linguistic one and the linguistic fact is that it cannot be given a definite answer under any condition as we know only that it is inclusive but not to what extent. The most highly-valued instances of irony are, of course, those structures which are sufficiently ambiguous to allow the speaker (to take only irony stemming from hidden identity) to speak as himself and as whoever he is thought to be. The dramatic excellence of *Oedipus Rex* stems not only from a plot which is ironic but from a carefully constructed linguistic heightening of that irony."

28. Jonas A. Barish, "Shakespeare's Prose," in Norman Rabkin, ed., *Approaches to Shakespeare* (New York, 1964), 245-263.

29. Bertram Joseph, *Acting Shakespeare* (London, 1960), 20-54. I am here developing Joseph's points on climax and antithesis.

30. In this connection, lines taken from early strata of the Vedas already contain this idea,

vácam astápadím aham návasraktim
rtaprsam indrāt pári tanvàm mame

"I have measured as thin from Indra the eight-footed nine-sided word attaining truth;" i.e., I have accounted as inadequate to, and imperfect by comparison with, the god Indra, the verbal expression which may attain to truth, though it may have eight feet (of metrical length?) and nine aspects." Delbrück, *Altindische Syntax*, as cited by W. P. Lehman, "Contemporary Linguistics and Indo-European Studies," *PMLA*, October, 1972, 985.

31. Even if one argued, as Geoffrey Hartman does ("The Voice of the Shuttle: Language from the Point of View of Literature," in *Beyond Formalism*, New Haven, 1970, 337-355) that there is something fundamentally binary, and also fundamentally mediating, in any poetic act, still Shakespeare's practice constitutes (obviously) a case of so extremely intense a manipulation of linguistic resources as to make them glory at every moment in doing what they may ultimately be said to be doing by virtue of being a case of poetry generally. "The power of the phrase lies in its elision of middle terms and overspecification of end terms." This definition sharply applies to "Or memorize another Golgotha," while one would have to have recourse to the (perhaps silent) overall bearing of the poems to assert it of "They fle from me who sometime did me seke." And indeed, the tendency of poetry to center on normative terms, horse and sun, tree and road, speak and weep and hold, goes counter to this specification. Shakespeare's shuttle is so fast as to blur with the sense of his overall bearing at every point.

32. F. P. Wilson, "The Diction of Common Life," British Academy Shakespeare Lecture, 1941, reprinted in Anne Ridler, ed., *op. cit.*, 113. Wilson calls attention (109) to *Politeuphuia, Wit's Commonwealth*, an anthology of *sententiae* published in 1597.

33. The intricacy and extensiveness of Shakespeare's recourse to proverbs is amply demonstrated in M. P. Tilley, *A Dictionary of the Proverbs in England in the 16th and 17th Centuries* (Ann Arbor, 1950). It is also discussed in C. G. Smith, *Shakespeare's Proverb Lore* (Cambridge, Mass., 1963).

34. Thomas Carter, *op. cit.*, 418.

35. Olga Bernal, *Language et fiction dans le roman de Beckett* (Paris, 1969), 153.

36. Bernard Weinberg, *op. cit.*, I, 68. Jacopo Mazzoni, *Della difesa della Comedia di Dante*, summarized in *ibid.*, II, 631, distinguishes between true and false, and then between dramatic and narrative, producing four categories, the *dramatica phantastica* and *dramatica icastica* being the two that include drama.

37. If *refined* is a middle between the extremes of *drab* and *golden*, we are given an equivalent for verse of the ancient classification of styles into *low, middle* and *high*, with middle, or Attic, as the honorific term. But these classifications are provisional as well as loose. J. V. Cunningham ("Lyric Style in the 1590's" in *The Problem of Style*, New York, 1966, 159-72) breaks drab or plain into two, *moral* and *flat*, finding a metrical marker, a fourth-syllable caesura, as an indicator of the moral:

> The life is long/that loathsomely doth last,
> The doleful days/draw slowly to their date.

38. Scaliger, *op. cit.*, as discussed by Geoffrey Hartman, *op. cit.*, 45-46.
39. Richard Carew, *The Excellency of English*, in G. Gregory Smith, *op. cit.*
40. Puttenham, *op. cit.*, III,iii; VIII.
41. Sister Miriam Joseph, *Shakespeare's Use of the Arts of Language*, New York, 1947.
42. The terms are those of Michael A. K. Halliday in Seymour Chatman, *op. cit.*, 330-368. Halliday defines them by many occurrences, by statistical preponderance in a sample. One can argue however that any single word or stylistic trait is "foregrounded" in the very fact of its one occurrence.
43. One way to rephrase the power of the poetic connection is to schematize its designations, whatever form they take, into Lotman's gratuitous binary sets, added by the poem to structure its constituents of ordinary language. (Yuri M. Lotman, *Analyz poetycheskogo teksta, struktura stycha* Leningrad, 1972).

    Such a definition meets the requirements of economy and elegance for assigning functions to elements in a lyric poem, as Lotman does, from the syllable through elements of diction to the distribution of persons (lyric poems having a heavy alternate tendency to mediate between "I" and some other). The dramatic tradition of the English Renaissance, however, avails itself imperiously of the full range of lyric uses (in Greek drama these are to be found most intensively in the chorus; French classical tragedy has verse of a more austere control). Such schematisms are overthrown in the multiplicity of persons—where the rule for two-person dialogue in Greek drama or two plus one, and the tendency to the same in France, may be taken to reproduce the "natural" doubleness of structure in verse while amplifying it in the larger framework of speakers in an imagined scene. It may be said that the English practice permits a free range of poetic uses, and calls attention ostentatiously to the triumphant resources at its disposal, just because the poetry uttered by speakers can be ordered, as a comparison of tenor and vehicle in metaphor or of physical and spiritual in reference, into the binary sets that the intense cross-purposes and open futures of its engaged participants will evade. That larger and different order of action permits a more complex, and freer, invocation of all those other binary sets in the resources of poetic discourse. So does the golden style come off as more dramatic than the refined style, as well as richer in its range of lyric reference; it follows the trans-binary openness of ascending action more freely.
44. Colloquium, State University of New York at Buffalo, Spring 1969.

CHAPTER 6: ENDINGS

1. T. W. Baldwin, *Shakespeare's Five-Act Structure* (Urbana, 1947), *passim*.
2. Leslie Hotson, *op. cit.*
3. Enid Welsford, *op. cit.*
4. Gregory Bateson, *op. cit.*
5. Though *tiny*, it has been argued, tends to be preceded by *little*. See Horace Howard Furness, ed., *Twelfth Night or, What You Will*, Variorum Edition, *ad. loc.*, and the NED.
6. Shakespeare's manipulation of such ignorance, his plotting of dramatic ironies by which a "practiser" in the plays manipulates the ignorance of others, is elaborate enough to have occasioned book-length treatment in Bertrand Evans' *Shakespeare's Comedies* (Oxford, 1960).
7. Jean Duvignaud, *Spectacle et Société* (Paris, 1970), 80.
8. Ernest Kantorowicz, *The King's Two Bodies* (Princeton, 1957).
9. Charles Williams, "The Cycle of Shakespeare," in *The English Poetic Mind*, Oxford, 1932, 53-54.

CHAPTER 7: JUSTICE

1. The word occurs only six times in Shakespeare's works, "provident" only twice and "providently" only once. I do not subscribe to the special "*argumentum ex silentio*" which would find the most pervasive concepts unformulable in a particular word. Rather, Shakespeare perhaps felt the course of enacted events carried its own force, without reading the overwhelming ideological prescription. "God" occurs 796 times and "grace" 601; a fair share of those carrying something like the sense "favor of God"; so that the notion equivalent to providence finds expression, while keeping the network of diction relatively uncommitted to views about the sequence shown.

   Shakespeare, in his adjectives 'alone,* inclines specially to definitions of order: the most frequent one he uses is "good," and of all his contemporaries, he alone would seem to include "noble" definitely among the top ten (it is his eighth), sharing with Donne a high reliance on "true" (his fifth). Of his abstract nouns, "nature" and "reason" involve a large, comprehensive, philosophical, theological, juridical, and popular tradition that asserts a final coherence among the laws of the physical universe, the progression of human and other life, eternal norms, and immutable faculties of mind. And there are hosts of related others—*quality, chance, justice, mercy, pity, law, counsel, art,* *bond, grace, degree, duty, service, fortune, honor, conscience, affection, election, measure, faith.*

The terms, already large in their reference, tend to define one another, as terms do in a philosophic system: the action produces definitions as it goes along.

*This data on Shakespeare comes from Marvin Spivack, ed., *A Complete and Systematic Concordance to the Works of Shakespeare*, Vol. VI. (Hildesheim, 1970). For Shakespeare's contemporaries, the analysis of long samples of selected poets is as reported in Josephine Miles, *Style and Proportion* (Boston, 1967), 144-145.

2. The very nature of the historical material Shakespeare addresses will not yield easily to the pattern of a single play—and therefore lends itself fairly readily to treatment on a longer span. As Herbert Lindenberger says (*Historical Drama*, Chicago, 1975, 99): "The very fluctuating quality of royal fortunes makes it impossible to isolate a typical historical 'structure' in Shakespeare as one can a tragic or a comic structure."

3. Willard Farnham, *The Medieval Heritage of Elizabethan Tragedy*, (Berkeley, 1936).

4. J. V. Cunningham, *Woe or Wonder*, 15-19.

5. The Hope Theatre, E. K. Chambers, *The Elizabethan Stage*, II (Oxford, 1923) 449-472.

6. E. K. Chambers, *The Medieval Stage*, I (London, 1903), 21.

7. Sigurd Burckhardt, *op. cit.*, 176.

8. This aspect of the Elizabethan attitude towards Rome is well summarized in Laurence Michel, *The Thing Contained*, (Bloomington, 1970), 60-61. Their admiration was qualified as T. J. V. Spencer shows in "Shakespeare and the Elizabethan Romans," *Shakespeare Survey X*, 1957, as reprinted in Frank Kermode, *op. cit.*, 400-419.

9. Thomas McFarland, (*Tragic Meanings in Shakespeare*, 131) substantiates this vividly: "Likewise the play's landscape, though nominally England, bears none of the comforting insignia of historical England. The bareness of Stonehenge is everywhere, though even the familiarity of Stonehenge itself is absent. The land has no cities, no towns, no villages; neither inn nor church, neither guildhall nor blacksmith's forge, meets our eyes; there are no stores, nor the tradesmen concerned with them, as there are no farms or farmers."

10. Lionel Abel, *op. cit.*, 29.

11. Laurence Michel, *op. cit.*, 34.

12. Antigonus, even in the process of giving his oath, makes a show of substituting pity for justice, pretending that he is powerless to act while accepting the commission to be an agent:

> I swear to do this; though a present death
> Had been more merciful. Come on, poor babe:
> Some powerful spirit instruct the kites and ravens
> To be thy nurses! Wolves and bears, they say,
> Casting their savageness aside, have done
> Like offices of pity.* Sir, be prosperous
> In more than this deed does require! and blessing
> Against this cruelty fight on thy side,
> Poor thing, condemn'd to loss!
>
> (II,iii,183–191)

Antigonus goes through all the motions—of a counsellor's advice among methods of execution (1) of hoping that the tales, instancing sentimentality and extravagance, of wolf children and the like will lead beasts of prey to turn kindly, (2) of imitating his wife in chiding the king whose order he is obeying, (3) in appealing to providence to bring about what he will not, (4) and disclaiming cruelty while aiming to execute it.

Camillo, another loyal counselor, has already given him an example of harder and swifter assumption of the commands of a higher justice: instead of following the order to kill Polixenes —though the king's word should normally have been enough to establish that Polixenes was guilty of the .adultery with the queen which in the law of this time was technically treason— Camillo quickly judges the conditions not to be normal, informs the victim, and escapes with him, to return sixteen years later, and marry the widow of Antigonus.

Antigonus has time to repent and the freedom to do so. But he does not. Even his escape from a gathering storm at sea as he lands on the seacoast of Bohemia does no more than substitute the sensationalism of a psychic experience for the imperatives of justice, leaving the infant exposed to a storm from which he will himself run away. The self-indulgence of his pity seems tender enough.to turn him away at any point in his long speech, which must be quoted in full to show the subtle tissue of contradictions in its feigned sympathy and deflective inferences:

> Come, poor babe.
> I have heard, but not believ'd, the spirits o'th'dead
> May walk again. If such thing be, thy mother
> Appear'd to me last night: for ne'er was dream
> So like a waking. To me comes a creature,
> Sometimes her head on one side some another—

---

*As numbers of items in *The Short Title Catalogue* attest, the English of this period were inordinately curious about prodigies of nature, stories of strange births, and the like.

I never saw a vessel of like sorrow,
So fill'd, and so becoming; in pure white robes,
Like very sanctity, she did approach
My cabin where I lay; thrice bow'd before me;
And, gasping to begin some speech, her eyes
Became two spouts; the fury spent, anon
Did this break from her: 'Good Antigonus,
Since fate, against thy better disposition,
Hath made thy person for the thrower-out
Of my poor babe, according to thine oath,
Places remote enough are in Bohemia,
There weep, and leave it crying; and, for the babe
Is counted lost for ever, Perdita
I prithee call't. For this ungentle business,
Put on thee by my lord, thou ne'er shalt see
Thy wife Paulina more.' And so, with shrieks,
She melted into air. Affrighted much,
I did in time collect myself, and thought
This was so and no slumber. Dreams are toys;
Yet, for this once, yea, superstitiously,
I will be squar'd by this. I do believe
Hermione hath suffer'd death, and that
Apollo would, this being indeed the issue
Of King Polixenes, it should here be laid,
Either for life or death, upon the earth
Of its rig⊦ ⌣ father. Blossom, speed thee well!
There lie, and there thy character; there these,
Which may, if fortune please, both breed thee, pretty,
And still rest thine. The storm begins. Poor wretch,
That for thy mother's fault art thus expos'd
To loss and what may follow! Weep I cannot,
But my heart bleeds; and most accurs'd am I
To be by oath enjoin'd to this. Farewell!
The day frowns more and more. Thou'rt like to have
A lullaby too rough; I never saw
The heavens so dim by day. A savage clamour!
Well may I get aboard! This is the chase;
I am gone for ever.

(III,iii,15-58)

He believes neither in dreams nor in ghosts; yet he accepts their
evidence, if only partly. Shakespeare believes in both, and all
that is predicted in this dream comes true—including the last
statement of the dream figure, the death that Antigonus seems
to feel he can escape. But if what the dream-Hermione says is
to be believed, he is powerless to save himself. And the retribution that the dream predicts belies the phrasing of exoneration

in which Antigonus delivers her message. Hermione, of course, is not dead, as we must wait to learn. But the Apollo of the oracle has pronounced her innocent of adultery, not guilty, as Antigonus all too willingly believes, although the wife to whom he has seemed to defer in this, like the audience and all the good characters, has gone on the assumption that the queen is in fact innocent. Actually he calls her both innocent and guilty here, mixing up Apollo's evidence and Apollo's consistent command.

The psychology of all this moral hypocrisy leads to a capital evasion—for which the retribution of providence is swifter than the slow retelling of the dream could have predicted. We soon see that more than a storm causes his fright: "*Exit, pursued by a bear.*" So much for the gentleness of wolves and bears; so much for Antigonus' earlier protestation that maybe they would cast their savageness aside. The mariner who was "glad at heart/To be so rid o'th' business" (13–14) will presumably have got aboard, and so been shipwrecked. But Autolycus' lingering to indulge himself in what he takes to be the dream's exoneration has brought his death (he would have died on shipboard anyway) by painful dismemberment. Nor does Shakespeare spare us the details (or have this action admit of any brutal, misplaced laughter at the bear's entrance):

> to see how the bear tore out his shoulder-bone, how he cried to me for help, and said his name was Antigonus, a nobleman .. and how the poor gentleman roared, and the bear mock'd him, both roaring louder than the sea or weather . . . the men are not yet cold under water, nor the bear half din'd on the gentleman; he's at it now.
>
> (95-105)

13. Northrop Frye, *A Natural Perspective* (New York, 1965), 105, 123-137.

14. "As this [*A Woman Killed With Kindness*] was acted, a towneswoman ... finding her conscience ... extremely troubled, suddenly skritched and cryd out Oh my husband, my husband ... she told them she had poysoned her husband ... whereupon the murdresse was apprehended." Thomas Heywood, "An Apology for Actors," (London, 1612).

15. The point is made by Emrys Jones, *Scenic Form in Shakespeare*, 3-40.

16. Johan Huizinga, *Homo Ludens: A Study of the Play-element in Culture*. Shakespeare pays particular attention to this question. See E. K. Chambers, *The Elizabethan Stage*, III, 123-125.

17. C. L. Barber, " 'Thou That Beget'st Him That Did Thee Beget': Transformation in *Pericles* and *The Winter's Tale*," *Shakespeare Survey*, 22, 1969.

INDEX OF NAMES

INDEX OF PLAYS